D0924347

LOST IN THE USA

WOMEN, GENDER, AND SEXUALITY
IN AMERICAN HISTORY

Editorial Advisors:
Susan K. Cahn
Wanda A. Hendricks
Deborah Gray White
Anne Firor Scott, Founding Editor Emerita

A list of books in the series appears at the end of this book.

DEBORAH GRAY WHITE

LOST IN THE
USA

AMERICAN IDENTITY FROM THE
PROMISE KEEPERS TO THE
MILLION MOM MARCH

**UNIVERSITY OF
ILLINOIS PRESS**
Urbana, Chicago, and Springfield

© 2017 by Deborah Gray White
All rights reserved
Manufactured in the United States of America
1 2 3 4 5 C P 5 4 3 2 1
∞ This book is printed on acid-free paper.

Library of Congress Cataloging-in-Publication Data
Names: White, Deborah G. (Deborah Gray), 1949– author.
Title: Lost in the USA: American identity from the Promise
    Keepers to the Million Mom March / Deborah Gray White.
Description: Urbana: University of Illinois Press, 2017. |
    Series: Women, gender, and sexuality in American history |
    Includes bibliographical references and index.
Identifiers: LCCN 2016044849 (print) | LCCN 2016045840
    (ebook) | ISBN 9780252040900 (cloth : alk. paper) | ISBN
    9780252082382 (pbk. : alk. paper) | ISBN 9780252099403
    (ebook)
Subjects: LCSH: Group identity—United States. | Social
    movements—United States. | Social action—United States.
    | Political activists—United States. | Social reformers—
    United States.
Classification: LCC HM753.W45 2017 (print) | LCC HM753
    (ebook) | DDC 303.48/4—dc23
LC record available at https://lccn.loc.gov/2016044849

In memory of my brother,
Otis

Contents

Acknowledgments

This book has taken an awfully long time to write—just short of twenty years, to be exact. I want to thank everyone who had anything to do with it, and apologize in advance to those who I might forget to mention, for twenty years is a long time.

I cannot, however, forget my indebtedness to Darlene Clark Hine for the small packet of source materials that she distributed during a 1998 conference commemorating the first anniversary of the Million Woman March. That packet was my first encounter with the rich testimonies that appear in this book. After reading them I asked a number of graduate students (who are now professors) to collect more. I thank Marsha Barrett, Crystal Frazier, and Stephanie Jones Rogers for their assistance.

I also benefited from the careful reading that various people gave chapters and the entire manuscript. I thank Carolyn Brown, Natalie Byfield, Venus Green, Wanda Hendricks, and Donna Murch for their kind and careful critical reading of the many chapters that they read out of the context of the entire manuscript. It was always a pleasure to get their feedback, and they even made it fun. Many thanks also to Carol Faulkner, Alison Parker, and Elizabeth Payne for their editing of the early renditions of parts of this manuscript. They helped me streamline my thoughts and clarify my arguments. I owe a debt of gratitude to Annelise Orleck, who read the entire manuscript for the Press and offered an extremely important critique. Among other things, she reminded me of the importance of brevity and why the book needed an introduction, which it did not originally have. Thanks also go to Dawn Durante at the University of Illinois Press, who believed in the manuscript from her first reading and to Anne Rogers for her meticulous and superlative editing of my endless references.

Institutional support has been essential. I could not have been at a more supportive institution than Rutgers University. The School of Arts and Sciences and the History Department gave me ample research funds and time off. I would never have been able to continue to publish other works and serve my undergraduate and graduate students had Rutgers not been so supportive. On more than one occasion I presented papers at the Rutgers Center for Historical Analysis, and the feedback I received was unparalleled. I can say the same for the paper that I presented at the Rutgers Institute for Research on Women. The year I spent at the Woodrow Wilson Center for International Scholars was equally fruitful. I am also indebted to the support received from the John Simon Guggenheim Foundation.

Lastly, I want to thank my daughters, Maya Pascual and Asha Reynolds, for their love, companionship, and support. A writer herself, Maya put aside her creative talents to do some of the tedious work that this manuscript demanded. Besides that, she helped with other projects, and in so doing gave me time to spend on this book. Once she had an assignment, she never failed to deliver the most amazing product. Asha's steadfast presence at events that honored me and my contribution to the profession was and is so valued. I thank her so profusely for driving and flying across the country to be by my side as I accepted various honors. I want her to know how deeply I appreciated her presence.

This book is dedicated to my late older brother, Carl Otis Gray Jr. His friends called him Carl, but in our house he went by Otis to distinguish him from our father. My brother was unabashedly gay, and he died of AIDS in 1993. Writing this book about the 1990s deepened my understanding of, and love for, him and his life, which ended way too soon. Long before I had any thoughts about writing books, he dreamed of being a writer. *He* was the writer in our family, and, as a card-carrying member of Mensa, he was also the family genius. I so wish he were alive today. I imagine us sharing and debating (no, arguing about) everything. It would have been great.

Introduction

Searching for Identity

In the late fall of 1998 I traveled to Michigan State University to take part in a conference commemorating the first anniversary of the Million Woman March. It was organized by Darlene Clark Hine and as a preview to that event she sent presenters a packet of sources that she had compiled as a tribute to the organizers of the march. In her opening note to readers, Hine said that the compilation was offered as an antidote to the tendency to "obscure, ignore, diminish, and silence Black Women." She ended the note the same way she opened it: "Not this time!"

I marveled at the sources in the packet. I was especially intrigued by the personal stories that detailed why women went or did not go, what they sacrificed to be in Philadelphia for a day, what they expected to find, how they expected to feel, and what dreams were realized or deferred on march day. Having worked in the archive and written about the absence of black women and their silenced voices, I was actually surprised that the articles were so rich in testimonials, for black women, tutored by years of slander, are usually reluctant revealers of their inner feelings.

As I read these sources I realized how important the Million Man March of 1995 was to so many of the women marchers who compared themselves, and their needs and goals, to the men who had gathered two years earlier. I felt that I could deepen my understanding of these women if I looked at articles on the earlier march. Lo and behold, some of the Million Man marchers referenced the Promise Keepers, and black gays compared the Million Man March to gay gatherings. Before I knew it, I was looking at sources on all of the mass gatherings of the 1990s and the first year of the new millennium. Each one led me to another.

This is how *Lost in the USA* got started and how I came to cover the Promise Keeper gatherings and the Stand in the Gap March of 1997, the 1993 March on Washington for Lesbian, Gay and Bi Equal Rights and Liberation, the 1995 Million Man March, the 1997 Million Woman March, the Millennium March, and the Million Mom March of 2000. As I read the sources the marches generated, I realized how little anyone knew about the masses of people who assembled at these outdoor gatherings, and how important it was that none of the attendees' realties be obscured, ignored, diminished, or silenced.

But this is not just a book about the identities of turn-of-the-century marchers. Though it began as a way to discern and define the identities of those who marched, the deeper I got into the sources, the clearer the common thread became. All of the marchers were uncertain of who they were and nonplussed by an America that had changed so much as to be unrecognizable and uncomfortable. I realized that Americans were marching as much *for* identity as they were to *reify* their identities. This book, then, argues that beneath the surface of the prosperity and peace that marked the 1990s, Americans were struggling to adjust and adapt to the forces of postmodernity—immigration, multiculturalism, feminism, globalization, deindustrialization, and the revolution in information technology—that were radically changing the way they understood themselves and each other. The marches/gatherings were a symptom of that struggle, and to examine them is to witness the changing definition of freedom and the messy business of remaking American citizenship.

This book argues that Americans were at a crossroads. They were between the twentieth and the twenty-first centuries; between modernity and postmodernity; and between—or, more properly, amid—identities. Nothing was fixed, much was uncertain. Historian Daniel T. Rodgers has described the era as "the age of fracture," and scholar Todd Gitlin has written about it as an era characterized by "the twilight of common dreams." Both analyze the rise of the individual's concern with their identity at the expense of a larger American identity. This book takes as a given the postmodern condition that turned the average American's world upside down, and focuses on how Americans tried to adjust.[1] It explains how Americans took something that was familiar—marches and gatherings—and used them as much to try to restore and reconstitute their modern selves as to merge and reconcile their modern and postmodern selves. What marchers tell us about why they marched or did not march, who they wanted to march with and why, and what they thought their effort would accomplish is powerfully revelatory about sexuality, race, class, and gender relations. Marchers' testimonies also tell us a lot about how different communities used marches. In short, the marches tell us a lot about America and how Americans were personally redefining the meaning of liberty and citizenship at the turn of the twenty-first century.

Lost in the USA is, therefore, not about march leaders or the politics of the marches; that can be found elsewhere, as can what the marches say about left- or right-wing politics. *Lost in the USA* looks beneath the aerial photographs of the marches—those shots that only show the marchers' surface identities—and examines *why* millions of Americans spent a lot of money and time to go to open-air gatherings where they stood with others to exclaim their profound understanding of who they *thought* they were. It demonstrates how unstable marchers' identities really were and how that instability affected individuals as well as the groups they were part of. In other words, this exploration demonstrates how the marches served individuals as both balm and irritant: a balm in the sense that they helped participants adjust to postmodern realities by providing a safe place to express anxieties, but an irritant in the sense that what happened at the marches sometimes reiterated the very problems marchers were trying to escape or rectify.

Lost in the USA is a bottom-up examination that unmasks not only individual angst but also group tensions. In doing so it privileges the marchers' voices and quotes them at length as a way to describe the cultural changes afoot in America at the turn of the twenty-first century. It takes up the subject of masculinity by examining, in both contemporary and historical perspective, the different ways that the Promise Keepers, the Million Man marchers, and gay men approached the issues of masculinity. It probes the ways these men handled issues of race, faith, and sexuality. Similarly, it offers an analysis of the ways that different groups of women approached femininity, feminism, motherhood, and sexuality, and examines their historical and contemporary ability to work across race and class, gender and sexuality. It explores how African Americans navigated the new terrain of post-blackness, and how lesbians, gays, bisexuals, and transgenders negotiated their struggles with inclusion. As such, *Lost in the USA* reveals how intersectionality functions in the lives of local people and how it works and affects relationships and coalitions.

To access the voices of everyday people, people who were largely inaccessible to scholars before the Internet made it possible to access almost everything written on every march, I read thousands of articles, editorials, and letters in newspapers across the nation and culled them for the participant's opinions, feelings, and ideas. Little did I know that I was embarking on what would subsequently be called a *digital humanities project*. When gaps appeared in what I could access on the Internet, I traveled to archives that held newspapers and articles in private papers. Very slowly, the story, or, more properly, stories, unfolded—stories about unhappiness, unsettledness, community, and individual search for change and fulfillment. In *Lost in the USA*, these stories are presented and analyzed in conjunction with the research of scholars, especially historians, who study American culture and society, women, gender, sexuality, and race.

Despite the richness and wealth of sources, as with any research project, the archive still presented problems. The sheer abundance of material forced me to impose boundaries; hence, *Lost in the USA* covers only about ten years. It begins with the first gathering of the Promise Keepers in 1991 and ends on Mother's Day in 2000. Although mass marches and gatherings continued into the first and second decade of the new millennium, because I could not give these marches—the sources of which expanded exponentially with the explosion of social media—the same intense examination as those examined here, I make only casual observations about the latter marches in the epilogue. I am satisfied, though, that the attention given to the last decade of the twentieth century has a logic all of its own. Sandwiched in between the end of the cold war and 9/11, the prosperous, relatively peaceful '90s was a period of national and individual introspection. Like the 1950s, however, these years of outward calm masked deep dilemmas that time would subsequently reveal. *Lost in the USA* examines what I believe is a unique period in American history.

Also, as expansive as the archive is, it is weighted, as so many things are, toward heterosexual men's activities. Although this book originated with the Million Woman March, that march was hardly covered by the press and has the least written about it. Similarly, the 1993 March on Washington for Lesbian, Gay and Bi Equal Rights and Liberation was not well covered, and quite often those who wrote about the Million Mom March were more interested in the National Rifle Association than the Million Moms. In contrast, journalists, scholars, and other commentators published volumes on the Promise Keepers and the Million Man March. Hopefully, my skills as a historian, developed in the trenches of black women's history, where silence and absence is itself a source, have helped balance out the imbalance of the archive.

A warning, however, is in order. *Lost in the USA* has an oxymoronic quality about it. It highlights groups but is really about individuals, and identifies multiple identities as the cornerstone of group representation and postmodernity. One will read here about "black America" even while being asked to understand that "black America" is not a solid entity. Though I lump lgbts (lesbian, gay, bisexual, and transgender) together, I use this abbreviation, like the phrase *black America*, as much as a way to simplify the writing as to have a point of departure for the disaggregation done here.[2] Another aspect of this oxymoronism is the use of the term *postmodernity* itself—a totalizing term for the fragmentation that characterized the era.

Yet, the central point of this book should be clear. It is that identities were in flux during the postmodern 1990s, and the mass gatherings of the decade were therapeutic places where people did not just express their identity but where they sought new identities as well. People went to the marches and gatherings because they felt lost and were seeking a more settled place in the country they called home. Some found what they were looking for; others did not.

CHAPTER 1

A New-Age Search for Order

O n May 14, 2000, hundreds of thousands of parents, most of them mothers, gathered on the Washington Mall to express their discontent. They were there to protest the deaths of so many Americans by gun violence, but their complaints spoke to more than that. "There has been an erosion of ethics in this country," said supporter Jeanine Gould-Kostka, of Rockville, Maryland.[1] Like so many others who had traveled to the Washington Mall in the decade leading up to 2000, Gould-Kostka felt the nation had lost direction and its sense of purpose. She would not have disagreed with William McCartney, founder of the Promise Keepers, the organization that brought hundreds of thousands to the Washington Mall in 1997. He believed that "America is suffering from a severe shortage of integrity."[2] Nor would Gould-Kostka have differed with Lois Frankel, a Florida state representative and founding member of the state's Commission on Responsible Fatherhood. When she discussed ways to rescue children from the chaos of family breakup, she proclaimed that "it's time to change the culture."[3] Twenty-year-old Andrew Clawson, an African American supporter of the 1995 Million Man March, looked at the gang violence in his community and the often uneasy interracial environment of his workplace. Echoing the sentiment expressed by Gould-Kostka, McCartney, and Frankel, Clawson concluded, "There's a lot of healing that needs to go on in this world."[4]

These expressions of dissatisfaction belie the notion of the 1990s as the decade of the "golden age" in American history.[5] Despite the economic boom that left individuals and the government wealthier than ever; despite record-low unemployment rates, the expansion of homeownership, and the democratization of computer use and Internet access; despite a decade that found no American troops extensively deployed in overseas warfare, Americans in the 1990s expressed the same kind of malaise that President Carter talked about in his classic 1979 speech, when there were comparatively few positive indicators. Americans were just four years past ignominious defeat in Vietnam and five years past the shame of Watergate. Stagflation, brought about in large measure by deindustrialization and dependence on foreign oil, defined the '70s. Americans were less hopeful than ever and the economic woes fostered what Carter called "a crisis in confidence," a crisis that seemed to prevail even through the "wild nineties." Indeed, at the turn of the millennium, the National Opinion Research Center at the University of Chicago reported that only 32 percent of Americans said they were very happy.[6]

Why so few? Why the continued malaise at the end of one of the most prosperous and peaceful periods in American history? Although some might point to the gap that grew between the rich and the poor during the nineties, the increased indebtedness of the average American, the growth of the prison-industrial complex, the increased cost of health care, and the burdens imposed by an intrusive technology, experts on happiness also emphasize psychological and emotional factors. They argue that once people obtain basic financial security, peace and tranquility of mind play a more important role in people's sense of well-being than material possessions and money.[7] Nobel Prize–winning economist Robert Fogel stressed this as well. As he looked back over American history, he identified the quest for "self-realization, the desire to find a deeper meaning in life," as one of the defining prerequisites to happiness in the new millennium.[8]

This is the point of departure for this book. Using thousands of personal testimonies gathered mostly from the nation's newspapers, it looks at what ordinary Americans tell us about why they traveled to Washington, DC, or to a neighborhood sympathy march. It echoes the findings that emotional issues bothered average Americans. It also underscores the idea that people seek happiness and are most happy when they are with people perceived to be like themselves.[9] Taken in conjunction with scholarly research put forth by humanists and social scientists, this "bottom-up" look at Americans shows that people marched and gathered not so much to make political statements or demands on the government—although many such statements and demands were articulated—but more so to find a better way to be in the world, a world that was rapidly changing. Subsequent chapters take a close look at what these marches tell us about politics, race, class, gender, sexuality, religion, and faith, but this first chapter establishes what people felt about their lives and why they were searching for a new order at the end of what many call the American Century.[10] It reveals a people who felt lost in their own country and who were in search of renewal and happiness. It shows that many Americans felt they had lost control over their personal and the nation's destiny and that they wanted to assert more authority over both.

Loneliness, Alienation, Anger

Obviously, not everyone experienced the '90s the same way. Race, gender, class, sexuality, and religion positioned everyone differently. Hence, there were several mass marches and gatherings, each ostensibly representing a different group and a different cause. Black men; white men; black women; mothers of all races; lesbian, gay, bisexual, and transgender (lgbt) men and women; black and white Christian men—all had different reasons for marching. These so-called identity marches were decried for this very reason. Rather than bringing Americans together, they were seen as divisive. They seemed to reify America's differences. They were, it was said, part of the problem and not part of the solution. And yet, Americans marched on Washington to find solutions to the problem of their unhappiness with the people they felt most comfortable and happy with. They marched to achieve or restore their happiness.

They did it with people who seemed to share the same outlook because these people offered safety and companionship in a culture increasingly judged to be alien. Sandra Rogers, a Boston participant in the Million Woman March, expressed what so many others felt about their lives when she said, "We have lost track of one another. . . . We have been too busy trying to pay the phone bill, the light bill, and the gas bill." About women she said, "We have been too busy looking for a man if we don't have a man, and if we have one, too busy trying to keep him." Plaintively she asked, "When do we have time to fellowship with one another?"[11] Almost never, was the answer that came from the Reverend Donna Schaper of the United Church of Christ. Writing in support of the Promise Keepers, she complained about the culture. "Whenever my husband and I argue that one is doing less than the other, we try to remember that we are both giving 100 percent. Even 100 percent each is not enough to hold down two jobs and rear three children. We are already doing too much and even that is not enough." She concluded, "Something is wrong somewhere."[12] What made things right for one black man was standing in a stadium bonding with Promise Keepers, men he perceived to be like himself. "Brother, you haven't lived until you've sung 'Amazing Grace' with a stadium full of men."[13]

As different as the marchers were, as differently positioned in society as they were, they nevertheless felt similarly alone and isolated, and this feeling propelled them to find others to be with. Tammy Baldwin, an openly gay congresswoman from Madison, Wisconsin, told those gathered for the 2000 Millennium March why she marched on Washington in a gay pride march in 1987 and then again at the 1993 March on Washington for Lesbian, Gay and Bi Equal Rights and Liberation. She marched, she said, "to replace my fear with courage, my isolation with belonging, my anger with hope." After a young gay man in northern Wisconsin called her to express his isolation, she decided to keep on marching so that he could likewise overcome his feelings and conquer his fears.[14] For thirty-three-year-old Louie Cortez of San Antonio, Texas, the 2000 Millennium March was also about overcoming isolation. "We wanted to build a sense of brotherhood," he claimed. Like it was for fellow Texans Caryl Cunningham, Luis Quintero, and Andrew Ornes, the Millennium March was a godsend for Cortez because it meant that for one day he would be in the majority and would be able to express his political views in an arena that was not closed to people like himself.[15]

Others marched for similar reasons. Million Man marcher Darryl Larkin, a UPS delivery man from Newark, marched because he said black men, "the most despised people in this country, . . . have to address our hurts and our wants."[16] Similarly, a thirty-eight-year-old white Wisconsin male planned to attend the 1997 Promise Keeper (PK) gathering in Dallas because it gave him a chance "to talk to guys about our deepest feelings and needs and fears." In this, he confirmed what Hal Jensen, the head of the Arizona Promise Keepers, testified to. "Men are lonely," he said. The Promise Keepers "provides men with a masculine context where they can go and share their heart and get some encouragement on struggles they are facing such as marriage or raising children."[17]

If isolation, racism, and the pressures of relationships and parenting gave way to anxiety and emptiness for some, for others it was the perception of community breakdown. This was especially the case with African Americans. "We're in crisis, and we've got to do something," said the Urban Institute's senior research associate Richard Majors as he spoke about the imprisonment of so many black men and the need for responsible parents.[18] According to Pulitzer Prize–winning journalist Eugene Robinson, the end of the twentieth century and the beginning of the twenty-first ushered in "disintegration."[19] The expansion of the black middle class, the increased isolation of the black poor and the incarcerated, and the infusion of biracials and, after 1965, of black immigrants transformed African American culture and left many black people feeling unmoored. Philadelphian Phile Chionesu, one of the local organizers of the Million Woman March, referred to this when she noted the "confusion and disharmony" that black people, especially black women, experienced with each other.[20] The Reverend Willie Barrow, a Chicago civil rights activist, alluded to it as well when, from the podium during the march, she cautioned marchers not to let anyone "tell you we are divided." As she saw things, "We are not as divided as we are disconnected."[21] Jacci Davis of Dallas used the word *disillusioned* to describe black women who were "sick and tired of the way things are."[22] Similarly, John P. Stewart, a navy budget analyst from southeast Washington, DC, supported the Million Man March for reasons having to do with connectedness. He planned to bring his five sons, fourteen grandsons, and his great-grandchildren to the Million Man March as a way to reinstate a sense of community. "We have lost something as a people," he claimed, "We need to achieve this oneness."[23] The Reverend Curtis Jones of Baltimore agreed. Speaking of the rather amorphous objectives of the Million Man March he said, "I know there's no real agenda for the march, no platform and no clearly defined plan for the future, but there is a real need for us to come and stand together in each other's presence. Hopefully, something will come of it."[24]

Promise Keepers were likewise concerned about the breakdown of community. All of their gatherings, especially their 1997 Stand in the Gap March on the Washington Mall, were a direct response to the fourth promise, to build "strong marriages and families"; the sixth promise, to "reach beyond racial and denominational barriers"; and the seventh promise, "to influence his world."[25] The 1997 march's reference to God's indictment of Jerusalem for its devolution into moral decay and God's search for someone to "stand in the gap" to save it from God's destruction made clear the PK concern over societal dissolution.[26] PK men believed they had to "stand in the gap" to save their families, communities, and nation. "There's no unity anymore," was a persistent complaint of Promise Keepers who saw disunity as a by-product of the perceived breakdown of the family, an excess of individualism, and racial disharmony.[27] Like Million Man and Million Woman marchers, Promise Keepers put more stock in personal responsibility than in the ability of institutions, including the government, to cure what ailed America. Standing together signaled progress to them. Grover McCoy, an African American member of Seattle's First AME Church and a retired chief of facilities painting for Metro Transit, planned to go to the 1996 Seattle PK meeting for this reason. "If we can do this among ourselves, we can pass it on to our children, grandchildren and our neighbors—how to get along and embrace each other."[28] Saint Louis commentator Tim Pettus felt likewise: "We have more crime, more fatherless children, more separation, more bitterness, and more anger." Government programs, said Pettus, had not solved the nation's problems. "Promise Keepers," he claimed, "is doing the only thing that will truly be effective in unifying our land. It is transforming the hearts of men."[29]

Million Mom marchers against gun violence were similarly concerned with societal decay. In 2000, as in most years of the 1990s, America had the highest rate of gun violence in the developed world. In 1998, the Centers for Disease Control reported that ten children and adolescents a day were killed by firearms. Though down from a high of sixteen deaths a day in 1994, it was, for the concerned, ten too many.[30] "Columbine was the last straw," said supporter Bethany Karn, speaking of the 1999 Colorado tragedy in which two white suburban high school males used semiautomatic weapons to injure many and kill twelve students and a teacher. Like Karn, Million Mom marchers pronounced it "an egregious stain on the American character."[31] In this pre-9/11 era, when security for most Americans was associated more with internal domestic violence than foreign terrorist attacks, gun violence presaged national failure and shame. To most it signified cultural breakdown. "It's not just about changing gun laws," said Maggie Escobedo Steele of California, "it's about changing society."[32]

Like Promise Keepers, Million Moms also wanted to bridge the racial and class gap in America. Many white suburban moms felt that they had for too long labored under the false consciousness that their neighborhoods made them safe. Whereas incidents like the 1999 shooting in Grenada Hills, California, where a gunman opened fire on preschoolers, elicited empathy for inner-city mothers whose children were vulnerable to random drive-by shootings, the many Columbine-like incidents sensitized them to the problems of America's troubled youth. Said Southern Californian Kathy Friedman to black urban mothers, "You buried oh, so many babies from gun violence, while too many of us did nothing. We were safely detached as we watched the violent scenes unfold on television."[33] Said Jeanine Smolarek of western Pennsylvania, "We have been very happy in our little suburban homes, and now it's come knocking on our doors."[34] Unlike the Promise Keepers or the Million Man and Woman marchers, Million Moms called on the government to act to keep Americans safe. "We have enough to worry about already. . . . We should not have to be afraid our children will be killed by guns,"[35] they said as they called for gun control and gun-safety laws.[36] As we will see in a later chapter, this sentiment was held by those opposed to gun control as well. Both Million Mom marchers and their opponents looked at the violence in America's inner cities and suburbs and indicted "the culture." This indictment only added to end-of-century angst and was one reason for the marches and vigils that sprang up around the nation. For the friends and relatives of gun-violence victims, the Million Mom March and local gun-control vigils offered comfort. Said Los Angeles police chief Bernard Parks, an African American whose granddaughter was shot just shy of her twenty-first birthday, "There's strength . . . when you realize that there are lots of other people suffering."[37]

Americans who despaired over gun violence were similarly disheartened by the change in the nature of the family. Many, if not most, drew a connection between the two. Indeed, Americans entered the new millennium with a family structure that differed substantially from that which existed at mid-century. Divorce rates were up, as were single-parent households. There were blended households of divorced and remarried adults, unmarried partners, new single-sexed households, and an increased number of interracial marriages as well. While some marchers called for a return of the "traditional" two-parent household, most stressed the need to adapt to the new order.[38] In general, Promise Keepers and Million Man and Woman marchers called for a return of the two-parent family with an understanding that the new socioeconomic order called for different gender roles; lgbt marchers insisted that same-sex marriages brought stability to communities and security to children who might otherwise be lost in orphanages or the foster-care system; and Million Moms thought that less violence would make life safer and easier for everyone.

Even though different marchers focused on different aspects of the American family and proposed solutions for different communities and neighborhoods, all thought less individualism and more familial and communal consciousness would make for less troubled youth, a more stable environment, and happier citizens. Pittsburgh bus driver Marion Reynoso, for example, went to the Million Woman March because she thought mothers could do a better job nurturing and rearing children. "The hand has come off the cradle, and the cradle is being rocked by itself," she said. "We have to go back and establish that hand on the cradle again."[39] *Pittsburgh Post-Gazette* writer Monica Haynes, a supporter of the Million Mom March, argued that Million Moms had to "stand in the gap for those children whose parents are not equipped to give them the moral foundation, time, attention and love that every child needs and deserves." She cautioned Americans not to assume that rich kids had no problems or that poor children were beyond help. Her solution to some of the nation's problems was to "love them all, care about them all, do for them all."[40] Although the concerns of gay families were enmeshed with the very complicated and contested issues of same-sex marriage, Dolores Lesnick, president of the San Diego chapter of Parents, Families and Friends of Lesbians and Gays, argued that same-sex families were like all families in that they comprised the basic unit of society and gave its members the love, understanding, and commitment necessary to survive. "We march," she said, "to show that we want what every parent wants for his or her child—to grow, be educated, work, play and pray in safety."[41] The men of the Promise Keepers and the Million Man March also recommitted themselves to the family as a way to improve themselves, their communities, and their children. Promise Keeper Stu Weber looked at the numbers of American children who were without fathers, 40 percent by his count, and proclaimed it a "national crisis." Men, he insisted, had to become closer to their own children and reach out to those without fathers.[42] Weber was not very different from a Million Man marcher who was adamant as he declared that "we dammed well had better get on the stick and take care of our kids. . . . They're all we have left. . . . By any means necessary, we will make our boys become good fathers to their children."[43]

In sum, the voices that emerged from the 1990s marches reveal much about what many were feeling during this decade. Americans gathered to overcome loneliness and isolation, to feel part of a majority, if only for a day. Ironically, although they searched for belonging with people who appeared to be like themselves, marchers from different walks of life felt similarly about what ailed them and the country. They did not single out or even name deindustrialization, globalization, information or scientific technology, or multiculturalism—the relatively invisible forces of postmodernity that dictated the course of their lives. Instead they dealt with that which was close: their busy schedules, their separation from each other, the changes in the family and community, the violence that forever altered their lives. They dealt with their disconnectedness by literally connecting with people; by joining hands and singing and crying and commiserating with them. In this way they tried to make sense out of what had, for them, come to be a senseless world. While some called on the government to fulfill what they thought were its obligations, many took the neoliberal approach of emphasizing personal responsibility as a way to exercise some control over distant impersonal forces. All refused to externalize societal problems. They would not hand them over entirely to a religious or government institution or their representatives. They went to a march. They vowed to change themselves and their families and communities in order that they might be happier and more fulfilled. Some might judge this naive or shortsighted, a limited or conservative response to problems that demanded grander solutions. Others would argue that the marchers were grasping at anything that would keep alive the hope of the American promise of the good life premised on freedom, democracy, and comfort, what Lauren Berlant calls "cruel optimism."[44] Still others would argue that marchers had somehow been manipulated into thinking that their problems had no political solutions or that they were the product of an individual's poor choices.[45] However this was processed by individual Americans, attending a march and gathering with others was evidence of the marchers' personal revolt against their new environment. If not a display of actual internal transformation, marching and gathering demonstrated a desire for a new internal self and a new future. Even those who demanded legislation—the Million Mom and lgbt marchers—sought to cope with their personal grief, fear, and loneliness by building community and changing themselves.

Another "Search for Order"

It is helpful to remember that this was not the first time that Americans had been confronted with monumental changes that seemed to gobble up everything that was familiar and comfortable. In fact, it is instructive to think of these marches in the same way that many historians have seen other such sea-change periods. In short, we learn much when we put 1990s marchers in historical perspective and see them as part of America's age-old search for order.

In fact, over forty years ago, historian Robert Wiebe characterized the turn-of-the-twentieth-century movement that has come to be known as Progressivism as a "search for order." In his now classic opus, Wiebe describes how Americans responded to the expansion of the market economy and the resultant breakup of small insular communities. As railroads facilitated migration to ever-expanding, overcrowded cities; as commercial agriculturalists replaced small farmers; and as finance capitalists like J. P. Morgan and corporate giants like John D. Rockefeller made a mockery of Horatio Alger–like individual enterprise, the world most Americans knew fell apart. During this time of explosive urbanization, industrialization, and incorporation, when things foreign, be they people or methods of distribution, changed people's perceptions of who they were, Americans searched for "peace and unity in Protestantism." According to Wiebe, "countless citizens in towns and cities across the land sensed that something fundamental was happening to their lives, something they had not willed and did not want, and they responded by striking out at whatever enemies their views of the world allowed them to see." They fought, he says, "to preserve the society that had given their lives meaning." While some, especially white Southerners, railed against and resisted the new racial order that made their lives unrecognizable, others, particularly the new eastern and midwestern middle class, adapted. They professionalized and bureaucratized everything. They made governments more efficient and responsive; they regulated housing, factories, and railroads. They tried to impose a scientific rationality on everything, from family life to banking to foreign policy. They believed that if they could control the impersonal forces of modernity, they "would bring opportunity, progress, order and community."[46]

But for many, this imposed order only intensified the problem. Modernity itself had made people's lives unreal.[47] Already the clock, and not the rising and setting of the sun or seasonal change, determined the course of one's life. Already the would-be small entrepreneur had surrendered his independence and taken a middle-management corporate job. By the middle of the nineteenth century, the fear of hell and God's wrath, and the forgiveness of sin as embodied in Christ, had ceased being the compass that guided people's lives. Rather, the mantra of the new era was self-control. The centerpiece of Victorianism, the precepts of self-control and individual will replaced the idea of God's grace as the key to personal and national progress. As described by historian T. J. Jackson Lears, this secularization of values had the most profound effect upon late nineteenth-century Americans: "They sensed that familiar frameworks of meaning were evaporating; they felt doomed to spiritual homelessness." As Wiebe's account of the period demonstrates, many Americans responded to this "homelessness" by trying to impose order on the chaos that was their new environment. But, according to Lears, many turn-of-the-century Americans responded differently. In a variety of ways they tried to retrieve what they perceived they had lost—their personal autonomy, their independence, their personal moral responsibility. Some tried to turn back the clock and preached "regeneration through preindustrial craftsmanship and a pastoral 'simple life,' or posed the violent lives of medieval warriors as a refreshing contrast to the blandness of modern comfort." Others tried to escape "the emotional constraints of bourgeois life" and their banal spiritual existence by "exploring the joys and terrors of medieval or Oriental religious belief." Antimodernist responses, argues Lears, were varied, but all were concerned with a "preoccupation with recovering intense experience." "In a secularizing culture, where larger frameworks of meaning were fading, the antimodern quest for 'real life' often focused on the self alone." Rather than reverse or slow down modernity, the focus on the self, argues Lears, "helped ease the transition to secular and corporate modes of modern culture."[48]

This history is instructive. First, we should see the 1990s as part of an era like that just described, a time when Americans were faced with such profound societal disruptions that they were forced to do something to try to reconcile their desires and expectations with their new reality, or, as put by historian William McLoughlin, "overcome jarring disjunctions between norms and experience, old beliefs and new realities, dying patterns and emerging patterns of behavior."[49] And, second, we should put the 1990s marchers into McLoughlin's context. We should see them as people whose world had been turned upside down and who needed to make sense of their new environment and restructure themselves to accommodate the new culture in order to make life more satisfying.[50]

The New American Reality

Children born in the 1990s would experience a totally different America than their parents or grandparents, who between them had lived through the rights movements of the 1950s, '60s, and '70s; the technological and scientific innovations that altered the individual's relationship to human life, time, and space; the immigration of new people, languages, and customs; the HIV/AIDS epidemic that by the 1990s had claimed over 40,000 lives; and the transformation of the economy that so changed the nature of work that gender roles and familial relationships were transformed. Some scholars call this phenomenon *postmodernism* and analyze it in much the same way they analyze modernism, the period discussed in the previous section.

As citizens, Americans were faced with high taxes and unemployment, low productivity and declining wages, and inflation caused partly by high energy prices. In the '70s and '80s, the rise in OPEC oil prices hit Americans hard. While trying to adjust to a service-oriented economy that saw manufacturing jobs migrate to countries where labor costs were lower, Americans also had to digest the reality of a labor force expanded by immigrants whose numbers increased from 4 percent in 1970 to 11 percent by 2000. As native-born Americans struggled to find a place in the new economy and understand the new people who, with the Immigration Act of 1965, came mostly from Latin America and Asia, they hardly found much solace in the lower cost of consumer goods purchased from foreign producers because the lower price tags had been traded for their depressed wages and high unemployment.

The nation's shift from a producer to a consumer or service economy and the export of jobs overseas made for fundamental changes in American society and culture, many of which were well under way before the seismic shift in the economy. For example, in the 1940s and '50s, racial, ethnic, and sexual minorities and women had begun to challenge laws and customs that put them in the lower echelons of the social and economic hierarchy. In the 1950s, '60s, and '70s, they ratcheted up their quest for equal rights. African Americans led the way with a grassroots movement that ended legal segregation, opened voting booths and the workplace, and expanded their opportunities for education and suburbanization. Hispanic and Native Americans, like blacks, fought against discrimination, police brutality, debilitating working conditions, and, in the case of Native Americans, the seizure by the American government of reservation lands. Women who participated in the feminist movement amplified the rights crusades by insisting on equality in every aspect of their public and private lives—from equal pay for equal work to the equal division of household labor that included washing dishes and taking care of children to sexual and reproductive freedom. Lesbians, gays, bisexuals, and transgenders insisted on living full uncloseted lives, challenged traditional ideas about gender roles and identification, and organized for medical research to find treatments and a cure for HIV/AIDS. All these groups insisted on learning their particular history, celebrating it, and inserting it into mainstream kindergarten-through-college curricula. When combined with the new languages and customs brought to America by immigrants who, unlike their predecessors, resisted acculturation in favor of celebrating their native culture, traditional ways of thinking and identifying were destabilized and became subject to reformulation.

For many Americans, change was not really an option. The manufacturing jobs that had made it possible for a single male wage earner with limited education to earn enough money to support a wife and children were disappearing. In the 1990s, the effects of the global nature of the economy were fully visible. As blue- and white-collar jobs were exported overseas and corporations downsized to be more competitive, layoffs in all sectors were common and job security disappeared. As industries computerized, jobs were lost or transformed and workers had to reskill. The decreased influence of labor unions made many workers all the more insecure. Increasingly, women entered the labor market to compensate for the lost earnings of men. Though the feminist movement had supplied an ideological basis for women's work outside the home by postulating all of the benefits that accrued to economically independent women, it was economic hardship that forced the majority to work to keep their families afloat.

Men, women, and families felt the pressure of the new economy and the social order that flowed from it. African Americans suffered disproportionately because racism made their lives more precarious than whites, many of whom resented having to compete with this newly empowered group. But whites suffered also. Young white families earned less in 1986 than comparable families in 1979, and they had little prospects for homeownership, a principal signifier of middle-class status. The thirteen-year period between 1973 and 1986 that saw real earnings for young men between the ages of twenty and twenty-four drop by 26 percent also saw the price of a mortgage for a medium-priced home rise to about 44 percent of an average male's monthly earnings. Alone, most men, especially racial and ethnic minorities, had a hard time purchasing and maintaining a home. On average, women fared the worst. Most did not enter the labor force as professionals, well-paid or not. Rather, they were fast becoming the nation's postindustrial proletariat, and poverty was increasingly feminized. As white women worked at jobs that made their unpaid homemaking more burdensome, many joined the majority of African American women who, after centuries of being stuck at the bottom of the labor ladder, still questioned the benefits of female labor force participation.[51]

The new economy played havoc with American culture, especially family culture. It demanded that men and women change their ideas about masculinity and femininity, about motherhood and fatherhood, and about the purpose and value of the "traditional" two-parent family. Once held together by the family wage that made women dependent on men's wages, men were the first to detether themselves from the economic burdens of their wives and children, followed by women who preferred singleness and single parenthood to unsatisfying and sometimes abusive relationships. Although feminism and women's self-sufficiency made it possible to imagine a truly democratic marriage in which household duties, child rearing, and emotional sharing became the responsibility of both parents, the reality was that it was hard to change the entrenched patriarchal patterns that by custom and institutional structure placed emotionally distant men at the head of the family. As divorce and rates of singleness rose, the end-of-the-century "traditional" two-parent heterosexual family became more unsettled and insecure. Households containing married couples with young children were fast becoming a minority. The blended household of divorced and remarried adults, single-mother households, and single-sexed households were becoming prominent. As one scholar put it, the family was a "contested domain," and the "postmodern family condition of diversity, flux, and instability" was a fact of end-of-century life.[52]

As their world spun out of their control, many Americans searched for ways to stop the tailspin. Many became less inclined to help the less fortunate and more sympathetic to politicians like Republican Ronald Reagan, who promised to lower taxes and cut back on the welfare state that was often scapegoated as the cause of all the economic woes. Out of fear of losing their jobs, many deserted their unions, sided with management, and voted for conservative representation. Fearful of competition from immigrants, many opposed bilingual education programs and supported English-only and other anti-immigrant propositions. Many sought religious guidance through the new cultural maze and took their cues from the church rather than government. In general, most Americans looked askance at the government. Voting reached all-time lows in the 1980s and '90s, and even the Democratic party, who since Roosevelt's New Deal had been known for its confidence in the government to bring about social change, pulled back from its support of social-welfare programs and government regulation of business. With Bill Clinton at the helm, it retreated to fiscal conservatism. While some railed against their new competition and supported measures that kept women tied to the home, minorities tied to low-wage labor, and sexual minorities closeted, others just increased the numbers of hours they worked per day, decreased the amount of time they took off, and hoped that they could make ends meet and keep pace with the new order of things.[53]

These changes in American life and culture were catalysts for the mass gatherings of the 1990s. Critics bemoaned these gatherings as identity marches because they seemed to emphasize the differences that separated Americans rather than the commonalities that brought them together.[54] Indeed, Americans did gather in distinct groups to try to congeal around what they considered the most important part of their identity. But they did so, ironically, not to be divisive but in an attempt to make sense of a world that was increasingly unfamiliar. They gathered with people they perceived to be like themselves because they needed to feel safe as they worked through their new circumstances. They gathered with the hope of finding stability in a world where a new economic order had combined with a series of rights movements to make, among other things, class mobility uncertain, gender roles confusing, and "community," however previously conceived, precarious. Promise Keepers used their maleness and Christianity to anchor themselves in the ever-changing turn-of-the-century environment. Million Man marchers found their moorings in their maleness and blackness and, along with Million Woman marchers, sought shelter in the black community they believed had piloted them through previous troubled times. These groups gathered to explore and pronounce a new understanding of their gendered and raced selves. They did not grumble excessively about the new structure of the economy, nor did they petition the state for help, but rather turned inward and embraced a self-help ethic. With some important exceptions, they were supported by their respective communities and the people close to them. Though lgbts and supporters of the Million Mom March did petition the government to act on their behalf, the journey marchers took to these gatherings was extremely personal and likewise grew out of a perceived new relationship to American society. Often driven by their need to have their subjectivity affirmed by a newly restructured American society, sexual minorities and Million Moms, like the Promise Keepers and Million Man and Woman marchers, gathered as much to express their identity as they did to find it.

Finding Identity:
Personal Responsibility and Inner Change

Although personal responsibility is usually touted by analysts as the neoliberal retreat from social-welfare government programs, 1990s marchers did not look at themselves that way. They just wanted more control over their lives and wanted to be happier. Marching and gathering, in fact, were just one part of a panoply of pushbacks intended to reassert personal autonomy. For example, in the 1980s, work arrangements like flextime (where workers vary their hours or days of work) and telecommuting (where workers perform all or part of a job at home or at a site other than the company premises) were considered disruptive. By the 1990s, however, with surveys showing that employees were wary of eighty-plus-hours-a-week jobs, that many despaired of forty-hour jobs—even those that came with more money—most companies adopted these and other quality-of-life practices as a way to improve employee morale.[55] Americans took other actions to improve the texture of their lives. A 1995 survey by *U.S. News and World Report* stated that during the preceding five years, 48 percent of American adult wage earners had cut back on hours of work, declined promotions, reduced their commitments, lowered material expectations, or moved someplace offering a quieter lifestyle.[56] Behind these actions was a desire for self-realization. Americans, says economist Robert Fogel, needed time to "enjoy the things they have, time to spend with their families, time to figure out what life is all about, and time to discover the spiritual side of life."[57]

Like those at the turn of the twentieth century, late twentieth-century Americans also wanted more intense experiences, and sought out alternative therapies to that end. Surveys show that during the 1990s, the use of herbal medicines, massages, megavitamins, self-help groups, folk remedies, energy healing, and homeopathy increased substantially. By 1997, out-of-pocket expenditures relating to these therapies were conservatively estimated at $27 billion, which was about equal to out-of-pocket expenditures for all physician services. In other words, Americans sought nontraditional solutions to the problem of their unhappiness. Not only did they expand beyond medical doctors but they sought spiritual counselors beyond traditional religious institutions as well. According to historian/psychologist Eugene Taylor, late twentieth-century Americans were protagonists in a "modern psychospiritual revolution." The revolution, says Taylor, "is occurring in the minds and hearts of millions of individual people whose biographies cut across all categories of type and culture. It is a revolution based on the expression of a new breadth and depth to contemporary experience that goes far beyond the ability of traditional institutions to address."[58]

The marches were part of the 1990s "psychospiritual revolution," and this helps explain the anti-institutionalism of so many of the marchers. They believed that their inner growth depended on their personal involvement in change. They believed they had to take individual responsibility for what was missing in their everyday world—something their traditional institutions had not satisfactorily addressed—and this compelled them to go or want to go to a march. Many used the marches to find out "what life is all about" or "to discover the spiritual side of life." They sought individual transformation and they believed it could be found in the group they chose to march with. Because some of the marches had an unmistakable religious quality about them, they bear a striking resemblance to the open-air revival meetings of America's Great Awakenings where leaders outside the marcher's everyday orbit proposed new ideas about new needs and inner change. Even those marchers who sought political change also sought spiritual renewal, renewal they had not found in their traditional religious, political, or social institutions.

Take, for example, the Promise Keepers. Of the marches explored in this study, only PK gatherings were explicitly religious. Founded by William Mc-Cartney, a controversial conservative football coach turned lay clergyman, it brought together Christians of all denominations in very nontraditional religious venues—sport stadiums. They sang, prayed, testified, and listened to sermons about transformation through God's grace.[59] They also renounced their current way of living and sought renewal. Although many PK organizers were ministers and its leadership claimed that they worked not to take men out of churches but in tandem with them to bring men to God, even critics and skeptics traced the origins of the Promise Keepers to the failure of the church to minister to men. Said Meg Riley, a Unitarian Universalist minister who challenged PK conservatism, "This is a real testament of how the mainstream churches have failed men; it's a wake-up call for us."[60] The Promise Keepers, wrote the United States Conference of Catholic Bishops' Committee on Laity, Marriage, Family Life, and Youth, may "be filling a spiritual and pastoral vacuum." As the committee offered strategies on how to get men more involved in the Catholic Church, it also cautioned priests not to outlaw Catholic participation in PK events. PK, it believed, provided "an awakening experience" that the church had to "receive, organize, chan-nel and develop." "Catholic men," it conceded, "may be finding in *Promise*

Keepers something they are not finding in their own church, namely, a viable and attractive ministry to men."[61]

In fact, this is what made the Promise Keepers so attractive to its followers. Not only Catholic men, but also male Protestants of all denominations found in PK a unique place to express and explore their desire for individual reformation, something inseparable from their ideas about manhood and masculinity. The complex gender, race, and class issues embedded in all of the marches are addressed at length in subsequent chapters. However, apropos the "intense experience," the "hunger and thirsting after the deep things of life,"[62] are the testimonials that bear witness to the transformative spiritual content of Promise Keeper events. "I cried my head off," said a forty-five-year-old civil engineer who attended the 1997 Stand in the Gap March. "To see so many men struggling . . . that was just powerful. That's why you see the crying. For the first time in our life, we could be real men of God." "I just felt lifted," said a forty-year-old program manager. "I felt an energy I didn't feel before. . . . This is not about religion; it's about the connection with God." Men are attracted to the Promise Keepers, said another attendee, "for the love that the men show for each other."[63]

Though not explicitly religious, the 1995 Million Man March was for many men similarly transformative. For most of the marchers it did not matter that the event had been organized by Nation of Islam minister Louis Farrakhan, who was associated with anti-Semitism, anti-Christianity, sexism, and homophobia. One would hardly have expected him to have attracted so many marchers to the nation's capital. But it was the message, not the messenger, that was paramount. The message was "atonement" and "reconciliation." Political in only the subtlest way, Farrakhan challenged black men to build black neighborhoods, save black children, and to be responsible, unifying heads of families. He called for inner change: "It is only when we are at one or at peace with ourselves and our Creator that we are fortified with the ability and the capacity to successfully reconcile our differences with each other," said Farrakhan in his "Vision for the Million Man March."[64] As with the Promise Keepers, attendees were not followers but communers. "Farrakhan made the call, but the march belongs to us" was a typical marcher refrain.[65] The mayor of Baltimore, Kurt Schmoke, underscored both the religious and communalist quality of the march. It evoked such church-like feelings in him that when it was his turn to speak, he did what his brother, a minister, often asked his congregation to do—to hold hands and greet one another. He asked them to say to each other, "Brother, my brother, let's get busy." For Schmoke, the march was not about Farrakhan or any of the leaders but about the marchers, their interaction, and their psychic needs: "The most important messages conveyed that day were the ones that they [the marchers] spoke to one another—not the ones they heard from a distant stage."[66]

The messages were varied but in addition to addressing the needs of African Americans—a subject taken up in detail in a later chapter—they spoke to personal renewal, change, and joy. "I just want to be here," said Charlie Crump, a forty-seven-year-old carpenter from Port Chester, New York, who had arrived at 4:30 a.m. "This is the most positive energy I have felt in my entire life. I wouldn't want to be anywhere else today. If I have to stand for 12 to 14 hours, I'm going to be right here."[67] Said twenty-seven-year-old Travis Fowler of Oklahoma, "I've never been in the company of so many men. . . . It gives me a feeling of greater trust."[68] Thirty-five-year-old Kenneth Gaines walked to the march from Philadelphia with seventy other recovering addicts. It took five days to make the 160-mile trip. "This has been a spiritual cleansing," he testified, "I've hurt my women, my children, myself. Now it's time to make amends."[69]

Like the Promise Keepers, Million Man marchers expressed a desire to change things themselves and not rely on institutions to do the work they felt that they should do, work that inner change compelled them to take responsibility for. Whereas Promise Keepers believed that citizens had strayed from what had once made America strong, Million Man marchers saw self-help as a black nationalist tradition that had helped the race survive. Thus, despite the complaints that the "atonement" purpose of the march "blamed the victims" of racism,[70] for many marchers the Million Man March was like an exorcism; it liberated black men, and by extension black people, from dependence. Said Florida accountant Dan Collins, "If we reach down to grab a brother and pull him up, we won't have to look to others."[71] "If one million of us can put up $10, we can do for ourselves what we've been begging others to do for us" was the opinion of Muslim minister Rahim Muhammad of San Diego.[72] Comparing the Million Man March to the 1963 March on Washington, Saidi Enguui, a fifty-three-year-old housing development manager from Newark, New Jersey, summed up this kind of thinking this way: "That day, there were a lot of good white people who helped us during the civil rights movement. Today, it's just us. In some ways, we've matured. We no longer need white people to fight for our freedom. It's up to us."[73]

The Million Woman March mirrored some of the same phenomena as the Promise Keepers and Million Man March. Though not nearly as controversial, Phile Chionesu and Asia Coney, the march organizers, were nontraditional leaders rooted in black Philadelphia. Like PK events and the Million Man March, the Million Woman March had the feel and flavor of a revival, and the official purpose issues of the march—"Repentance, Restoration and Resurrection"—expressed the similar theme of spiritual metamorphosis.[74]

The Million Woman March spoke directly to the issue of black women's unhappiness. In 1997, a Centers for Disease Control (CDC) study found African American women to be the unhappiest people in the country. Their "negative mood" rate was "nearly three times higher than for white males." Even when education was taken into account, it was determined that black women were less happy than white men, white women, and black men (in that order).[75] The CDC was evasive on the reasons for black women's unhappiness, but in his report on the study, journalist Courtland Milloy asked, "Could it be that black women actually are being treated worse than any other group? Has their willingness to shoulder the weight of the race and make whatever sacrifices necessary to save their families taken an unseen emotional toll? Do they, as mothers of children most likely to die before the age of 21, simply experience the world differently?"[76] Political scientists Ange-Marie Hancock and Melissa Harris-Perry would answer yes. Hancock argues that black women suffer from the public perception of black women as welfare queens, "a dominant mother responsible for the moral degeneracy of the United States."[77] Harris-Perry argues that, historically, African American women have been required to be strong and hide weakness behind a façade of strength. "To be true to the race a black woman must not fall into depression, allowing herself to be weak, pitiful, or needy. These are defined as the attributes of white women." According to Harris-Perry, "without her strength a black woman must discover a new standard against which to judge the value of her humanity, not just for herself, but in relation to her family, church, race, and nation."[78]

For many black women, the Million Woman March was a step toward that self-discovery. "This is an awakening march," said Washington, DC, organizer Wessita McKinley. "We hope to renew ourselves spiritually, mentally, physically and financially."[79] Although there is no way to tell whether the marchers knew of the CDC "negative mood" study, many women did address it indirectly by stressing how they marched to become more positive. For example, Jacqueline Walker, a thirty-three-year-old administrative clerk, marched to become "more positive, more productive and more loving,"[80] and Ericka Winn, a twenty-three-year-old saleswoman, marched to gain "a positive mind."[81] Others stressed their need to heal. "Once we heal ourselves and each other, then we can heal our families, our community."[82] "There are a million plus reasons to be here," said Ms. Bartell, a thirty-seven-year-old owner of a printing company and clothing boutique, ". . . but I think healing is the number one thrust that has jelled the women to say I want to be a part of this."[83]

As it was with Promise Keepers and Million Man marchers, Million Woman marchers looked inward and took personal responsibility for change. This was ironic because the decline in well-paying jobs and withdrawal of government support systems, first with the Reagan and Bush administrations and then with Bill Clinton's rollback of welfare in 1996, seemed to be a conscious and unconscious reason for the march in the first place. Nevertheless, marchers overwhelmingly believed that the government could not give them businesses to run, could not teach family values, and could not bring about the sisterhood that they craved.[84] "The solutions to our problems," wrote Laurian Bowles, a junior at Pennsylvania State University, "need to come from us, not Congress, nor those who have not walked in our shoes."[85] A federal government worker put it this way: "Charity starts at home and before we can help others, we have to get ourselves together. This is about taking responsibility."[86]

Neither the lgbt marches nor Million Mom March echoed this theme of anti-institutional, nonpolitical, personal responsibility. If anything, these marchers believed that the government *could* make their lives easier and happier and that it was their personal responsibility to apply political pressure to make the government respond to their needs. Lgbts demanded antidiscrimination and civil rights laws and Million Moms demanded gun control. Their issues politicized them and they wanted to be recognized as political beings. Besides attending a march, they petitioned their legislatures, took out media ads, and sponsored or opposed legislative referendums. And when they marched, they marched in part to demonstrate their political strength. "I will vote with my feet this Mother's Day," said Mary Winter, who intended to go to the local Denver Million Mom March in May 2000 to advocate for gun control.[87] Another Denver mom was so energized by the gun issue that she marched right into the Colorado secretary of state's office and filed a petition to run for the Colorado House of Representatives. Said Paula Busey in response to Second Amendment arguments against gun control, "I believe in the Constitution, but I believe it should protect everyone, not just gun dealers and gun manufacturers."[88] Similarly, for gay activist Glen Paul Freedman, the 2000 Millennium March was just one part of his political agenda: "After the march, we intend to carry empowerment and energy back home to register voters and be a powerful force for issues important to us. . . . We will be voting for candidates who support the gay community just as seniors vote for candidates who support Social Security."[89] Joe Wilson of Iowa expressed the consciousness of many sexual minorities when he said, "Just being there and being visible in front of the Capitol was political, I was proud to be there."[90]

Notwithstanding the political orientation of the lgbt marches and Million Mom March, and in some cases because of it, marchers used the events to express personal renewal and individual transformation. This was especially the case for those lgbts who used the 1993 or 2000 marches to come out or to connect with others like themselves. Here it is important to reiterate how the marches helped many lgbts deal with their isolation. As is discussed in a subsequent chapter, the 1993 march, and especially the 2000 march, was fractious. As with all of the 1990s marches, there was controversy over the march's leadership and purpose. Still, many expressed the need for renewal. Twenty-two-year-old Michael Flanagan, for example, had been discharged from the marines because he was gay. "I felt like my entire world was being torn apart," he said. "For the longest time, I didn't think I had anything to live for." For him, the march was a turning point because it ushered in "a meaningful future."[91] The same was true for Ron Swanda, the National Gay Pilots Association's first executive director. For him, the 1993 march was a "life-changing event." It was the first time he was out to everybody and, according to him, "being 'out' like that wiped away a lot of unfounded and internalized fear." "It was liberating," he claimed, and allowed him to be "even more open to the amazing power of this event."[92] Over and over marchers testified to the hope and internal change that the march inspired. Mostly it was the "belonging" that the march instilled. "It's empowering and . . . after you've been to one you don't feel like you're alone anymore," claimed David Deay after the '93 march.[93] For many, "being yourself" meant living truthfully, something so many found rejuvenating.

Million Mom marchers also spoke in the language of internal transformation and change. As noted earlier, many had not given a second thought to gun violence until they were touched by an incident that was either figuratively or literally close to home. Often, a suicide or criminal shooting of a friend or loved one or someone they could identify with left them bereft and in search of answers and support. The grieving process provoked questions and compelled action that involved a personal metamorphosis that in turn fed the Million Mom March and movement.[94] Typical was the testimony of an Albuquerque mother whose life was altered the morning she learned that her son and two of his friends had been shot twelve to eighteen times at point-blank range with an assault rifle. "We have friends who hunt," Mary Hunt told a reporter, "but I never thought about a gun as a weapon to kill a person, especially not my son. Not my baby." Hunt's grief sent her screaming to her knees and to the march. But it also caused her to read up on gun laws, educate herself, and, as she put it, "make a difference." She planned to begin lobbying the New Mexico state legislature for tighter gun-control laws after the march.[95]

Political action, therefore, did not preclude or preempt a desire for what historian T. J. Jackson Lears calls a "thicker" experience. For some, becoming political was a prerequisite to self-realization, their way to take responsibility for their personal happiness. Like those who espoused self-help, they wanted a more meaningful life. They wanted to change the culture, something that first required inner change. In sum, though not the only reason to march, the conscious and unconscious search for renewal drove Americans with different politics and of different faiths, sexualities, genders, and races to the mass marches and gatherings of the 1990s.

Marches Matter

In her study of marches on Washington, historian Lucy Barber argues for the significance of marches. She claims that they have forged an American political tradition and created "national public spaces" where people can "build support for their causes" and "act out their own visions of national politics." Marches on Washington, she argues, transform the capital into a place where ordinary Americans can perform citizenship and expand it beyond just a place for politicians and officials. Barber makes her case knowing that many dismiss marches as inconsequential, distracting, and an outmoded tactic of yesteryear.[96] For example, distinguished journalism professor and *Time* magazine writer Lance Morrow compared the marches of the 1990s to the 1963 March on Washington for Jobs and Freedom. He called the latter solemn and dignified but the former he ridiculed as an "art form (happening, circus, pep rally, Chautauqua, media spectacle, political threat)" that had "devolved into special-interest pleading."[97] Sandy Grady of the *Philadelphia Daily News* dismissed the Million Man March, the Millennium March, and the Million Mom March as "media carnivals that pass in a noisy blur."[98] Ordinary citizens held similar opinions. Of the Million Man March, Robert Malone, a black nursing student at Los Angeles Trade–Technical College, wondered about the march's impact. "What is this march really going to do? Tomorrow, we'll all be back in the same position. I don't have a job now and I won't have one tomorrow after the march. Progress is about jobs and money, not marching."[99] "We don't need marches to save our community," said a woman who opted out of the Million Woman March. "We marched throughout the 60's, and that had its place. . . . It's like our leaders have run out of ideas."[100] Another citizen swore off the Million Man March for a similar reason: "I thought marches were for protest, not atonement. When you march on Washington, aren't you supposed to be demanding something of Washington?"[101]

As we have seen, Americans did march to demand something from Washington, but they also marched to request something from and for themselves. In fact, the marches of the 1990s reveal more about Americans than their politics, and the gatherings speak to more than the political tradition of marching on Washington. Americans were hurting in the 1990s, and the marches demonstrate this. Life seemed out of control and the culture was unsatisfying. There had been so many deep changes. Americans of all walks of life felt stressed, and many marched on Washington and Philadelphia or went to a sport stadium or their local town square to show their discontent. They were doing what Americans a century before them had done. They were searching for order; they were looking for renewal. They wanted to take control of a culture that had spun so out of control as to be unrecognizable. In this they showed not only that the American tradition of marching on Washington was alive and well, but they also breathed life into the tradition of awakenings. In fact, rather than diluting basic Americanness by dividing the nation along identity lines—something critics bemoaned—marchers paradoxically confirmed their Americanness by reaching back and replicating some age-old American customs. In the process, marchers demonstrated that the American "bootstrap" tradition of self-reliance was still sound. Although they started from different corners of the American experience, marchers were on the same page in looking for ways to channel the forces of postmodernity. They all wanted to get more in touch with their real selves; they wanted a new purpose in their lives and a more meaningful existence. This negates the idea that the 1990s marches were media circuses and political spectacles. Indeed, for many who felt lost in the United States of America, the marches opened a door to self-discovery.

CHAPTER 2

Looking for a Few Good Men

The Transformation of Manhood

When the controversial minister Louis Farrakhan addressed the masses of black men assembled on the Washington Mall on October 16, 1995, he had few words of consolation. His address was filled with rebuke and chastisement, aimed mostly at an America that had mistreated its black citizens, but also at black men for forsaking their responsibility to rescue their families and communities. "We cannot continue the destruction of our lives and the destruction of our community," he preached. "There must be repentance." Until black men felt "remorse or contrition or shame for the past conduct which was wrong and sinful," black America and the American nation could not be redeemed.[1] Almost two years later, on October 4, as a group of mostly white men prepared to gather on the same landscape, another controversial leader, William McCartney, founder of the Promise Keepers (PK), delivered a similar message. "America is suffering from a severe shortage of integrity and men are behind some of its worst manifestations." Things would not change until "men seek God, confess their sins and begin making the necessary changes, as God empowers them."[2]

Although Farrakhan, the leader of the black nationalist Nation of Islam, and McCartney, a Christian former football coach turned proselytizer, had much to disagree about, when it came to end-of-century manhood they found common cause. McCartney founded the nondenominational Christian Promise Keepers in 1991, which by 1996 had held twenty-two stadium revival-like conferences that had brought out over a million participants. By 1997, when PK held its signature Stand in the Gap gathering on the National Mall, it had drawn nearly two million men to its gatherings, and although attendance declined after it eliminated its entrance fee in 1997, by 2000, Promise Keepers claimed to have reached over five million men in states as geographically and politically distant as Texas and New York, Washington and Georgia.[3] The message at each Promise Keeper rally was the same: the nation was a moral wasteland; its communities had lost their way; crime, materialism, and immorality had become endemic; families were in disrepair; and men who had failed to lead families and communities had to accept responsibility for the mess their abdication of responsibility had created. The Nation of Islam preached a similar gospel. When Farrakhan called for the men's-only Million Man March, he ingeniously took the message of men's responsibility to African American men, a group that Promise Keepers had been trying, with limited success, to court.

The eagerness of so many men to attend these gatherings—and in the case of many Promise Keepers, attend them over and over again as well as go to locally organized, small, intimate sessions where men shared with each other their innermost feelings—attests to men's receptivity to the Promise Keeper and Million Man March message and the transcendent quality of the events. Journalists like Greg Freeman, of the *St. Louis Post-Dispatch*, called the camaraderie black men experienced at the Million Man March "magical," a once-in-a-lifetime sensation.[4] William Willimon, minister at Duke University, marveled at the men who, he said, were seeking a "thicker spiritual experience."[5]

When journalists, theologians, and social science scholars sought reasons for these men's gatherings, they almost universally agreed that the cultural shifts resulting from the changed economy, immigration, and the rights movements of the '60s and '70s had forced men to seek new ways of being a man. Masculinity was being remade in the '90s, and the process forced men to rework their attitudes and behavior toward women, the family, and children, as well as toward their work, other men, their communities, and the nation.[6]

This chapter uses the Promise Keeper gatherings and the Million Man March to explore the new masculinity. Aerial photos of the Million Man March and the Stand in the Gap gatherings look very similar, as do the messages that emanated from their respective podiums. The feelings expressed by attendees of the separate gatherings were likewise similar. From a distance the marches look alike, and it is impossible to see how and why the mostly white men of the Promise Keepers and the mostly black men of the Million Man March had, from their radically different historical backgrounds, arrived at this same place with similar messages. But a closer examination reveals profound differences that tell us a lot about how race, class, faith, and sexuality intersected and affected men's feelings about themselves in the 1990s. As the men gathered to express their thoughts and ideas, the historical forces and the contemporary reality that brought these men to Washington at different times in separate marches became evident. This chapter examines the message of the gatherings in the historical context of American masculinity. It looks at how end-of-century manhood differed from what went previously and how and why black and white men heard similar messages differently.

The Promise Keepers

It is impossible to be precise about Promise Keeper demographics because, unlike an institutionalized church or denomination, the numerous nationwide stadium gatherings made PK "membership" difficult to assess. Attendees ranged from hard-core supporters to casual sympathizers. Nevertheless, several surveys found them to be mostly married (at least 80 percent), mostly white (at least 80 percent), middle-income fathers who were fairly well educated and who self-identified as politically moderate to conservative Republicans or Independents. From one-fifth to a quarter of the attendees had been divorced. While less than 4 percent had not graduated from high school, most had a high school diploma and some college, or a college or higher degree. More than 80 percent identified themselves as "born again" or affiliated with an evangelical denomination.[7]

These characteristics put PK men into several demographics about which much has been written. As deindustrialization and globalization decreased domestic manufacturing, sent companies and jobs overseas, and made it difficult for a family of four to survive on the single income of a male breadwinner, white men like the Promise Keepers endured substantial change and loss. Between 1974 and 1999, real wages for male high school graduates dropped 24 percent. In the late 1990s, 3.1 million manufacturing jobs were lost.[8] Late twentieth-century white men also matured in a society that was different from that of their fathers who, buttressed by a relatively stable post–World War II economy, the bargaining power of labor unions, and the educational and homeowner benefits of the GI bill, were able to pursue dreams, find work, and support their families in an economy that privileged them. In contrast, late twentieth-century white men competed in a more diverse labor force and also in an economic milieu where corporations showed little loyalty to workers, where unions were comparatively weak, where salaries barely kept pace with inflation and did not always include pensions and benefits, where divorce rates along with single parenting was higher than ever, and where homosexual males were beginning to challenge hegemonic heterosexual definitions of manhood.[9]

In the last decade of the millennium, everything about manhood was up for reinterpretation. It was not enough to be the family breadwinner, something made more difficult by the changed economy; one also had to be an emotionally involved husband and parent. The increased number of women in the workforce meant that men were expected to do household labor as well as do more child nurturing. Fathers were expected to provide the latest consumer goods for their families, and spend quality time with them so that their children grew up with their emotional and intellectual development intact and so that their wives and lovers were buoyed by their sensitivity. Said one historian, the new demands left "fatherhood fragmented, and fathers uncertain."[10]

According to some scholars, the changed requirements of fatherhood and masculinity left many white men angry. With the median white male income reported to have declined 22 percent between 1976 and 1984, and with women and minorities representing most of the reported labor force growth in the late 1980s, white male baby boomers were said to feel betrayed, jilted, and discriminated against by a nation that seemed more responsive and accessible to everyone but them.[11] Although they still controlled the nation's politics, accounting for 77 percent of Congress (though only 39 percent of the population) and 92 percent of state governors; although they comprised 70 percent of tenured professors; and still headed most Fortune 500 companies and comprised the wealthiest demographic in America, white men still had what scholar Michael Kimmel called a "wind chill" mind-set—how well they were doing did not matter as much as how they *felt* they were doing.[12] And they *felt* they were doing badly. Affirmative action that opened colleges, universities, and the workforce to women and minorities; advertising that left the impression that blacks and women had exceeded the social economic standing of white men; and the increased proportion of marriages that ended in divorce made them feel like failures.[13] According to scholars, '80s and '90s media images that featured independent women like Murphy Brown and happy upper-middle-class African American families like the Huxtables of *The Cosby Show* fueled white male resentment and convinced them that they were being left behind.[14]

While there is evidence that some white Promise Keepers fell into the "angry" demographic, there is reason to pause before describing the PK masses as such. First and foremost are PK testimonies that show them to be more bewildered than angry by the new reality and the demands being made of them. No doubt confusion sometimes gave way to anger, but their confusion deserves the kind of consideration that Promise Keeper founder Bill McCartney gave to men. At fifty he experienced the kind of bewilderment that sent so many white men into a tailspin. The successful coach of the University of Colorado's football team, he seemed to have it all: material wealth and the respect of his peers. But his family was in trouble. His unmarried teenage daughter had had two children fathered by different African American Colorado football players, and he blamed his "workaholism" for what he considered the breakdown of his family. "I watched my family suffer as I poured myself into my career," he said. "I was letting go of my most basic responsibility." His life was not one to emulate, it was "full of holes," he lamented. The men he admired were the ones "who wash the dishes, change the diapers, take out the garbage." After intense introspection he came to believe that the men who put their families first got "the greatest return on their investment." He founded the Promise Keepers so men could use Christian teachings to redirect their lives and be happier.[15]

Another reason to pause before putting PK men into the angry white male category is that a small but significant number of Promise Keepers were not white and the PK organization worked hard to foster interracial cooperation. After 1995, anywhere from 15 to 20 percent of the Promise Keepers were minorities. While social scientists have focused on the white majority, these mostly black participants—who by definition do not fall into the angry white male demographic—add the perspective of race and gender intersection.

There is also the sixth promise. Promise Keepers adhered to seven promises that, briefly stated, committed them to the following: (1) to honor Jesus Christ; (2) pursue vital relationships with other men; (3) practice spiritual, moral, ethical, and sexual purity; (4) build strong marriages and families; (5) support the mission of the church; (6) *"reach beyond any racial and denominational barriers to demonstrate the power of Biblical unity"* (italics added); and (7) influence the world. Like all Promise Keeper promises, the biblical origins of the racial reconciliation pledge were highlighted and explained in the *Promise Keepers Men's Study Bible*, a King James version of the Bible with extensive clarifying notations following relevant passages. For example, following John 17:20–23 there is a half-page, single-spaced explanation relating Jesus' prayer that all in the church "may be made perfect in one" to the principle of racial reconciliation.[16]

A discussion of Promise Keeper men, therefore, must explore how race, gender, *and* faith came together with end-of-century economic and social realities. While such an exploration does not nullify the "angry man" characterization, it takes us beyond it, into a deeper understanding of how some American men handled the everyday issues of postmodernity.

What Promise Keepers Wanted,
Needed, and Experienced

Promise Keeper events were very much like religious revivals. They were held in sport stadiums, but instead of cheering for their favorite team, attendees cheered for God and each other. Raucous conviviality was replaced with weeping, hugging, praying, and testifying. At the men's-only gatherings, anywhere from 30,000 to 70,000 attendees held their hands high, swayed back and forth, sang at the top of their lungs, admitted their shortcomings, confessed their sins, and promised to accept responsibility for high divorce rates, for estrangement from their families, for community disorganization, and for their own unhappiness. At the large gatherings they listened to sermons that assured them that Christ would forgive them of their past misdeeds and fulfill those who lived their life according to the seven promises. They also were assured that they would leave the stadium with their heterosexual masculinity intact. "You don't come here and feel like you're losing your masculinity because of your faith," said a thirty-one-year-old pastor of a United Methodist Church while attending the 1995 RFK stadium event in Washington, DC.[17] Whatever else can be said about these men, their attendance at Promise Keeper gatherings and subsequent small accountability group meetings evidenced a level of commitment to understanding and meeting the changed requirements of end-of-century manhood.

The revivalist atmosphere of Promise Keeper events was central. Promise Keepers created and structured a place and space where men who had been taught to stifle their feelings could, in a Christian context, express their anxiety about their society, absorb and contemplate the meaning of their emotions, and "try out" new ways of being a man. Todd Rich, of Charlottesville, Virginia, was, as he described, "totally unprepared for the experience." "What I didn't realize," he said, "was that the Holy Spirit was about to take hold of my heart and show me the power of God's grace as I had never imagined. The sight of 50,000 men singing praises to Jesus and confessing their sins in the presence of so many others was overwhelming." Rich, who attended the June 1997 Washington, DC, Promise Keeper gathering at RFK stadium admitted to a reporter that his life had been so "laden with sins of all sorts and sizes" that he thought he was "far past the point of being accepted into the body of Christ." But, said Rich, "as we sang 'A Mighty Fortress' I felt the power of the spirit working in me, and the redeeming love of the Lord."[18] Rich's experience was repeated many thousand times over. What Steven Clemm of Batavia, New York, described as "supernatural," Tom Walker of Beaumont, Texas, described as "awesome," Charles Sanderson of Vista, California, described

FIGURE 1. At stadium events like this one, Promise Keepers could express joy and sadness; they could "let go and let God" without thinking about who might judge them and without fear of reprisal. *Photo by Karl Gehring/Denver Post via Getty Images.*

as "incredible," and Jay Comeaux, of Houston, Texas, characterized as "a real inspiration and a great blessing."[19]

What happened to men at PK events was unlike what happened to them in church. Promise Keeper gatherings were held in sport stadiums or arenas because PK leadership understood that the very unfamiliar message they were delivering, and the very unfamiliar emotional response they were eliciting, and the very unfamiliar behavior they wanted Christian men to model, had to be introduced in a setting that was familiar to them. PK leaders judged stadiums to be safe spaces for the transformation of Christian men from the detached, stoic, competitive, independent, emotionless, breadwinning tower of strength many thought they had to be to the sensitive, sharing, community-minded, nation-building man that postmodernity demanded. Said the Reverend Mark Horst of the Park Avenue United Methodist Church in Minneapolis, Promise Keepers gave men what they didn't get in church, "a safe place to cry and laugh at themselves."[20] Said Chad Cook of Grand

Rapids, Missouri, "Christianity was religion in my brain, but it never got to my heart until I came to my first Promise Keepers event."[21]

Men not only needed lessons on how to be more expressive, but they also needed to feel okay about showing emotion, something they were accustomed to doing in stadiums but seldom in church. Ken McGeorge, a PK Canadian hospital management executive who retired from his career at age fifty, expressed what many of his American counterparts felt about the different ways they and their fathers' generation experienced manhood. "Men aren't Marlboro machos. The truth is that underneath, we are all struggling with conflict, and stress and insecurities."[22] Men, said African American Houston firefighter Garry Blackmon, "have not been taught to relate. In our lives we have been taught to be stoic, to hold back pain."[23] That wasn't working for a thirty-five-year-old factory supervisor from Turtle Lake, Wisconsin, who, after attending a PK gathering, realized that "I don't have to be this macho person who can do everything and control everything."[24] Being an end-of-century American man was a "lonely experience," said Morris Kennedy, a *Tampa Tribune* columnist. People moved more than they used to, small towns accepted fewer newcomers, and men and women were sorting out "new ways to relate to one another." Said Kennedy, "It looks to me as though a lot of men are just trying to fit into the family at all, to just find a place at the table."[25]

PK showed men where and how to look for that place in a space where many of the status issues that consumed men had been eliminated. This was essential for the fulfillment of the second promise: "to pursue vital relationships with a few other men, understanding that he needs brothers to help him keep his promises."[26] Because Promise Keepers strove to replace masculine individualism with communalism and brotherhood, stadium events were designed to be competition-free. As leaders encouraged men to hold hands, sing, pray, and confess their sins together, clothes, jobs, cars, and homes diminished in importance, something that did not happen in church. The male-exclusive PK rallies also eliminated the need to impress women or compete with other men for their attention. Freed from the necessity of performing manhood for female consumption, men could show and practice compassion without fear of being perceived by women or other men as weak. "Men feel more at ease without the presence of women," said a Canadian Promise Keeper.[27] Two Florida PK interviewees agreed. "Men can be more open with another man than even their spouses." "Some need another man to reach them."[28]

For a lot of men, PK was transforming, not the least because conscious dependency was so new to them. "There's an intimacy," said Tampa Floridian Norsky Mendez.[29] If PK testimony can be believed, intimacy was not some-

thing the 1990s man was comfortable with, either with women or men. For
Rico, a Connecticut Cape Verdean, sharing confidences with another man
was like "one man asking another man to dance." Men did not have very
good friendships "because friendship meant exposure and exposure means
vulnerability."[30] Many Promise Keepers found that once they let themselves
be dependent on another man, or, as PK would have it, build brotherhood
with another man, they became happier people. "I really did feel like I had
some splinters taken out of my soul," said the once-skeptical Bruce Eber-
stein of Bowie, Maryland, who added that if he had been introduced to the
Promise Keepers three years earlier, he would not be divorcing.[31] For many
PK men, it came down to having friends: "Whatever you're going through,"
said divorcee Bill Butterworth of the Denver area, "you were never intended
by God above to go through it alone, you need friends."[32]

As we will see in the next chapter, the exclusion of women raised the
suspicions and ire of many women's groups, but PK built its defense on this
need to create brotherhood. Male camaraderie would, PK leaders argued,
teach men to depend on each other and be less independent and competitive, and this would help them better relate to women. The result would be a
society with fewer divorces and less violence. One Promise Keeper described
the process this way: "By talking [with other men] the struggles men have
held in their heart for two or three years can come out. It gets men to start
talking with their wives. When a man becomes transparent with [his] wife
and family, the relationship changes."[33]

Men were not only taught how to relate and share with their wives but they
were also instructed to serve them as a way of reinserting themselves in the
household as full-fledged, responsible husbands and fathers who were active
family participants and leaders. The fourth promise committed men to build
"strong marriages and families through love, protection and Biblical values."
They were to do this by leading their families. Leadership was defined as
service, something PK leaders understood was hard for men. "Men don't like
to serve," said one Promise Keeper. "In our culture, we believe it is only the
weak who serve." But men could learn to lead through service if they followed
the example of Jesus Christ, who demonstrated his love, his leadership, and
his servanthood when, after the last supper, "with all of His authority, with
all of His power" he knelt before his disciples and washed their feet.[34] PK
taught men to lead through humility, that family leadership was not exercised
by proclamation or by dictatorship or by demanding subservience from
women and children.

This aspect of PK was a problem area for women's groups and their
supporters since the idea of husbands serving wives was seen by many as

akin to putting women on a pedestal to better enable male dominance. "I've known plenty of men who treated women like queens because they could not treat them as equals," said skeptic Andrew Herrmann, a columnist for the *Chicago Sun-Times*. However, he found it hard to argue with PK advice that "your mate is your equal, your adult partner, and should be treated as such. . . . To honor your mate is to tell her she is equally capable of calling the plays—that means not only encouraging her to have a say in running the team, but to listen to her viewpoint and try the plays she calls."[35]

Despite the objection of some feminists, the servant/leader appealed to many thousands of Promise Keepers. Once Ken Kemper of Kansas City made a promise to honor his wife, he spent more time with her and less time watching TV. "I can't honor her while channel surfing," he said. Another Kansas Cityite admitted that he changed the way he related to his nine-year-old son, who was afraid of thunder. Instead of insisting that he "grow up and be a man," he "tried to deal with that fear," and "talked about who created thunder and that fear was a natural emotion."[36] New Orleans resident C. J. Acosta testified that PK saved his marriage. When he started attending the small PK gatherings at his church, he and his wife had been separated twice. The group helped him deal with his work and home life, which in turn strengthened him spiritually. By his admission, "I was as far away from the Lord as a person could get. But today I'm just thankful that I'm on the right track. . . . It's because of Promise Keepers that my wife and I are together today," he said.[37]

The masculinity endorsed by Promise Keepers made them unlike their precursors, who in the early twentieth-century search for order had also turned to Christianity to help them meet the changes modernity had imposed. Confronted with urbanization and the replacement of physically demanding work with office jobs, middle-class white men called "muscular Christians" rebelled against what they perceived as the feminization of their society—the glorification of the "female traits" of nurturance, refinement, and sentimentality over the "male traits" of strength, courage, and endurance.[38] The rise of the corporate economy had, they argued, diminished the importance of physical strength, made men too intellectual, overcivilized them, in fact; women had become too influential in a church that had become too emotional and less stern. If men were to save themselves from effeminacy and female dominance, thought muscular Christians, they would have to restructure American institutions, including schools, churches, and families, so that men did not become too domesticated but retained some of their God-given boorishness. Early twentieth-century muscular Christians encouraged men to be crusader-like in the service of Jesus Christ, and strong and virile in their service to the church and community. Christ was imaged as a warrior, and his power and strength were stressed over his service and forbearance.[39]

In contrast, late twentieth-century Promise Keepers encouraged a softer manhood that enabled men to adapt to a society in which women were their workplace colleagues and demanded more familial presence from them. Though some dubbed the Promise Keepers "testosterone Christianity,"[40] PK actually wanted men to show their more feminine side and be more sensitive and emotion-filled. They wanted men to be less like Old Testament warriors and more like the New Testament empathetic Jesus.

There were some exceptions, however. One was the oft-cited African American Promise Keeper Tony Evans, who, in the 1994 edition of *Seven Promises of a Promise Keeper*, ranted about the "feminization of the American male," a phenomenon he thought produced "a nation of 'sissified' men." Men, the Dallas pastor proclaimed, had abdicated their leadership of the family to women and the only way for them to reclaim their manhood was to reconstitute themselves as head of the household. Here he was emphatic. "I'm not suggesting that you ask for your role back, I'm urging you to *take it back*" (emphasis his). Evans expected women to resist. After all, he reasoned, women who had been accustomed to shouldering all the parental responsibilities would probably not surrender control easily, but he advised men not to compromise: "If you're going to lead, you must lead." And to women he advised, "Give it back! For the sake of your family and the survival of our culture, let your man be a man if he's willing."[41]

Although Pastor Evans provided fodder for those who saw the Promise Keepers as a masculinist Trojan horse, Evans was actually the exception that proved the rule. Few other PK men publically echoed his ideas, and by the 1997 Stand in the Gap gathering on the National Mall, Evans himself was moderating his tone. He called for spiritual familial leadership but refrained from using language castigating feminized men. Interesting also is the fact that although Evans is listed as an author on the cover of the 1999 edition of the book *Seven Promises of a Promise Keeper*, his '94 article was excised and none of his writings appear in the book, suggesting that he was indeed an outlier and that the Promise Keepers took their servanthood seriously.[42]

Where women were concerned, Promise Keepers did take issue with the church for providing for the needs of women over those of men. The church, the 1990s PK felt, had not helped men develop skills suitable for postmodernity. Speaking of the church that he had grown up in, thirty-eight-year-old Dwight Benjamin of Prince George County claimed that "I didn't find a lot of male figures there."[43] "There are lots and lots and lots of organizations for women," said a Missouri Promise Keeper who was searching for a group that would help him bond with men, "but it has been hard to keep a men's group going."[44] In New Bedford, Catholics planned their own Wake-Up Call for Catholic men—an exclusive revival-style gathering of men at which Mass would be celebrated. Though Catholic and evangelical theology differed, as noted earlier, Catholic clergy reasoned that they had to adopt some Promise Keeper tactics because PK had responded to men's spiritual issues and given Catholic men a chance to bond and a ministry that taught men how to trust each other so that together they could refashion manhood.[45]

Not disassociated from a brotherhood aimed at refashioning masculinity was PK's emphasis on racial reconciliation. PK leaders taught that men of all races and conditions were brothers in Christ and therefore had to find common ground with each other. Only then could they become more Christlike and fulfill the masculine task of nation-building. As put by Raleigh Washington (African American), Glen Kehrein (white), and Claude V. King (white) in their 1999 article in *Seven Promises of a Promise Keeper*, the cultural isolation that characterized the lives of most Americans made the nation weak. First Corinthians 12:21–26, they noted, teaches that the parts of the human body are mutually dependent, and when one part suffers the entire body suffers. African Americans, Hispanic Americans, Asian Americans, and European Americans were different parts of the national body. Despite their different histories and experiences they were mutually dependent parts of the body politic that were equally important to the health of the nation. "We must be intentional in developing sensitivity to the needs of other members of the body," instructed Washington, Kehrein, and King, who warned that "failure to recognize" the needs and contributions of all would hurt all. "If we don't know a person's background or experiences, we won't understand his attitudes, actions, and beliefs. We won't know his pain and suffering, and the body of Christ will lack the health it could have."[46]

Just as PK believed that the church had failed to help men adapt to new gender needs and had thus weakened families, the backbone of the nation, it also believed that the church had failed to build interracial brotherhood. "The main institution of segregation is our churches. We do it every Sunday morning," said Clint Wright, a Polk County, Florida, school superintendent, who saw in PK a blueprint for racial unity.[47] For Ellis Casson, the pastor of the First African Methodist Episcopal Church of Seattle, the racial reconciliation message of the Promise Keepers would bear fruit all around. "If we can do this among ourselves we can pass it on to our children, grandchildren and our neighbors—how to get along and embrace each other." Casson had attended the 1996 Promise Keeper ministers' conference held in Atlanta's

Georgia Dome, one of several ministers' conferences held exclusively to teach ministers how to expand the PK message to their congregations. The 39,000 male pastors who attended learned how to make racial reconciliation and the other six promises part of their male ministry.[48]

Much has been made of the resistance generated by the racial reconciliation promise, but before turning to that resistance, it is important to note that the Promise Keepers organization worked assiduously to attract minority participants. For example, at least one-third of the PK staff and officeholders were minority, as were the speakers at Promise Keeper stadium events.[49] African American bishop Phillip Porter Jr., founder of the All Nations Pentecostal Church of God in Christ in Aurora, Colorado, was the national chairman of the Promise Keepers from 1994 through 1999. Also, PK often held events tailored to reach particular ethnic or racial groups. For example, preachers Daniel DeLeon and Ruben Duarte exhorted Hispanic men gathered at the 1996 San Antonio Alamodome event to be positive role models for their children. In what was titled *El Gran Despertar*, or mega wake-up call, Hispanic men, in the same revivalist style common to all Promise Keeper gatherings, pledged to forsake machismo and oppose gang activity in their neighborhoods.[50] Likewise, after having neglected Asian Americans for most of the '90s, in 1996 PK hired Louis Lee, a Lorenzo, California, Chinese American pastor, as a national ethnic ministry manager to Asian Americans. In August 1997, Lee convened an Asian American Promise Keeper event that attracted 800 attendees. Though tailored to Asian men's needs, the call for responsible manhood and relationship healing was much the same as it was at most PK events.[51]

Equally important is the fact many Promise Keepers tried to incorporate the sixth promise into their lives, and many found it fulfilling. Promise Keepers approached racism not as a systemic societal problem, but as a problem that rested with individuals. They saw racism as a sin, and triumph over racism, like triumph over any sin, could not be accomplished corporately but by individuals who, after establishing a personal relationship with God, deliberately worked at reforming themselves. In keeping with this approach, Promise Keepers directed men to establish friendships across race lines in order to exorcise their own racism. The story of the friendship that developed between Brian Walker (black) and Steve Wagner (white) from the Twin Cities area of Minnesota was the kind of relationship Promise Keepers believed would lead to lasting change. Wagner, a truck driver warehouseman, confessed to being prejudiced against blacks, and Walker, a Federal Express courier, was at one time a black nationalist separatist. Neither knew or had made friends with men outside their race. Both gave the Promise Keepers credit for changing their attitudes. Said Wagner, who attended his first Promise Keeper gathering in 1994, PK was "about Jesus and what Jesus is doing to change men's hearts. . . . He helped me to face my prejudices." Through PK he met blacks who shared their stories of prejudice with him. "I was appalled by what I heard," he said. "Through Promise Keepers, I've met 200 black men and not one that I did not like and love as a brother in the Lord. . . . God," he said, "has removed the fears and the stereotypes." Walker was equally transformed. "All this stuff Promise Keepers preaches about racial healing—well they mean it and it works," he insisted. His three children call Wagner "Uncle Steve." Said Walker, "He's family now. His family and my family do a lot together now." For both Wagner and Walker, the Promise Keepers made a big difference in their lives. It helped them strengthen their families, their faith, and their friendships. It made the nation stronger by fostering a strong interracial friendship. And it made Walker and Wagner happier.[52]

In fact, most Promise Keepers emerged happier after an encounter with PK. Like many men at the end of the twentieth century who found themselves financially and emotionally dislocated by the impersonal forces of deindustrialization, economic globalization, multiculturalism, and feminism, they sought new ways of relating to family and society. The Promise Keeper organization promised that if men changed themselves they would be happier; it taught men that by abandoning traditional masculine traits and by taking personal responsibility they could lead their families and communities, and through them, the nation, out of despair. It did not try to replace the church but helped the church minister to men. It did not attack the structures that had changed their lives but helped men develop new relationship skill sets. Through the Promise Keepers, men learned new ways to relate to their wives and children and other men, some of whom were of another race.

Million Man Marchers

If pollsters are correct, the black men who gathered on the Washington Mall on October 16, 1995, were generally older, wealthier, better-educated, and more religious than most African American men.[53] This onetime event that in many cases necessitated extensive travel expenditures (unlike the Promise Keepers, which in any given year held local stadium events that were accessible to men of moderate means) naturally attracted those with more disposable income than the average African American. Specifically, Million Man marchers had an average median household income of $43,000, as compared to $19,333 for all black households. Seventeen percent had household incomes between $50,000 and $74,999; 11 percent had incomes between $75,000 and $99,999; 8

percent had household incomes of $100,000 or more. A third of the marchers were aged eighteen to thirty; 42 percent were thirty to forty-four; 20 percent were forty-one to sixty; and 4 percent were sixty-one years of age or older. Very few (5 percent or less) had less than a high school education; 22 percent had completed high school and more than 70 percent had some college, were college graduates, and/or had a postgraduate education. Consistent with data that showed the black middle class to be disproportionately dependent on government employment, at least a quarter of the marchers worked for local, state, or federal governments. Forty-seven percent were employed in blue-collar skilled and unskilled jobs, and 44 percent did white-collar and/ or professional work. The percentage of Million Man marchers who were married (42 percent) almost matched those married in the general black population (43 percent). Similarly, the percentage of those divorced (10 percent) almost matched the 8.8 percent of divorced American black men.[54] Forty-six percent of Million Man marchers were single, and 60 percent said they attended church or religious service at least once or twice a month. This last statistic is remarkable since a 1992 study of church attendance showed that only 30 percent of black men attended church on any regular basis.[55] An earlier study done by the National Organization for Research at the University of Chicago found that between 1986 and 1989, only one of five black men attended church once a week.[56] This made Million Man marchers more religious than most black men and more comparable to Promise Keepers (who still registered a 20 percent higher church attendance rate). Like Promise Keepers, most marchers were Protestant (52 percent), though 7 percent were Catholic, 6 percent were Muslim, 5 percent belonged to the Nation of Islam, and 14 percent reported that they had no religious affiliation.[57]

Marchers gave a variety of reasons for participating in the Million Man March but generally speaking it boiled down to their concern about the state of the black family, the state of the race, and racism in America.[58] Although most marchers fell into the demographic characterized as relatively stable working or middle class, they were deeply concerned about the 14.9 percent of black households that by the end of the decade reported income of less than $10,000. Journalist Eugene Robinson calls these blacks "the Abandoned"— the youngest black Americans who lived in core urban neighborhoods and the rural South.[59] Marchers were also concerned about the decline in marriage among blacks. Between 1979 and 2001, marriage rates fell for all Americans but especially for African Americans, and especially for young, less educated black men (they fell from 25.9 percent to 13.3 percent). The same time period that saw a decline in marriage saw an increase in single-family households headed by women. The increase was so stark that by the time of the march, the majority of black children were being raised by single female parents in father-absent households. The economic and family statistics were not unrelated. Poverty directly correlates to the number of working adults in households and particularly to the number of working men, who on average make more money than women because their employment generally commands higher wages. For African Americans, poverty also correlates to homicide and incarceration rates.[60] In 1988, nearly 5,000 African American males, age fifteen to twenty-nine years old, were murdered. The chances of a black male being murdered were four times higher than for a black female, seven times higher than for a white male, and twenty times higher than for a white female.[61] Besides the rise in the number of black males murdered, the 1990s saw a phenomenal increase in the number of black males imprisoned for nonviolent crimes.[62] Many felt that something had to be done. "The situation in black America is so bad now that it almost doesn't matter what that something is as long as it's some kind of action," said Al Brown, a community worker from Chicago's West Side, a black neighborhood reeling from these problems.[63]

As much as they were concerned about less fortunate blacks, it would be a mistake to think that Million Man marchers cared less about their own circumstances. In fact, they marched as much for themselves as they did for "the Abandoned." Like Promise Keepers, they too fell into a demographic described as angry. After the 1992 Los Angeles riot—a riot ignited by the exoneration of four white police officers whose beating of a prone black man named Rodney King was captured on videotape—the Center for the Study of Urban Poverty at the University of California at Los Angeles conducted surveys to measure "ethnic alienation from American society."[64] Social scientists were astounded to find that discontent was highest among black households whose incomes were $50,000 or more, the income range of many Million Man marchers. In his 1993 study, journalist Ellis Cose described this demographic as "rageful." His 1993 book, *The Rage of a Privileged Class: Why Are Middle-Class Blacks Angry? Why Should America Care?*, helps us understand why so many black men gathered on the Washington Mall in October 1995.

Chief among the sources of black anger was the strategy and consciousness of color blindness. According to Cose, black people were angry that many whites—the very powerful and the not so powerful—had pronounced America to be color-blind, when every day they experienced racism that impacted their happiness and determined their life chances. By pronouncing the death of racism, whites had effectively silenced their protest and made their criticism of racist job relations hazardous to their employment, promotion, and interactions with coworkers. Cose found countless black men who had to ignore racist comments and policy, lest they, as black men, be perceived as someone who was not a team player and thus not worthy of promotion or meaty assignments. African American men and women, wrote Cose, were tired of having to keep their bitterness to themselves, tired of feeling that they didn't belong, tired of having to always prove their competence, tired of having to second-guess the role race played in a hiring or promotion or something as innocuous as an invitation to a boss's dinner party. They were tired of having to dress up to do simple things like shop, lest they be mistaken as shiftless and targeted as a shoplifter. Middle-class African Americans felt that they were always held to higher standards when a job or a bank loan was at stake, and they chafed and grew rageful when they saw whites with less talent, less ability, and less intelligence soar ahead of them in rank, salary, and status. Through interviews and social science studies, Cose unveiled the deep resentment felt by middle-class blacks for what they termed the "black tax"—the toll paid for being black in America. Although they had accustomed themselves to being excluded from social events hosted by their white colleagues; had learned how to drive themselves to work harder and ignore comments suggesting that their success was only due to affirmative-action programs; had developed coping skills for being excluded from, or being outright denied, the privileges granted to whites who had graduated from the same or lesser institutions of higher learning, they were angry.

Cose's study also revealed the ambivalent relationship that existed between the black affluent/middle class and the so-called black underclass. In short, the former group was angry that whites did not differentiate African Americans, but viewed all blacks through the same lens. In addition to being resentful that blacks of means, no matter how tenuous, were held responsible for rehabilitating the black underclass, they were also angry at this class for coping so poorly and not overcoming as they had done. Whites, they felt, could be evaluated individually, but because all blacks seemingly represented the race, middle-class and affluent black men felt that in any interaction with the police they could not assume, as could white men, that they would be presumed innocent until proven guilty. They blamed both white racism and black lower-class irresponsibility.

And, according to Cose, middle-class/affluent blacks were angry because the future did not hold the prospect that things would get better. Being helpless to change America's public or private perception of African Americans, they were forced to raise their children to believe that they would compete on a level playing field, all the while knowing that their children would likely be hampered by the uneven plane created by race. Even more anger-provoking for middle-class and affluent blacks was the fact that no one—either poor blacks or whites—thought they had anything to complain about. From the lower-class black perspective and from the white perspective, middle-class/affluent blacks were doing well. They were living the American dream and, despite their protest to the contrary, their "success" made color blindness not a myth but a self-evident reality. They should have been happy.

But they weren't, and the Million Man March (and, later, the Million Woman March) proved it. On October 16, 1995, many gathered in Washington, and despite the controversy over the march's organizers (an issue taken up in a later chapter), these mostly middle-class African American men used their emotion, their words, and their performance to express their grievances about being black and male in postmodern America.

What Million Man Marchers Wanted, Needed, and Experienced

Like Promise Keeper gatherings, there was a revivalist quality to the Million Man March that imbued the men with a spirituality few had experienced before. In fact, Joseph Lowery, the head of the Southern Christian Leadership Conference, called it "the biggest revival that I've ever attended."[65] Men prayed together and held hands in demonstrations of unity and brotherhood. Expressions like "It's a holy day," "This is a spiritual day," "God's with us now," and "Only God could be behind this" were common.[66]

Like Promise Keeper leaders, organizers of the Million Man March structured the gathering space so that men could commune and bond around common concerns. Although some women did attend the march, organizers explicitly requested that women stay home. They also established the theme of "atonement," with its attendant promise of forgiveness and redemption, as the ecumenical spiritual foundation on which black men of different faiths and economic standing could unite and be compassionate in their dependence on each other. As a concept, atonement was broad enough to bring men of different viewpoints together and also ground the masculinity being proffered. Atonement made messages like the one delivered by the Reverend Jesse Jackson palatable and congruent with manliness. He asked, "What must a million men do?" To his rhetorical question he answered, "We can reduce divorce rates, stop self-destructive behavior, drive out guns and drugs, see the ten ethical commandments as the keys to educational and economic empowerment. We can pay alimony where there is no matrimony and become upbeat dads rather than deadbeat dads. . . . [We] can lead the charge to stop domestic violence, to stop wife battering, to spare our children from seeing the trauma of a pleading mother and a mad and abusive father." Before words of conclusion that cautioned against letting the "forces of oppression break your spirit," Jackson told the gathering men to set an example because "a million men could set a moral tone for the whole nation."[67]

Just as there were many who objected to the men's-only format, there were many who objected to the atonement theme. Like the Million Man marcher who complained that the march was meaningless because it did not protest or demand something from Washington (see chapter 1), journalist and author Earl Ofari Hutchinson asked, "Atone for what?" He and many others thought the march's leaders let policy makers off the hook by "blaming the victim," making march organizers no better than whites who ignored the structural roots of inequality while stereotyping and oppressing blacks.[68]

But atonement and the men's-only environment registered differently with others. Like Promise Keepers, in order for some men to accept atonement as a masculine trait, they needed to do so in the absence of women. The strategy was especially effective with men who felt they had let black women down. It allowed them to express sorrow, regret, sin, and repentance in an environment in which men were not competing for the attention of women. Wayne Wilson, of Los Angeles, put it this way: "I believe that there are certain times when it is appropriate for men and women to be separated. These are times when men and women can 'let their hair down' and not feel constrained to maintain their egos and/or their special interests."[69] And indeed, released from the masculine requirement of being strong in front of the so-called weaker sex, many men cried and broke down in empathy for black women who they felt were carrying too heavy a load for the race. Said Don Collins, an accountant from Saint Petersburg, "For so long, black women raised our families. We want to carry our 50 percent of the load in the family, and in the church and in the community."[70] Los Angeleno Danny Bakewell put it differently: "Our atonement is to our black mothers, daughters and sisters. We want them to know that we apologize to them for all that we have allowed them to take." He added, "Sit down, Sister. Thank you for leading us for so long. We've grown up now."[71]

Most marchers did not disassociate black fatherhood from the relationship between black men and women. They were concerned about the decline in black marriage but they did not talk about being better husbands as much as they talked about being better fathers. "The most critical consequence of the family falling apart is that it leads to a failure in rearing children," said the Reverend Frank Thomas, pastor of New Faith Baptist Church in Madison, Illinois.[72] The need to take better care of black children was on the minds of many who expressed concern over failure to pay child support. Said Denver organizer Alvertis Simmons to his fellow marchers: "Brothers . . . if you know

FIGURE 2. Million Man marchers pledged to be better fathers and leaders of black America. Many men brought their sons to the march as testimony of their commitment. *Photo by Richard Ellis/AFP/Getty Images.*

a brother who is not paying child support, cut him off because he should be taking care of his kids."[73] A group from Boston called Fathers Inc. wore T-shirts with the words "By any means necessary, be a father to your child." One member told his interviewer that the members had brought their sons with them because "our kids are the future. They're all we have left" and they had vowed that they would go to any length to "make our boys become good fathers to their children."[74]

Million Man marchers also tied their paternal responsibilities at home to their responsibility to their communities. Thirty-four-year-old Ron Hunt, a Kansas City, Missouri, father of three, who worked with an anti–drug and alcohol program, and who described the march as a "spiritual awakening," said, "I believe I've got to continue to work hard in my community . . . but I also need to start with my own kids."[75] Like Hunt, who pledged to reinvest in his home and neighborhood, many men accepted responsibility for allowing black communities to deteriorate, not necessarily because they personally had disappointed black women or children, but because they had failed to help less fortunate black men, and had therefore failed to build black neighborhoods. Going to the Million Man March gave them a second chance. Like a baptism, they could be forgiven and start anew. At least that is what a forty-eight-year-old postmaster from Atlanta, Georgia, felt: "If there's one regret that I have in my life," he admitted, "it's that I've been so busy taking care of my family that I've neglected brothers who have been less fortunate."[76] Like Shelton Williams, a twenty-four-year-old Saint Louis resident, the postmaster planned to go home and help other black men. "We've got to take it home and get it across to our friends and family, sort of like a revival."[77]

While some atoned for not helping black communities, others had something in their personal past they wanted to put behind them, and still others just wanted a new beginning. At the Million Man March black men learned that asking for help to start over and begin anew did not diminish, but enhanced, their manhood. Like the thirty-two-year-old recovering addict from Bladensburg, Maryland, who said that "a lot of us have been out there drugging and doing whatever it is," many wanted to start over.[78] For thirty-five-year-old Kenneth Gains, who traveled to the march from Philadelphia with seventy other recovering drug addicts, the march was, as he put it, "a spiritual cleansing." "I've hurt my women, my children, myself. Now it's time to make amends."[79] Others were like forty-eight-year-old Derrill Johnson, a steelworker with thirteen children who admitted to having "a lot of animosity in my heart." Sounding a theme that echoed that of many a Promise Keeper, Johnson said, "I will have a different outlook on dealing with kids or womenfolk—dealing with life in general."[80] In short, the Million Man March allowed men to say a thunderous "I'm sorry," and not only keep their manhood intact, but feel manlier for doing so.

The march also allowed black men to be in each other's presence without tension, and especially without violence. African American journalist Gregory Freeman understood the significance of this. "Black men often look upon other black men with suspicion," he reported. At the march, "No one was robbed. No one was drinking. We were enveloped in a sense of peace and security."[81] Most attendees found the brotherly love that pervaded the march almost unbelievable. Stanley Banks, of Bedford-Stuyvesant, New York, felt the need to demonstrate it when he turned to a nearby white man with a notepad (probably a journalist) and offered proof of the peacefulness. "You can turn to anyone and say, 'Hi,' even strangers," he said. To prove it he turned to the stranger next to him, stuck out his hand, introduced himself by name, and said "How you doing, brother?" In response, the Cincinnati resident clasped his hand, introduced himself, and said, "Real good, real good." From Banks's perspective, "You can't do nothing better than that. You're not going to be able to go anywhere in the world and do better. . . . It has to start with us."[82]

The significance of the expression of love for each other, of brotherhood, cannot be overstated because Million Man marchers were aware of the harmful toll black male violence was taking on black communities. Black-on-black male crime was so rampant that many marchers gave it as a reason *not* to attend. Others were like John Edwards, a thirty-five-year-old Department of Agriculture manager, who went hesitantly because, he said, "I was a little afraid of my own people."[83] There were many there who were like Jesse Patty from the Tampa, Florida, area, and Curtis West of Chicago. They attended the march, in part, to pay tribute to their sons, both of whom had been killed by other black males. West carried a sign that read "We Are Our Brothers' Keepers." When speaking about his tremendous loss he said, "Instead of killing my boy, those other boys should've been looking out for him." He attended the march to "talk about the killing." "We've got to stop the killing," West said.[84] A former Chicago gang member who attended the march was ready to listen to West. "To stand shoulder to shoulder, with no animosity, no anger, no pre-judgements, no egos, and gang-banging is powerful," said Shannon Blunt, who had gone door to door gathering friends to come with him to the march. "I feel reborn," he said.[85]

Black men standing peacefully united, bonded together in love and respect, was not just something Million Man marchers needed to start the work of healing themselves; it was needed, and deliberately designed, to reconstruct the image of the black male, which historically has been associated with criminality.[86] During the late eighties and early nineties, the image of black men as naturally violent permeated America. Several incidents played into their villainization. At the time of the march they had yet to dispel the fear induced by George H. W. Bush's Willie Horton presidential campaign ad. The ad pictured Horton, a convicted murderer, who kidnapped a white couple and raped the woman while out of prison on a furlough plan once supported by Michael Dukakis, Bush's Democratic rival. As black and brown men were shown going through the revolving doors of America's prisons, they entered the American imagination as monsters.[87] The Central Park jogger case, in which five teenagers—four black and one Hispanic—were convicted of mugging and raping a young white female in New York's Central Park, had the same effect. Although their convictions were vacated in 2002 when another man confessed, during 1989, the year the incident happened, and 1990, the year they were tried and convicted, story after story characterized the five as participants in a kind of animalistic ritual of "wilding."[88] By 1994, when O. J. Simpson was arrested for killing his white wife, Nicole Brown Simpson, and her friend, Ronald Goldman, the centuries-old stereotype of the black brute beast had been reinforced and validated. The Million Man March had to work against the fear these images instilled as well as the nihilism promulgated by the commercialization of "gangsta" hip-hop.[89]

Although the Million Man March did not eliminate the negativity associated with black manhood, a million stalwart hand-holding men gathered peacefully and prayerfully with tearful eyes created a viable counterimage that both blacks and whites could celebrate and black men could emulate. For thirty-one-year-old corrections officer Charles Griffith of Baltimore, a softer, kinder black man was a necessary model for the generations of black youth he saw daily in the Washington, DC, jails. He thought it was important to show that black men and conflict were not synonymous. "I know the system isn't fair to us but I still see these black kids coming in and everyone wants to be the hardest of the hard. . . . They think they have to live up to some image. . . . It hurts to watch it," he said.[90] For two nineteen-year-old white female students from George Washington University who stood on the sidelines, the quiet solemnity was actually shocking. "It's amazing," they exclaimed, "the fact that a million and a half people are here, and they are all unified, and there is no violence, and now they are holding hands." "It's very profound," one of them said.[91]

In sum, in an age where things seemed so out of control, where marriage rates among African Americans were historically low and incarceration levels historically high, where more black children than ever before were being raised in single-parent female-headed households, the Million Man March came up with a prescription that allowed black men to take personal action, and thus take back some control over their fate. They were not directed to bear arms or demonstrate against the government, nor were they told to depend on governments or other institutions to fix what was wrong with them. Like the Promise Keepers, they did not take aim at the structures that

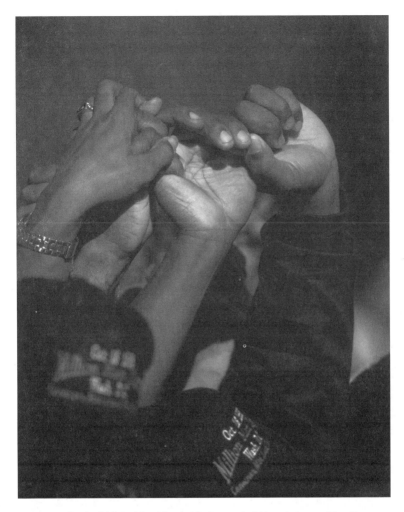

FIGURE 3. At the Million Man March, black men held hands in a self-healing process and pledged to help each other and their families overcome the problems in their communities. *Photo by William F. Campbell/The Life Images Collection/Getty Images.*

ₗmade their lives difficult. They were told they could remake themselves into different kinds of men and thus effect change. At the Million Man March, in an atmosphere made holy by their behavior, black men looked introspectively at themselves and said "I'm sorry." They asked for forgiveness, and promised to give and accept help from other men.

The Promise Keepers and the
Million Man March Compared

Admittedly, the Promise Keepers and the Million Man March do not present us with an easy one-to-one comparison.[92] PK was avowedly Christian while the Million Man marchers had a higher-than-average percentage of black men who by their church attendance and testimony mostly identified as Christian. The Promise Keepers had a mass march on the National Mall in 1997, but their events stretched over the decade while the Million Man March was a onetime event. However, there are several similarities that compel a comparison. Among them are the facts that they centered on masculinity and were both organized around men who valued "men-only" congregation and accepted Christian concepts of sin, repentance, forgiveness, and redemption. There are also the facts that they were attended by the most financially fortunate of their respective groups, by men described as angry who gathered en masse in revivalist fashion. Finally, since both groups gathered during the 1990s—a period of outward calm but of internal turmoil—a comparison extends our knowledge of the race, sex, and gender dynamics at work in turn-of-the-century America.

Demographics suggest some of what we need to know. Both Promise Keepers and Million Man marchers hailed primarily from the middle to the more privileged economic class of their respective white and black communities. They made more money and they were better educated. And yet the difference between their ages and marriage rates tells a back story. Eighty percent of the Promise Keepers were married, almost double the 42 percent of Million Man marchers. Also, from one-quarter to one-fifth of the former were divorced compared to only 10 percent of the latter. The greater youthfulness of the Million Man marchers (a third of them were between eighteen and thirty years old) probably accounted for some of the singleness among black men, and the higher number of unmarried among them helps explain the higher divorce rates among PK men. However, Million Man marchers' greater singleness was also a reflection of black men's higher rates of homicide, incarceration, and poverty. Since experts agree that men who are married generally are happier than men who are not, and also that men who do not feel secure in their ability to provide for a wife and children abstain from relationships that require them to do so,[93] it is reasonable to assume that although Million Man marchers were among the more privileged men of black America, in comparison to white Promise Keepers they were more insecure and unhappy.

Historical knowledge about race in America fills out the story that the demographics hint at. For example, the higher marriage rates among the Promise Keepers help to explain why PK men spoke more about their relationships with their wives and children while Million Man marchers talked more about their mothers, sisters, and daughters or generalized about "womenfolk." But history tells us more. Nearly forty years ago, historian Herbert Gutman explained the historical difference between native-born white and black families. While white families of the eighteenth, nineteenth, and early twentieth centuries elevated the nuclear family to normalcy, African Americans were as likely to venerate extended family and fictive networks as the husband-wife family. Prohibitions against legal marriage, the sale of slaves as property, the need of slaves and then later of migrants to "create" family (fictive kin) in its absence, and male un- and underemployment after enslavement forced African Americans to expand family membership in order to have enough people from which to draw economic and psychological support.[94] Given this historical context, it is easy to understand why Million Man marchers spoke about women more generally while their PK counterparts spoke more specifically about their wives. Not only was the marriage rate among Million Man marchers lower but they also probably had a broader concept of family than did Promise Keepers. Race had structured their historical lives differently and it made a difference in the 1990s.

The difference was also reflected in the way these white and black men defined the new masculinity. The difference was subtle but it was real. For example, PK men typically expressed a need to be softer and kinder. "We're free to be weak and we're free to fail," said Promise Keeper Joe Gelak of Springfield, Maryland.[95] PK men also wanted their sons to learn the value of a more loving, less macho manhood. They wanted them to learn to be more like Jesus Christ, the compassionate Father. Said one Colonia, Illinois, man about his own father, "I don't remember ever hearing 'I love you' from him or ever being held in his arms . . . but my Heavenly Father let me know that He would be my Father and hold me in his arms."[96] Fifteen-year-old Daniel Hutchinson, who traveled to a PK gathering with his father, got a firsthand experience with that kind of love. He learned, he said, that a man didn't have to talk "about bad things" to be a man. He found the male bonding soothing: "You get to unite with other guys and get hugs and that kind of stuff. It's pretty cool."[97]

By contrast, while Million Man marchers *performed* a manhood that was softer and gentler than the one projected by the media, they were more likely to stress the need for men to be more race oriented. Specifically, they used the words *unity* and *uniting* as adjectives, and defined them as masculine traits. "I feel like it's going to be good for America to see brothers, uniting," said Jeffrey Walker of East Columbia, Maryland.[98] "This is our chance to show unity in the black community," said Lloyd Dixon of Kansas City.[99] Thirty-eight-year-old Anthony Belton, a Houston, Texas, bus driver, brought his two sons to the gathering because he believed that "black men coming together in unity is a historical experience." He wanted his sons to "experience it, to learn from it and to move forward from it."[100] Even Earl Ofari Hutchinson, who chastised organizers for blaming the victim, praised the unity aspect of the march. "It sends a much needed message any time you can get a show of unity among African American men especially."[101]

The character traits implied by unity did not necessarily exclude softness, compassion, and kindness but they were different. Belton, the Houston bus driver, stood with his sons and other Texas men under a banner that read "Black men standing tall, unbent and unbowed."[102] Also under that banner was fourteen-year-old Omar Owens. He linked unity to nonviolence, cooperativeness, and altruism. African Americans would make it "not by fighting or by standing alone, or by looking out just for ourselves. But by looking out for one another."[103] Boys like Owens were on the mind of *Washington Post* columnist Courtland Milloy, who associated unity with the self-respect and self-control that it took to end black-on-black crime: "I like the idea of a million African American men just coming together and not acting like Hutus and Tutsis for a change," he wrote.[104] Related to Milloy's comment were those of Pittsburgh labor leader Nate Smith. Before the march he wrote that he hoped the Million Man March replicated the scene in Spike Lee's movie *Malcolm X*, where hundreds of well-groomed, unarmed black men in overcoats, white shirts, and ties and hats converged on a New York City police station. "Marching in straight lines, never speaking a word, totally disciplined. No one broke rank." For Smith, the scene, and the real-life episode on which it was based, "was more frightening . . . than blacks acting crazy and out of control." Indeed, said Smith, "the power of presence belonged to the marchers."[105]

The contrast between the Promise Keeper desire to be less macho and more emotional and the Million Man desire to be more disciplined and powerful is significant. For sure, their respective expressed concerns were not the sum total of their very complex thinking on this very complicated subject of masculinity. Furthermore, being more emotional and kind did not cancel out a desire to be disciplined; being disciplined did not necessarily mean that one rejected emotionalism. But the foregoing examples demonstrate that black and white men approached masculinity differently. To understand why, we need to understand their different histories.

Historically, middle- and working-class white men defined the parameters of American masculinity, and they usually used blacks and women as negative referents. For example, after the American Revolution, a man was defined by his independence and personal autonomy. As American white men they had refused to become the slaves of the British and vowed to have their liberty and serve only themselves. "We won't be their [Britain's] negroes," wrote John Adams. "Providence," he continued, "never designed us for negroes. I know, for if it had it would have given us black hides and thick lips . . . which it han't done, and therefore never intended us for slaves."[106] Black men, white men thought, could not be real men because as slaves they could not be self-made men. They were considered to be like women: submissive, dependent, and unfree. In the early nineteenth century, white men believed themselves to be manly because they controlled their own time and their own labor. They fought and obtained the right to vote because they owned themselves and, for that matter, the property of women. When industrialization and incorporation compromised their control over their time and labor, they gradually redefined manhood to fit late nineteenth- and twentieth-century realities. A real man was defined as a male who achieved success in the marketplace; who earned his wealth through diligent hard work or who banded together in solidarity with other men to define his labor force participation. A man was someone who controlled his emotions and desires, who was muscular and physically strong, virile though sexually restrained. Most important, white men defined a real man as someone who separated himself from all things female and all things black.[107]

This last fact is crucial. White men did not separate their gender from their race. Women were consigned to the domestic sphere and banned from voting in part because as the "weaker," "gentler" sex they were perceived to lack the intellect and the emotional and physical strength to manage the responsibilities that came with work in the public domain. At the 1893 World's Fair, for example, the white women's pavilion was separated from the white man's with the explanation, given by the *New York Times*, that "the achievements of man [are] in iron, steel, wood, and the baser and cruder products" while a "sublimely soft and soothing atmosphere or womanliness" pervaded the Woman's Building, which exhibited "the more delicate and finer products of the loom, needle brush, and more refined avenues of effort which culminate in the home, the hospital, the church and in personal adornment."[108] The ideals of a hard, solid, firm manhood, and a soft, delicate womanhood did not remain static throughout the twentieth century but changed depending on time, place, and circumstances. But women, especially white women, remained men's reference point on manhood. And usually white men cast women, if not the antithesis of manhood, as the polar opposite. Men, ideally, were perceived to be stoic (like the Marlboro Man), intellectual without being an egghead (like Teddy Roosevelt), athletic (like John F. Kennedy), and heroic (like Charles Lindbergh and World War II soldiers). They understood themselves as men by defining women as people they were not.

They also understood themselves as men by defining themselves as different from blacks. Throughout most of the twentieth century, African Americans and other minorities were consigned to servile labor. Perceived to be ruled by instinct rather than intellect, like women, blacks were thought to be weak and emotional and lacking in self-control. To most white men, black men were like the African porters whom Teddy Roosevelt wrote about in his travel narratives. They were primitive. Though "strong, patient and good-humored savages, with something childlike about them that makes one really fond of them, . . . like most savages and most children they have their limitations. . . . They are subject to gusts of passion and they are now and then guilty of grave misdeeds and shortcomings; sometimes for no conceivable reason, at least from the white man's standpoint."[109] In short, Teddy Roosevelt and countless white men throughout the twentieth century were able to understand themselves as men—as rational, self-controlled grown-ups—by projecting onto black men the traits that they did not want associated with themselves. As historian Gail Bederman put it so perceptibly, "To speak of the white man was thus to link white males to the power and evolutionary advancement of civilization and to link black males to unmanliness and savagery."[110]

This history was layered with the part of Christian thought that assigns negative characteristics to blackness. Early Christian literature, wrote black theologian Robert Hood, "identified the devil as the Black One or Dark One, so marked because of his falling from the light of God's grace."[111] This notion was alive and well when Englishmen first met Africans and made the consequential association between blackness and slavery, and whiteness and freedom. Because Africans were heathens and Englishmen were Christians, whiteness became synonymous with Christianity. For early white Americans, wrote colonial American scholar Winthrop Jordan, "the term 'Christian' seems to have conveyed much of the idea and feeling of *we* as against *they*. . . . To be Christian was to be civilized rather than barbarous, English rather than African, white rather than black."[112] Early Americans also associated black skin with the curse of Ham, wherein Noah cursed Ham's son, Canaan, for Ham's sin of looking on his father's nakedness when he was drunk. The curse condemned Canaan to be "a servant of servants . . . unto his brethren."[113]

Although this short detour into the nineteenth- and twentieth-century history of manhood does not tell us all, or most, of what we need to know about the history of masculinity in America, it does underscore two relevant points. The first is that ideas about race went hand in hand with ideas about gender. Whether dealt with consciously or unconsciously, race and gender were never completely separate categories. And second is the fact that ideas about black inferiority have a long history in American secular and religious history. These facts must be kept in mind in any comparison of the Christian Promise Keepers and Million Man marchers. Both groups of men addressed masculinity, but because they had traveled separate historical roads to the Washington Mall in the 1990s, they predictably handled the issue differently. Having always defined white men as strong, independent, self-made, and self-controlled Christians, end-of-century white Promise Keepers now sought release from an identity they found straitjacketing. In the 1990s they reworked their understanding of Jesus and his love and made him a model of compassionate manhood.

That black men did not embrace a manhood that validated emotionalism, fragility, and a softer manhood can be traced to their having been historically tainted as weak, soft, criminal, and primitive. That they did not embrace a manhood based on a redefined Jesus had not only to do with the fact that the Million Man March was not an avowedly Christian event, but also with the fact that historically a black man who was seen as Christlike was also often derisively cast as an Uncle Tom—the Harriet Beecher Stowe character who endured the brutality of his white master, Simon Legree, without fighting back, and who, like Jesus on the cross, died rather than save himself.[114] While white Promise Keepers had a history that allowed them to renegotiate their conception of strength, black men could not risk such a negotiation.

African American men had spent most of their history in America disproving negative characterizations of themselves. Because their masculinity had not been taken for granted by white Americans, black men had always had to prove and proclaim their manliness—to themselves and to others. Said Frederick Douglass when he beat his brutal master, Mr. Covey, the battle "revived within me a sense of my own manhood."[115] In 1829, when David Walker, a free North Carolinian, challenged enslaved men to copy the former slaves of Haiti and throw off the yoke of slavery, he asked, "Are we Men!! How could we be so submissive?"[116] During the Civil War and World Wars I and II, black men were challenged to fight, and challenged themselves, on the grounds that valor in war would demonstrate their manhood. From the former slave turned soldier in the Civil War who proclaimed "I feel like a man with a uniform on and a gun in my hand"[117] to the World War II army corporal who proclaimed "I went into the army a nigger; I'm comin' out a man"[118] to the "I Am a Man" placards worn in 1968 by the striking Memphis sanitation workers that Martin Luther King gave his life supporting,[119] black men have had to prove and proclaim their manhood because it was never assumed to be their natural possession.

They especially had to distance themselves from women, not only to distinguish themselves as men, but also to prove whites wrong about their effeminacy. Obviously, this was hard since slavery and institutionalized racism established a hierarchy designed to emasculate black men by making it impossible for them to fulfill the prescribed masculine duty of economic support and aggressive defense of women. Nevertheless, inasmuch as proof of their fitness for race and gender equality hinged on demonstrating these manhood qualities (how black women handled gender conventions is taken up in the next chapter), black men adopted the same distancing technique as white men. Despite the realities that forced black women, first as slaves and then as free laborers, into the public arena of hard, backbreaking work, the nineteenth century was punctuated with remarks like those of the Reverend J. W. C. Pennington, who spoke against the ordination of woman with the argument that women were unsuited for "all the learned professions, where mighty thought and laborious investigation are needed" because as the "weaker sex" they were "incapacitated . . . both physically and mentally."[120] And throughout the twentieth century there were statements made like those in a 1970 position paper issued from the Congress of African Peoples proclaiming that "man is the head of the house. He is leader of the house/nation because his knowledge of the world is broader, his awareness is greater, his understanding is fuller and his application of this information is wiser."[121]

Another way that black men established themselves as men was by working on race survival and uplift. Self-help uplift was critically important at the turn of the twentieth century when African Americans were adapting to modernity. As blacks migrated to urban areas, filled the classrooms of historically black colleges, credentialed themselves in the professions, sought nonagricultural work and the franchise, they created African American organizations for help and support. The black men who helped create organizations like the National Association for the Advancement of Colored People and the National Negro Business League joined fraternities like Alpha Phi Alpha and Omega Psi Phi and fraternal orders like the Freemasons and Elks. They created and performed a masculinity based on service, property ownership, production, and respectability, and on the fight for civil and economic rights. In their organizations, men pooled their resources, built their meeting places, and took part in certain rituals, and thus practiced and performed a self-defined masculinity that they believed helped the race and demonstrated their manhood.[122] The same could be said of black men during the mid-twentieth-century freedom movement. Like the North Carolina A&T freshman who, with three other young men, sat still while whites shouted racial epithets and poured condiments on them, black male activists "created militant new models of black manhood" while also seeing their activism as "a rite of passage into manhood."[123] When asked about the Greensboro sit-in experience, one of the young men predictably responded, "I probably felt better than I've ever felt in my life. . . . I felt as though I had gained my manhood."[124]

Many Million Man marchers probably felt this way too, which is why racial uplift and unity—defined as disciplined, self-controlled, nonsubmissive manliness—was emphasized on October 16, 1995. Although the march is often compared to the 1963 March on Washington for Jobs and Freedom (something this book takes up in a subsequent chapter), it was more in step with the tradition of self-help racial uplift and activism. "Who will save the black man if not us?," asked a black physician from Louisville, Kentucky. "We're not going to get anywhere blaming white America for everything when we're responsible for ongoing atrocities in our own communities," said Jesse Thomas, a race relations consultant from Dunkirk, New York.[125] Self-help had provided sustenance when none was forthcoming from political parties, federal and local governments, or progressive whites, and it was a familiar guide at the Million Man March.

Understanding this history helps us contextualize Pastor Tony Evans's seemingly anomalous Promise Keeper attitude about men's leadership in the home. In the same article in which he chastised "'sissified' men," Evans spoke specifically about African Americans. "In the black community," he said, "women run the show to an alarming degree." Citing familiar statistics, Evans noted that 60 percent of black children grew up without fathers. Since most of their teachers and caregivers were women, Evans saw most black children growing up without men in their lives, which for him spelled ruin for black America. He blamed the "feminized male" for the eclipse of masculine influence in black neighborhoods, where gang violence and teenage pregnancy ran rampant. Harking back to the tradition of African American self-help, Evans proclaimed that "there is no sum of money—no federal, state, county, or municipal program—that can get us out of the ditch we've fallen into." Sounding very much like forebears Pennington and the Congress of African Peoples, Evans proclaimed that the only way to save African America was "by getting men to assume their responsibilities and take back the reins of spiritually pure leadership God intended us to hold. . . . Otherwise," he predicted, "our culture is lost."[126]

If Evans's approach to Promise Keeper masculinity is rooted in black history, this history, specifically the philosophy and tactic of self-help, also explains why so many black men eschewed PK. For many black men, self-help means staying away from white people. One black male editorialist proclaimed that he was not going to Washington if marchers were going to "complain about how THEY haven't built our communities" or "to demand yet more crumbs from somebody else's table,"[127] and Bishop H. H. Bookins of Los Angeles averred that "we did not come here for a handout from the white people on the Hill."[128] While this kind of thinking did not keep Evans away from PK, the ideology of black self-help was an impediment to cross-racial male bonding.

It suggests other differences between the white men of the Promise Keepers and the black Million Man marchers as well. For example, film clips of the two gatherings show controlled enthusiasm, men holding hands and hugging, and men chanting in unison. However, 1990s PK events were far more emotion-filled. In part, this can be attributed to the evangelical Protestantism that infused PK reflections on masculinity. But it is also an indication of the release white men sought in their embrace of new masculine values. Although most of the Million Man marchers were Protestants who hailed from an evangelical tradition, they were far less emotional than Promise Keepers.

Some of this has to do with what Hutchinson said about unity and African American men, and what the editorialist said about not going to the march if marchers were going to complain that "they" had not performed appropriately. Hutchinson's quote—"it sends a much needed message any time you can get a show of unity among African American men especially"—begs the same question as the editorialist's: Who is the "they," and to whom is the message Hutchinson talks about directed? Thirty-three-year-old Blake Boddie of Pine Top, North Carolina, also gives us food for thought. His comment, "It's a good thing to show them that all black men are not in jail or on drugs," forces us to think about who the "them" is.[129] No doubt for some men the "them" was black women, from whom they sought forgiveness. But Hutchinson had recently published *The Assassination of the Black Male Image*, which looked at the way black men had been slandered and psychologically emasculated since slavery. For him, the "them" was white America.[130] Boddie was a respondent to a *Washington Post* poll that found that most blacks thought the Million Man March was "an opportunity for black men to defy negative stereotypes" and make "a positive statement about the role of black men."[131] Boddie, therefore, was like Hutchinson. He wanted to experience respectable manhood but was aware of the value of the performance. So too was David Bositis, a white senior research associate at the liberal-oriented Joint Center for Political and Economic Studies. Significantly, when this white scholar was asked, before the march, about the probability of success, he said that it was "the conduct of the march—the way the speakers conduct themselves, the way the marchers conduct themselves—that will very much have to do with the long-term success or failure of the March."[132] In short, while Promise Keepers could "let go and let God" in the performance of a new gender role, many black men gathered with the double consciousness identified by twentieth-century historian and activist W. E. B. Du Bois. They had to objectify themselves and perform a new role that was not just gendered but raced. Boddie and Hutchinson let us know that they felt their "twoness." They were at once American men who found the end-of-century demands confusing, and they were also black American men who had been racially stereotyped.[133] Mindful that they were being watched, and angry because of it too, these mostly middle-class men performed a softer and gentler manhood—a nonviolent, disciplined show of unity—not only because they felt it the only way to succeed in postmodern America, but also because they needed to demonstrate black men's worthiness to white America.

And they performed this manhood with a profound sense of history that drew them close to previous generations of African American men. Notably, Promise Keepers' sense of history made them want to be different from previous generations of white American men. Million Man marchers however, expressed admiration for those who had gone before and achieved so much for the race. Many, like Michael McKinzy, compared the Million Man March to the '63 march, and got a greater understanding of the trials endured by that generation. "I wasn't even born back then," he said. "But this, now for me is something to look back on as a source of strength and something to build from."[134] Lloyd Dixon, who went to a local march in Kansas City, Missouri, felt similarly. "If people that came before me can sacrifice all their lives, certainly I can sacrifice one day."[135] Charles Sydnor III, who traveled to the march from Maryland with his father, said that the march made him feel things he had not felt by just reading about the '60s. He no longer had to wonder whether he would have been able to summon the courage to do what his father's generation had done. "Here's my chance to do something like that."[136]

In sum, if nothing else, this short comparison of the Promise Keepers and Million Man March teaches us that history matters. Though both groups of men went to the Washington Mall in the 1990s with masculinity issues weighing heavily on their shoulders, their respective histories forced them to approach the issue differently. For over three hundred years, black and white men had been each other's referent for ideal manhood. They had dissimilar familial histories and experiences with freedom. Their consciousness about the purpose of their marches was also not the same. The question that arises most poignantly from this comparison is: Could these differences be overcome? Could all that made them different trump what made them alike?

Reconciling Promise Keepers and Million Man Marchers

Putting the Promise Keepers and the Million Man March in historical perspective and seriously considering the intersectionality of race, faith, class, gender, and sexuality help us revision the Promise Keepers' attempt at racial reconciliation and consider the ways white and black men might reconcile.

Most analysts judge PK efforts at racial reconciliation to have been a failure, and there is ample evidence to support their conclusion. There is, for example, the white Promise Keeper who was angry that he drove two hundred miles to a PK gathering only to hear its leaders, as he put it, "talk about that crap."[137] About the racial reconciliation message another white Promise Keeper said, "It didn't come across right." Promise Keepers "were sawing off their own legs talking about how bad things were."[138] Comments like these made up 40 percent of the negative feedback PK leaders received.[139]

Even the positive steps taken toward racial reconciliation either did not work for the Promise Keepers or fell short in critics' eyes. For example, membership declined rapidly after the Promise Keepers eliminated the sixty-dollar entrance fee to stadium gatherings after the '97 Stand in the Gap gathering on the National Mall, a move taken to encourage minority men to attend. Much of the money allocated to underwrite minority participation (travel to conferences or special conferences for minority clergy) had come from the entrance fees, and its elimination unfortunately forced Promise Keepers to scale back all of its activities, including minority outreach and recruitment.[140] Then there is the fact that many Promise Keepers could embrace racial reconciliation only if they also minimized the impact of race in America or dealt with race as a problem of individual behavior rather than as a systemic problem. Sociologist Mary Stricker says that white Promise Keepers were so attached to the idea of black inferiority that they could only embrace racial reconciliation from a narrow color-blind perspective; that is, they could commune with black men only if they could do so while "seeing past the skin," or not recognizing the difference that race made in their respective lives.[141] A color-blind approach, says Stricker, allowed those Promise Keepers who embraced racial reconciliation to not see blackness—something they associated with inferiority—and thus feel they were not racists.[142] Sociologists Michael Emerson and Christian Smith argue that the PK approach to racism was inadequate because the organization's approach was rooted in a

Christian individualism that did not allow for an all-out attack against racism's structural roots.[143]

These scholars are right—the Promise Keepers' limited and color-blind approach did indeed keep black men from embracing PK. "A lot of men are hesitant about the Promise Keepers because [it's] viewed as being led by white Republicans," said Aaron Haskins, the African American reconciliation manager for the Northwest.[144] Since color blindness had become part of the anti–affirmative action rhetoric of the Republican Party, blacks were naturally suspicious. Also, black men did not want to be tokens; they did not want to go to onetime events and be the means by which white men eased their conscience about their racial sins, and they did not want to be patronized. Said a black Protestant air force chaplain who attended the Promise Keeper 1996 Superdome conference in New Orleans and heard the message of racial reconciliation: "What good will that be [the message of reconciliation] if I need a job on Monday, and you have one, and you stand on all your hallelujahs in church on Sunday and don't help me?"[145] Even some black conservatives rebuked the Promise Keepers. For example, African American media host Ken Hamblin, whose mantra was personal responsibility, blasted Bill McCartney and the Promise Keepers for being patronizing toward black Americans. "The last thing my people need is you and your organization mobilizing to reinforce the notion of how difficult and lowly it is to be dusky in the U.S.," he wrote. Protesting McCartney's many speeches in which he railed against people who do nothing about American racism, Hamblin reminded McCartney of the '60s freedom movement and the many blacks and whites who worked around the clock against racism. "We don't need a white male army of God's angels on earth rushing to our aid, overcome with missionary zeal to liberate us from the hellishness of being black in America. What we need is to be dealt with as equals, fully vested Americans."[146]

While Hamblin's causticity underscores the limited racial reconciliation achieved by the Promise Keepers, it also should make us marvel at the fellowship that *did* occur. When we consider white and black men's historic mistrust, the ways they served as each other's conscious and unconscious referent, the different ways they imagined and used masculinity, the different contemporary societal positions, and the different contemporary issues facing their respective communities, it is a wonder that *any* Promise Keeper gathering had *any* interracial hand-holding and commiserating. And yet, after 1995 anywhere from 14 to 20 percent of Promise Keepers were African American in an America where black people composed only 12 to 13 percent of the population—and men, presumably, half of that.[147] Given all that kept them apart, that there *were* black and white Promise Keepers in the 1990s, that the leadership of the organization was significantly integrated, and that racial reconciliation remained one of the seven guiding principles of the organization is remarkable. To the question "Is the glass half empty or half full?," a case can be made for the latter.

For starters, there were the many friendships like that cited earlier between Steve Wagner and Brian Walker. Alongside black men like Hamblin who found PK patronizing and white men who resented the racial reconciliation "crap," there were those like Houston firefighter Garry Blackmon, an African American who quit his job to join the staff of the Promise Keepers because, more than any other ministry, political agenda, or group, PK dealt with his inner pain.[148] There is Dale Layton, a Birmingham, Alabama, white man, who to the chagrin of his neighbors deliberately befriended black men in his city and invited them to fishing outings at his community's lake.[149] Like so many other Promise Keepers, Blackmon and Layton found gender and religion a way to bridge the racial divide. "The first step is for us to see each other as men—just men," said the African American Reverend Raynard Casimier of New Orleans.[150] Noting the power of Christ, another black pastor challenged Promise Keepers to "cross color lines" and make the secular world jealous. "They don't believe," he said, that "Christ can bring this body together."[151]

Like Million Man marchers, black and white Promise Keepers found common cause when it came to the masculinity issues of fathers being present and accountable to women and children and men taking responsibility for the moral condition of America. While recognizing that African Americans had legitimate reasons for being suspicious of Promise Keepers, the Reverend Tony Morris, an African American, attended a PK minister's conference because, he said, it had a vital message for all people, especially the African American community. Raised by a single mother, he believed that "it is a definite responsibility on fathers to be at the forefront of raising their children, giving them the value system that they need to have."[152] Morris would probably have agreed with the black male editorialist who wrote that as a Christian African American male he found a lot to like in both the Million Man March and the Promise Keepers. Though he approached both with caution, he felt that all men needed "to atone, take more personal responsibility and examine what it means to be men."[153] Robert Flennaugh, a black Seattle dentist who attended the 1996 PK gathering at the Seattle Kingdome, also appreciated the relationship message. Men being more loving to their wives and more involved in their children's lives had resonance for him: "There was a real sense of being true and truthful in all your relationships."[154] Responses like these demonstrate that the Promise Keeper mission to use Christianity

FIGURE 4. The sixth promise of a Promise Keeper was to reach across racial and denomination divides for the purpose of demonstrating biblical unity. Though many men found this difficult to do, others worked on it and some succeeded. *Photo by Porter Gifford/Liaison/Getty Images.*

and gender to bring white and black men together to heal themselves and families was appealing to some black men.

Also appealing was the focus on self-help. As already noted, to the regret of many, the Million Man March did not protest systemic racism but focused on individual and communal self-improvement. For some, the tradition of self-help uplift was an obstacle to interracial bonding; for others, however, it meshed with their Christian belief that salvation was an individual endeavor that came only through one's personal relationship with Jesus Christ. Individuals were responsible not only for their relationship with Christ, but also for Christlike living and Christlike relationships. Reform, Christians believe, starts with personal responsibility.[155] One white Promise Keeper put it this way: "If you really are not happy with the nation and want change, the first thing that needs attention is the man who looks back at you when you shave in the morning."[156] Another said that his pastor preached that the individual has "to be intentional about racial reconciliation." He himself believed that the "Bible is very clear about multiculturalism: Every tongue, tribe and nation will be together before the Lord." He thought that "to do it before the Lord, we'd better learn to do it here."[157]

Black Promise Keepers embraced the concept of self-help from both a black and a Christian perspective. They believed that community development began in the community and with individual improvement, including getting along with whites. For example, fifty-five-year-old Andrew Nelson was skeptical that PK could break down the walls of segregation that kept black and white congregations worshipping separately on Sunday mornings, but he was willing to make an individual effort to that end. He attended the 1996 PK gathering at the New Orleans Superdome because he thought it had to start with people like him. "God can change us," he said. "I do believe that, otherwise, I wouldn't be here."[158] The African American chairman of the Promise Keepers, Bishop Phillip H. Porter, summed up the feeling of countless black Promise Keepers with this observation: "Unless hearts are truly changed, you can pass legislation, march all you want, educate the mind, but you will still have nothing but a retreating. The inner man being unchanged will still act out his prejudices."[159]

While personal responsibility and self-help enabled some black and white Christian men to bridge the racial divide, heterosexuality was yet another bridge. Although rank-and-file Promise Keepers and Million Man marchers did not leave a large body of evidence of their feelings on this score, scholars have found that among both white and black men, religiosity and religious attendance has a high correlation with homophobia.[160] Since the Promise Keepers and Million Man marchers were among the most religious men of their respective racial groups, we can suppose that they conformed to scholars' findings. Additionally, both groups of men were led by leaders who opposed homosexuality. The Promise Keepers' founder, Bill McCartney, called homosexuality an "abomination against God Almighty," and in 1992 he actively campaigned against lesbians, gays, bisexuals, and transgenders (lgbts) when he supported passage of Colorado's Amendment 2, which would have prohibited lgbts from claiming minority status for legal protection against discrimination.[161] Steve Chavis, the African American national spokesman of the Promise Keepers, made clear the Promise Keeper stance of "hate the sin, love the sinner." Racial reconciliation was possible and a desired goal, he said, but "certain walls . . . won't come down. . . . We do have something to offer gay men," he insisted, "but it's not what they want to hear." About homosexuality being a sin, he claimed that "there's no gray area, because the Bible is quite clear."[162]

Minister Louis Farrakhan also opposed homosexuality. In one of his many attacks he described homosexuality as freakish, unnatural, perverse, and a deviation from the law under which Allah created man.[163] "God don't like men coming to men with lust in their hearts like you should go to a female. If you think that the kingdom of God is going to be filled up with that kind of degenerate crap, you're out of your damn mind," he inveighed.[164] At the Million Man March, no representative of black gays spoke from the podium.[165]

In all likelihood, Million Man marchers and Promise Keepers were reassured by the heterosexuality embraced by their respective leaders. Issues of late twentieth-century sexuality are discussed in detail in later chapters. For now, though, we need to remember that these black and white men, who were among the most religious of their respective cohorts, were being asked to embrace a masculinity that required a homosocial intimacy most were unfamiliar and even uncomfortable with. They were also being asked to atone, to assume an attitude of humility that necessarily required a shift in their understanding of manliness. In different ways, scholars and others remind us of how difficult it was for late twentieth-century men to feel comfortable with each other—to hug, embrace, and cry with each other—in a society that was gaining in tolerance for homosexuality. Rico, the PK Cape Verdean cited earlier, likened sharing confidences with a man to "asking another man to dance." Sociologist John Bartkowski would argue that the PK antigay sentiment put men like Rico at ease because its antigay stance naturalized heterosexuality and therefore rendered male intimacy "safe."[166] Both Eve Sedgwick and Ron Becker would argue that because homosexuality in the 1990s was beginning to be accepted and even normalized ("Don't ask, don't tell" became the official policy of the military in 1993, and the number of homosexual characters and subjects in the media increased exponentially throughout the nineties), McCartney's and Farrakhan's antigay ideology, along with the male-only camaraderie of the gatherings, eased the "panic" that heterosexual male companionship provoked among these religious black and white men. Men needed to feel, they would say, that there was nothing homosexual about men having and depending on male friends.[167]

In sum, then, this look at the Promise Keepers' efforts at racial reconciliation and the common concerns of Promise Keepers and Million Man marchers finds that black and white men have more in common than has been assumed and that the possibilities for racial reconciliation are hardly preposterous. For sure there were black and white men who could not, and never would, cross the racial divide, but there were enough who would and tried. Neither Promise Keepers nor Million Man marchers attacked systemic racism but looked inward and used the secular and Christian concepts of self-help and personal responsibility to help them forge a more functional manhood. Their ideas about fatherhood and relationships were also similar enough for black and white Promise Keepers to bridge the racial divide. Ironically, heterosexuality formed a potential bridge, suggesting that racial walls would fall but only while heterosexual barriers were being erected.

The Confluence of Class, Faith, Gender, Sexuality, and Race

This chapter does not tell us all we need to know about black and white men nor does it exhaust what can and should be noted about the Promise Keepers and the Million Man March. However, it does show that the 1990s found many American black and white men "lost in the USA." Though they congregated separately, the men who attended the gatherings were angry, unhappy, frustrated, and looking for a blueprint for change. They turned inward and asked more of themselves than they did of the government and institutions. Separately, they vowed to change themselves, and by doing so, their families and communities.

This story of the Promise Keepers and the Million Man March also shows us that this is not a one- or even two-dimensional story. It is not enough to analyze the Promise Keepers as a conservative white group that fought for racial reconciliation, or the Million Man marchers as a group of black men who gathered to affirm their black identity in a society increasingly hostile to black males. Nor is it enough to critique their turn to personal responsibility without considering how and why their approach made them happier. Promise Keepers and Million Man marchers were looking for more satisfying relationships. The more religious of their peer groups, they were also looking for more satisfying ways to be men in a society in which the rules of manhood were in flux. Their class mattered, their gender mattered, their race mattered, their faith mattered, and their sexual orientation mattered. These identity variables had mattered throughout history and history mattered in the 1990s as multiculturalism, globalization, feminism, and deindustrialization made life uncomfortable and unfamiliar.

There is plenty of irony here. It's ironic that these men, who on some level were angry with each other and who had such different experiences with manhood—different enough to march separately—should wind up with similar solutions to similar problems. Also ironic was their individualistic approach to problems even they recognized demanded communal solutions. Perhaps most ironic is that Promise Keepers and Million Man marchers looked for better ways to relate to women. Still, while they found it necessary to exclude women from their congregations, they were unsure of how to commune comfortably with men. More revelatory than ironic is that the race identity of these white and black men so defined who they were as men that the commonalties they shared on the basis of gender and sexuality were, while not obliterated, obscured.

Finally, this look at the Promise Keepers and the Million Man March shows that people's feelings count. In the 1990s, much attention was drawn to the gatherings' respective leadership. For different reasons, Farrakhan and McCartney were controversial, and at the time of the gatherings there was endless speculation about the political power that would accrue from the gatherings and how McCartney and Farrakhan would use that power. The focus here has been on the people whose nerves they touched and whose problems they hoped to solve. Clearly, there were many who were lost, and many of them looked to the Million Man March and the Promise Keepers to find their way.

CHAPTER 3

Standing By Their Men

What Promise Keeper and
Million Man March Women Wanted

On the morning of October 4, 1997, members of the National Organization for Women (NOW) greeted the hundreds of thousands of Promise Keepers (PK) who gathered for the Stand in the Gap assembly on the National Mall with shouts of "Ominous!" and "Dangerous!," and with placards that read "Patriarch Keeper."[1] It was a familiar sight, one that had been repeated at almost every Promise Keeper gathering since its founding. "They're a very sexist, racist and homophobic organization," said Sondra Sinke, the Nebraska chapter coordinator of the National Organization for Women, when the Promise Keepers gathered in Omaha in 1999.[2] Later that year, at the PK meeting in Hartford, Connecticut, the protest was the same. In an editorial titled "Much to Fear from Promise Keepers," Alice Lambert, the president of the Connecticut NOW, wrote, among other things, "We feminists believe that women control their own bodies and lives. Bill McCartney . . . opposes women's rights."[3]

Feminist opposition to the Million Man March was similarly insistent. Julianne Malveaux, the future president of Bennett College, asked, "When men are 'stepping up,' we have to ask, will the first step be onto a woman's back?"[4] Another black woman, Rhonda Williams, could also not support the march: "If it means that more men are capitulating to a type of thinking that says black families are simply broken and pathological, unaffected by economic and cultural change, and simply needing some more good ole-fashioned male supremacy—I can't sign on."[5] Neither could activist Jewel Jackson McCabe, who declared that African American "needs are not served by men declaring themselves the only 'rightful' leaders of our families, or our communities and of our ongoing struggle for justice." Justice, she said, "cannot be achieved with a march that offers a distorted racist view of black manhood with a narrowly sexist vision of men standing degrees above women."[6]

Whether they knew or felt it, these black and white women had a lot in common. For sure, they rejected both Bill McCartney and Louis Farrakhan, both of whom were associated with antiwomen, antifeminist, and homophobic positions. Even though both Farrakhan and McCartney at one time or another disavowed their critics' claims, they both drew heavy skepticism when they proclaimed the equality of men and women and men's responsibility to share parenting responsibilities.

Also, black and white feminists did not buy into the idea propagated by march leaders that these large gatherings gave men a chance to bond and thus be emotionally reborn into kinder, gentler human beings. Rather, to feminists, this was just another instance of what one scholar has called "male romance," the phenomenon that "involves men going off with other men, ritually bonding with each other, and being 'reborn' within a community of males," a process that throughout American history has allowed men to consolidate power while eliminating women from the centers of political, social, and economic control. Rather than allay feminists' fears, "the preponderance of tears and repentance . . . on the National Mall constituted a symbolic claim on the capital itself." Men's mourning, it was believed, signaled little more than a softer expression of male domination. According to *New York Times* columnist Maureen Dowd, when men explore their fragilities, "it usually leads to trouble."[7]

Most Promise Keeper and Million Man March women, however, rejected the view put forth by NOW.[8] On the morning of October 16, 1995, activist and self-avowed feminist E. Faye Williams had only good things to say about the multitude of black men who gathered in Washington, DC, for the Million Man March. "There is an African proverb that it is the women who hold up the sky," said Williams. "I have a feeling that from this day on, it's going to be a whole lot easier . . . you have come to help us hold up the sky."[9] Williams, a Washington, DC, lawyer and chair of the march's organizing committee, was joined in her support of the march by countless other black women who could be heard along the sidelines shouting, "Black man. Black man. We applaud you, black man. Black sunshine! Black sunshine! We love you, Brothers!"[10] For them, October 16 marked a new beginning. They were not offended by Farrakhan's instruction that women stay home and mind black children so that men could march alone. It would not, as Dowd predicted, lead to trouble, but to a new era where black men claimed leadership of neighborhoods and of families, where black men recognized the strength of black women, and where the abuse of black women was henceforth tolerated by no one.[11] So supportive were black women of the Million Man March that a *Washington Post* poll found that more black men than women objected to the exclusion of women. Only 18 percent of the black men polled said the march ought to be single-sexed while fully half of the black women polled supported the men-only restriction.[12] Similarly, black male academics were more likely than their female counterparts to think that black women should have been included.[13]

The elation expressed by these black women was not unlike that of the wives of most Promise Keepers. When Jeanne Parrott's husband left for a 1994 gathering in Boulder, Colorado, Parrott "prayed that God would open the floodgates and that Dale would come home touched by the Spirit in a new way."[14] She was overjoyed that he did. Karen Jensen felt the same way about her husband. "Women have gone through years of tears, and God is answering their cries," she proclaimed. "Promise Keepers is teaching men how to become servants to their families, and to society," she said.[15] Jensen's sentiment was seconded by syndicated columnist Suzanne Fields, who found a lot to admire about both the Promise Keepers and Million Man marchers. "It's unfair to call them anti-feminist because they don't bash women or women's issues, but like the Million Man March participants, insist on meeting without women . . . to reevaluate themselves from within, with other men."[16]

Why did these women support these male-centered gatherings? Why were they not threatened by them? Because the Promise Keepers are a predominantly white group and the Million Man March was a predominantly black event, answering these questions allows for a rare comparison of the way these two select groups of black and white women view men and male-female relationships. It also allows for a look at the different ways that feminism figures in the lives of these black and white women. Besides exploring why feminist arguments like that promoted by NOW missed the mark with these women, this chapter explores the similar and different needs and desires of these black and white females. It looks at what was important to them and explores their perspectives in both historical and contemporary contexts. Finally, this chapter suggests that, as with their male counterparts, these women had more in common than we might expect, beginning with the fact that their responses to their men's organizing was calculated to help them cope with, and even overcome, the profound societal dislocations of the 1990s.

The Promise Keepers and the Women Who Supported Them

Like their men, Promise Keeper wives, female relatives, and friends were searching for a new order—new ways to relate to society. Though the family itself was transforming under the weight of postmodernity, PK women ironically put enormous faith in the ability of the family to help them prevail against the very forces that were changing the family.[17] They thought the two-parent heterosexual family was the core unit of American society and believed that the dislocations of the '70s and '80s had weakened it but that it could be strengthened through the cooperative efforts of husbands and wives. No doubt they were disturbed by the decline in marriage, including the almost 10 percent drop in white women's marriage rate between 1950 and 2000 and the corresponding increase (nearly 10 percent) in the divorce rate.[18] But, like PK men, they thought that the family was in trouble because men had emotionally abandoned the unit. They believed new gender roles could rejuvenate the family and they supported Promise Keeper efforts to steer men toward those new roles.

Most PK wives felt their men became more sensitive and loving once touched by the organization's teachings. They believed that by showing men how Christ loved his disciples and other people, PK showed Christian men how to befriend other men in supportive, thoughtful ways and in so doing taught them how to relate to their wives and children. This is the message that comes through the strongest in PK wives' testimonials. For example, Jennifer McDonald of Wayzata, Minnesota, thanked her husband for attending a PK convention and "learning how to be a better husband and father and sharing your faith." Fellow Minnesotan Allyson Jelinski likewise thanked her spouse for making "our family the top priority in his life." Although another Minnesotan, Kristine Harley, dissented, finding all the rant about men making family a priority akin to endorsing a "benevolent tyranny," others, like Sally Becker of Milwaukee, found it the salvation of their marriage. "Now there's more give and take. . . . He's more understanding of my needs and I'm more understanding of his."[19] Connie Schaedel of La Mirada, California, was similarly thankful of PK: "Our relationship, our marriage, became even more complete, even more whole, as a result of the way he felt he could express himself."[20]

PK wives found that Promise Keeper teaching led to a marked improvement in the way their husbands related to their children. Veronica Gonzalez, for example, said that her husband Efrain, a Kansas City pastor, "spends more time with their five children and they love it."[21] Minnesotan Sarah Richards reported that her husband, Brian, came home from a rally determined to spend more time with their three- and five-year-olds. Although his job as a CPA forced him to bring work home, PK taught him the value of "making more time for the family."[22] Likewise, African American Houston firefighter Garry Blackmon, whom we met in the previous chapter, was married twelve years and had four children before he attended his first Promise Keeper gathering. According to his wife, Kintra, it was that first meeting that made him "more sensitive to the needs of the family." "Every husband needs to be part of Promise Keepers," said Kintra Blackmon.[23] Michigan insurance agent Ron Bodine's wife agreed. Promise Keepers, she maintained, "opened up more time for talking with [his thirteen-year-old son] and doing things with him."[24]

Most PK wives wanted men in the household because they believed it made the family stronger and changed the family chemistry. In short, they thought that men and women are fundamentally different, particularly in matters of relationships and emotions, and this difference balanced the family in a positive way. Karen Tucker, for example, felt that her husband needed to build relationships with men in order to better communicate with her. "Men are just not as good at building relationships as women are."[25] Annette Cox of Liberty, Kansas, felt similarly: "It is easier for women to find other women. It seems harder for men to find each other." Kimberly Francisco of Kansas City saw men and women in complementary ways. She thought that women, more than men, often put more effort into finding ways to improve themselves, their spiritual lives, and their families. "Men find value in their jobs, and women find value in the way someone treats them."[26] The Reverend Peggy Jones, a black woman who had nothing but praise for the Promise Keepers, thought PK was a blessing because she knew "how difficult it is for them [men] to open up."[27] And when her friends suggested that she would be made subservient if she continued dating her Promise Keeper boyfriend, Kathy Finnell of Kansas City scoffed as she expressed the essentialist idea that "men need to be leaders." She added, "To the extent that you are in a relationship with a man, if you don't trust his decisions and yourself in his hands, you need to look elsewhere."[28]

At first glance it seems that these women had conceded decision-making autonomy and assumed a subordinate role in the household in return for masculinist protection, something NOW leaders decried.[29] That the Promise Keepers projected a kinder, gentler—in fact, gallant and chivalrous—masculinity did not mask, they argued, the fact that PK men wanted women to play subordinate roles in the households so that they could assert their authority through their role as protector. Political scientist Iris Marion Young explained

FIGURE 5. Feminist protestors often demonstrated outside Promise Keeper gatherings, or what PK called conferences. These protestors demonstrated at the Stand in the Gap March on Washington on October 4, 1997. *Photo by Porter Gifford/ Liaison/Getty Images.*

this very well when she argued that feminine women are more likely to concede to masculine dominion when men are loving and self-sacrificing and not selfish, violent, and aggressive. Since the feminine woman wants healthy, safe homes, and because "masculine protection is needed to make a home a haven," the logic of masculinist protection is the submission of women.[30] Scholar Deniz Kandiyoti calls this dynamic the "patriarchal bargain." Women, she argues, consciously and unconsciously weigh their life chances against the patriarchal system of their society and constantly strategize according to the benefits that accrue from submitting to male domination. Even when that system does not yield economic or emotional security for women, their perception that it does or their sense that resistance will not empower them is enough to keep the patriarchal bargain in place.[31] Critics of PK wives supposed this kind of bargain was at work. To them, these Christian women were making a deal with patriarchy that was just as bad as making one with the devil.

And this was maddening. "They want to subjugate women," said Mary Celeste, a spokeswoman for the Colorado Legal Initiatives Project.[32] "SMART WOMEN DON'T BUY YOUR PROMISES" read a banner that flew over the 52,000 men who met in a stadium in Boulder, Colorado.[33] Diana Butler, an editorialist who attended a Los Angeles PK rally, put the argument succinctly. She found the Promise Keepers to be unobjectionable on the level of individual transformation. The overall ethos and agenda, however, was objectionable because PK "implicitly and sometimes explicitly opposes women's leadership in the home and in the church." Butler took exception to one PK minister who interpreted Ephesians 5:22, "Wives, be subject to your husbands as you are to the Lord," claiming that "he urged men to 'outserve' their wives." To Butler, there was something wrong with this Christian definition of marriage as a "competition in which the best servant wins."[34] Butler was also disturbed by what she thought was PK's greater sensitivity to racial matters than to sexism. That PK failed to denounce the sins of "pornography, demeaning women verbally, abuse, sexual sin, power manipulation, [and] lack of emotional support" was "belittling" to women. She summed things up this way: "Promise Keepers envision life as a football game. A great team on the field cheered by women on the sidelines."[35]

Most Promise Keeper wives disagreed with the likes of Butler, and they would not have acceded to the scholarly arguments of Young and Kandiyoti. They took exception to the idea that they were being submissive and would not abide the notion that they had somehow bought protection. "Critics don't understand. They're speaking out of ignorance," said Kathy Simmons of Independence, Missouri. "I haven't heard anything that suggests that the woman is inferior in any way."[36] Valerie Bridgeman Davis, a black woman who described herself as "a happily married womanist," had an entirely different interpretation of Ephesians 5:22. She and her PK husband, Don, read mutuality into the verse. "I believe in submission, but as us submitting to each other," she heard her husband say.[37] Laurie Beyer, a PK wife from Milwaukee, would agree with Davis: "To me there is nothing more equal than the way God designed marriage relationships and families to be."[38]

PK wives felt this way for several reasons. Intertwined with their sheer exhaustion from doing double duty as minimum-wage earners and as mothers was their understanding of equality, not in the sense of sameness, but as equal complementary roles. Since they believed that men and women were inherently different, it followed that men and women brought different qualities to the relationship and had different roles to fulfill in the household. "It's called teamwork," said Marilyn Kenaga. While some feminists might see female subordination written all over her directive that "men are to work

FIGURE 6. Although protestors often gathered outside Promise Keeper events, so too did supporters. Like the women in figure 5, these women met Promise Keepers as they gathered for their Stand in the Gap March on October 4, 1997. *Photo by Porter Gifford/Liaison/Getty Images.*

and provide for their families and bathe them in the word of God" while women "are to help the husbands by taking care of what God has given them," PK wives saw this as equality based on the complementarity of men and women.[39] This is how Kim Bruder of Milwaukee interpreted things. Her seemingly contradictory statement that "I do feel the husband is head of the household, but we're equal," makes the most sense if viewed in this light.[40] Similarly, this is what Texan Lynda Vaughan meant when she said, "Men are leaders of the family, but that doesn't mean they step all over us and we are doormats; . . . that means we work together."[41]Minister Donna Schaper summed this sentiment up this way: "We want our men to dance. We don't even mind being led—in fact, some of us want to be led. We don't want to be led everywhere and we won't be. We won't let ourselves be led out of the benefits of partnership marriage." Underscoring her feeling that the pressures of the new economy had almost overwhelmed women, who like men were searching for new relationships—a new order of things—Schaper said, "Women are tired of being both mother and father. We want strong men as much as men want to be strong. Strength in men is not a rival to our strength; it is a complement."[42]

This perception of equality rooted in complementarity was in direct rebuttal to the feminists' critique of the Promise Keepers. In this counternarrative, PK women were not duped into making a naive bargain with willful patriarchs, nor had they succumbed to a nationalist project that had them safely ensconced in the private sphere of the home, protecting the hearth for the good of the nation.[43] Rather, feminists were the problem. Feminists, they would argue, were uncompromising, man-hating, angry, shrill women who did not value the family or the communities that families made strong. Feminists were all about self, whereas they, Christian women, were about God, family, and community.

Even Promise Keeper women who were critical of PK distanced themselves from feminism. One woman, who described herself as an evangelical Episcopalian, agreed with feminists that PK "is dangerously close to reversing many hard-won gains." But she quickly added, "Not that I am a feminist." Sarah Peterson, a woman who sought a divorce from her husband because his Promise Keeper teachings led him to become too assertive, was also sure she was not one of those "strident bitter women who have placed their careers above all else." Said Peterson, "You do not have to be a feminist . . . to have some say-so in what happens in your own house."[44] Another woman, from Rhode Island, said she took her cues from the strong women in the Bible. When her PK husband tried to push her into a subordinate role, she screamed at him: "Did you miss Mary and Martha? Jesus told her to get out of the kitchen, and come sanctify herself at his feet. He told her Mary had made the better choice. Tell me where that is in these sermons you're hearing?" Yet another woman, quoting from her *Study Bible for Women,* took aim at those Promise Keepers who did not read mutuality into Ephesians. The verse in her study bible read, in part: "Rather than meaning the mutual acceptance and endorsement of woman and man, it has been used to evoke the idea of male dominance and female submission. Similarly, the terms 'equal but different' have often been twisted to mean 'unequal and hierarchical.'" When she finished reading she turned to her interviewer and pointed out what was obvious to her: "For goodness sakes!," she said of her study bible. "It's not exactly radical feminist!"[45]

The important point here is that Promise Keeper women believed in the equality of men and women but they did not want to be associated with feminism, especially with what some perceived as radical feminism. In this they were like the women from various denominations who in 1997 signed "A Christian Women's Declaration," a concise statement of theology that attempted to carve out a middle ground between Christian fundamentalists who advocated women's submission to men and feminist positions that were perceived to be anti-Christian. These women sang the praises of women of previous generations who made it possible for women to enjoy more opportunities and respect than ever before. They claimed as their foremothers the women who first bore witness to the risen Christ. They proclaimed equality with men based on the fact that Jesus Christ made "freedom and dignity possible for all human beings—for women as well as for men," as well as on the fact that women were created in God's image "and the grace of God is extended equally to women." These women affirmed the Triune God, meaning that although they addressed God by the name *Father*, they "acknowledge that God, who created sexuality, is neither male nor female." The human race, they claimed, was constituted, not by a continuum of sexes, but by two complementary sexes, both created in God's image and created to mutually serve one another. All that these women asked of their fellow Christian women they also asked of men. They were especially aggrieved because they were "conscious of how often women have been the targets of such disrespect, abuse, prejudice, and oppression." They pledged themselves "to stand in solidarity with all who have been denied justice, freedom and opportunity."[46]

Needless to say, in their declaration these Christian women took aim at what they perceived to be the faults of women they identified as radical feminists, particularly their endorsement of cultural trends they deemed harmful. Among the many faults they attributed to radical feminists were the latter's interpretation of gender as a social construct. They claimed that while they recognized the force of cultural influence on individual choice and on concepts of maleness and femaleness, they affirmed "that sexuality is rooted in the biological designation of the two sexes—male and female." These Christian women rejected what they claimed was the radical feminist notion of "equality" as "identical." They also rejected the idea that women have been "empty vessels" shaped by patriarchy and that women have been "victims," and they rejected the "exaggeration of women's suffering." They claimed that there have been "countless women of vision and tenacious faith who, through prayer and perseverance, overcame limitations of every variety to influence the shaping of human history." Rather than complain about the innate superiority, inferiority, or radical differences between men and women, these Christian women claimed to celebrate the commonalities of men and women as well as their "unique differences." Of course, in their view, radical feminists were to be faulted for the glorification of "sexual lifestyles without limits or consequences and views of marriage and family that contradict biblically-based faith and time-tested moral behavior." In other words, radical feminists had to be opposed because of their support of abortion, homosexuality, and same-sex marriage, cultural practices that they believed destabilized the family.[47]

Because Promise Keeper wives are a diverse group of women, it is impossible to know whether they all endorsed the "Christian Women's Declaration."[48] However, given the similarity of positions on the centrality of marriage and the family, the equality of men and women, the complementarity of men's and women's roles, the mutual service of husbands and wives, and the folly of radical feminism, the "Christian Women's Declaration" does help us position PK wives theologically and understand the religious principles that underpinned their support of their husbands. It is also helpful to understand that the women who supported the kind of equalitarianism endorsed by PK wives were considered to be to the left of Christian fundamentalists, who blasted the declaration. These critics excoriated women who "equivocate on the masculinity of God and the maleness of Jesus, neuter language, and separate the man from his proper office as head of the church and family." These more conservative Christians opposed what most PK wives supported. Above all, they believed that "among Christians rule is given to the man, who is to lay down his life for the woman, who for her part is to submit to him."[49] This is not the portrait PK wives presented in interviews and testimonials, a portrait made clearer when placed not just in the secular context many, including NOW leaders, placed them in, but also in the Christian context, where they appear far more liberal or progressive than their more conservative counterparts.

The work done by sociologist Judith Stacey on evangelicalism and feminism also helps us understand Promise Keeper women. During the course of her 1980s fieldwork in Silicon Valley, California, Stacey found that, with the exception of ideas about homosexuality and abortion, "feminist ideas and practices have diffused broadly throughout evangelical Christian discourse in the United States." Many of the evangelical women she came in contact with expressed sentiments similar to those of PK women. "We are not doormats," said one woman who espoused submission in the context of mutuality. Despite the diversity of the evangelical community, Stacey still found that Christian women and secular feminists had much in common. For example, Christian women's magazines took working outside the home for granted, counseled women against tolerating abuse, and held men as responsible as women for failed relationships. Using the term *postfeminism* to denote the fact that feminism had in fact transformed evangelical interpretations of the Bible such that ministers and journals provide "information on rape self-defense, criticisms on social pressures for thinness and youth, and reviews for books celebrating friendships between women," Stacey interpreted the choices made by evangelical women as a response to the unsettling disloca-tions imposed by America's new economy, an economy that, as she put it, has "intensified cravings for security and spirituality."[50]

Stacey's work dovetails with that of religious scholar R. Marie Griffith, who studied members of Women's Aglow Fellowship International, an evangelical women's organization dedicated to prayer and women's fellowship. Careful not to leave the impression that her subjects are feminists, Griffith nevertheless demonstrates the affinities between them and Aglow women. Both, for example, denounce the irresponsibility shown by many husbands toward their families and express distrust of men. Like feminists, Aglow women are woman centered and use their communities to help women build self-esteem and love for themselves independent of male relationships. In her words, "Both evangelicals and feminists . . . want to see women's cultural and social labor revalued, celebrated, and elevated in status." The difference, Griffith argues, is partly in the way Aglow members define womanhood. In essence, Aglow women ascribe different characteristics to women and men and they believe feminism forces women to act, unnaturally, like men. Like Promise Keeper women, Aglow women want women to be able to embrace power grounded not in the sameness of men and women but in a powerful womanness.[51]

What then can we conclude about why most female relatives of Promise Keepers supported their men's efforts to change themselves? For sure they espoused a nonfeminist and sometimes antifeminist position. But Promise Keeper women, like other evangelical women, were nevertheless profoundly wary of male supremacy and supremely confident in women's abilities. Yet, because they supported their men's efforts to change themselves, PK women wanted men back in the household in a meaningful way, not just as providers but as emotionally involved responsible husbands and fathers as well. They wanted to share responsibilities with them in the home, a home made stable by the equal complementary contribution of husbands and wives and mothers and fathers. This was their strategy for dealing with the high divorce rates, rising singleness, and other insecurities of postindustrialism. They were past deciding whether some of the basic precepts of feminism were good or bad; they needed a strategy for dealing with all the work they had to do in America's new postmodern culture and they were willing to work with men who looked to the Promise Keepers for help in navigating the new status quo.

Million Man Marchers and the
Women Who Supported Them

Like Promise Keeper wives, the black women who supported the Million Man March believed in the viability of the two-parent heterosexual family and the necessity of making it central to African American community life. Race and place, however, differentiated these women from their white counterparts. African American women did not talk about the family apart from discussions about the race, also understood as the "community." They believed that the family had to remain strong because, historically, it had been *the* bulwark against racism and its economic effects. Its weakening, they believed, had left black people more vulnerable than usual. Typical of the sentiments expressed were those of Linda Greene, a national fund-raiser for the march, who declared, "I knew this was going to restore family values in our fragmented African American race."[52] Freddie Groomes, executive assistant for Florida State University's Human Resources department, said something similar when she said that "I think that the strength of the black family equals the strength of the race."[53] Frances Murphy, the publisher of the *Washington Afro-American*, opined that "almost all of us agreed that the goal was to reverse the balance in the black family and create a partnership with our men, like it was originally, before slavery." Cora Barry, the wife of the former mayor of Washington, DC, went so far as to deny that the march was about "division by gender." Despite the call for a "men's-only" march, and despite the official exclusion of women, Barry declared the march to be about "the liberation of our people."[54]

Barry was, no doubt, thinking about the state of the black family and the literal absence of men.[55] This made E. Faye Williams's statement (quoted earlier) about holding up the sky more than a mere metaphor. As Williams subsequently elaborated, "Just the thought of a million black men coming together makes the job easier for me and other black women who are out there every day working. Maybe we do finally get to bow out for a little while and get a little rest." Williams took her support a step further when she suggested that black women, who have the highest rate of singleness in the nation, might finally be able to find a man and get married. "Just think," she said half tongue in cheek, "we could observe all these black men in Washington in October and be married by Christmas."[56]

Black women's support for the Million Man March was, therefore, steeped in a desire to reverse a particularly harsh postmodern condition faced by African American women. Chicago alderman Dorothy Tillman spoke for a lot of them when she said, "I've been on the front lines all my life. It does my heart well to see our men go forward."[57] A San Francisco woman had the same feeling. "I myself raised my three oldest sons alone for 10 years. There comes a time when you have to stand up and take responsibility. . . . Men can no longer sit back and say it's the white man's fault."[58] For the millions of women who had been the financial backbone of their families, Linda Greene's statement that "they are recommitting their lives to us as a provider of their families" represented the real hope perched behind black women's support of the march. For others, like Geneva Smitherman, a University Distinguished Professor at Michigan State University, Greene expressed their desperation. "The fact of the matter is we *can't* do it alone. Sisters have been climbing up the rough side of the mountain. . . . Unless we do something quick, this will be the plight of the next generation of African Americans in the 21st century."[59]

As steadfast as was most black women's support of the march, it was not uncritical. Just like the support that PK wives extended to their emotionally absent Promise Keeper men, black women were angry that black men had abandoned their familial responsibilities and had fomented so much of the violence in black communities. In fact, because so many black women agreed with the goals of the march—the atonement of black men for their sins against women and the family—many did not hide their frustration. Alderman Tillman, for example, was pleased to see black men go forward, but she expressed anger over the fact that "the men are killing each other and the men in our community need to address that."[60] Two Cleveland-area women hinged their support for the march on what happened when the men returned home. One woman, the associate director of the Interchurch Council of Greater Cleveland, warned, "This better not be a case where they feel all this emotion in Washington and go back home and do the same things that cause problems when they get back home." Another woman, activist Grace Jones, thought it would be a wasted effort if when the men returned home they did not "seriously address the problems of the African-American community." If the march turned out to be just a "symbolic march," she said, "they can all fold their tents and go away as far as I'm concerned."[61] A forty-nine-year-old New York woman who attended the Million Woman March was like-minded. When she compared the Million Man and Woman Marches, she found the difference in each march's purpose: "The brother's march was atonement; the sister's march is affirmation," she declared. Expressing that affirmation, she said: "We didn't do anything wrong. . . . We've got nothing to atone for, we were there keeping the family together while they were out doing whatever they were out doing."[62] Even a fifteen-year-old had imbibed this opinion. About the Million Man and Woman Marches she said: "We didn't need this march as much as the men did. Women always stick together. But men, if they got into it today, tomorrow they'd talk about killing each other."[63]

This criticism is significant since, historically, African American women have been cautious about criticizing black men for fear of being accused of dividing the race. The trope of the black woman as race traitor has a history that goes back at least until the 1830s when Maria Stewart, an African American activist, was forced to leave her Boston community for publicly questioning the effectiveness of black men's leadership on the question of slavery and abolition. When women like Sojourner Truth argued for female suffrage on the grounds that they did not want to be subject to any man, white or black, it seemed again that some black women were willing to sacrifice race unity and, worse yet, sacrifice black male suffrage, which was seen by many as the key to African American citizenship. Whether cast as a Mammy—an overweight black woman who loved her whites more than her blacks; a Jezebel—a woman who never refused the white man's sexual advances; or a Sapphire—a woman who usurped the black man's power in the home and community, the historical stereotypes of black women revealed them as women who could not be trusted to support black men. Several high-profile events of the 1990s, most notably the testimony of professor Anita Hill against Supreme Court nominee Clarence Thomas, seemed to reinforce the notion that black women were not loyal to the race.[64]

Obviously, this trope circumscribed black women's responses to the Million Man March and helps to account for the complexity of their feelings. Although support for the march did not preclude criticism, that criticism was tempered with understanding. The same woman who supported the march because she was pleased that black men were finally proactive could be angry about black men's past failures and yet still find reason to absolve black men of responsibility for those failures. For black women who supported the Million Man March, race and racism made all the difference. Promise Keeper wives believed that men and women were different because God made them so. Black women believed that too, but they also believed black men and women to be different because racism made it so.

This sentiment extended across the generations and was overwhelming. Twenty-nine-year-old Chicagoan Kristen Anderson said, "I think the black men in this country deserve my support. . . . [They] have an entirely different set of problems that are unique to both their malehood and their race."[65] An older woman, Pauline Tarver, Cleveland's NAACP executive director, expressed the very popular view—the one that surfaced effectively during the 1991 Clarence Thomas Supreme Court hearings—that, historically, racist measures were directed mostly at black men. "You have to understand that, historically, black men have been held down while black women have been held up as the positive, strong force in black households."[66] "Black men as a whole are in more of a crisis right now," said Crystal Herrod of Silver Spring, Maryland.[67] In professor Charshee McIntyre's opinion, the crisis was racism. She supported the march because she thought young black males had been targeted for extinction.[68] As if to agree, the day after the march, sixteen-year-old Jamilla James told her Washington, DC, high school class about her efforts to keep her brother occupied with house cleaning and homework to keep him away from the drug dealers who stalked her neighborhood. Her classmate, Martrelle Pyatt, chimed in with stories of how her family always made a "special effort to support the men in the family." When someone found a job listed in the newspaper that was in the suburbs, the whole family would chip in to get the male out to the job.[69]

The prevalence of these ideas demonstrates that political scientist Nikol Alexander-Floyd's observations about the black cultural pathology paradigm had a lot of currency among black women. Alexander-Floyd argues, convincingly, that in the past twenty-five years, contemporary black politics has developed a masculinist emphasis centered on "ideological assumptions about wounded Black masculinity (alternately described as the plight of the Black male/endangered Black male or the Black male in crisis) and the breakdown of the Black family."[70] According to Alexander-Floyd, assumptions about the black male crisis have caused both blacks and whites to endorse ideas about black family pathology and deviance, and to seek to reverse it by endorsing public policy aimed at restoring black patriarchy. Besides noting the similarity between conservative white politics, which likewise addresses patriarchy, specifically the absence of fathers, Alexander-Floyd posits that the combined black and white conservative agenda spells trouble for black women whose own particular personal and familial burdens are scapegoated, trivialized, or ignored.[71]

As indicated here, the Million Man March was indeed a perfect example of the heightened emphasis in black America on black masculinity. Not only did the march exclude black women but, as happened so often in the past, black women who pressed for inclusion were accused of being traitors to the race as well. And not just any traitor, but *feminist* traitors, out of touch with rank-and-file black Americans who did not have the luxury of concerning themselves with sexism because black male unemployment and homicide were wreaking havoc in their lives. Black women, cautioned Smitherman, "had to be wary of the seductive feminist trap." Black men might be sexist, she argued, but because white men held all of the power and control over the nation's institutions, black women needed to oppose them, not black men. To

oppose the march, "the first mass-based, sorely needed, long overdue, positive effort by black men, on the grounds of sexism is to engage," she said, "in
a misguided, retrogressive brand of feminism."[72] Abdul Allah Muhammad,
in the *Final Call*, the Nation of Islam newspaper, accused black women who
opposed the march of "merely parroting the white feminist party line."[73]
More scathing than Muhammad or Smitherman was writer Ishmael Reed's
commentary. He found black women critics in league with "right-wing white
males who controlled the media" and white feminists who were singularly opposed to black men, especially Mike Tyson, O. J. Simpson, Clarence Thomas,
and Mel Reynolds, black men who, he claimed, had been either excoriated
in the press or set up and denounced by black women in the justice system.
According to Reed, "Unlike the grievances of black mothers who must face
drastic welfare cuts, who can't afford to buy food, and the millions of working
poor black men and women, those of the college-educated academic black
feminists seem trivial." He added that feminists' complaints "must strike the
generation of black women, who were mauled by southern cops during the
civil rights movement, as a little silly."[74]

Reed's criticism of self-identified black female feminists harks back to
the nineteenth- and pre-twentieth-century civil rights era ideology that
held that black women who were privileged enough to escape the domestic
and agricultural work that circumscribed most black women's aspirations
were obligated to serve the race. As historian Stephanie Shaw has observed,
educated black women were "expected to . . . make a difference in the lives
of the many people in their communities who did not enjoy the advantages
that they did." Whether they attended one of the few integrated schools like
Oberlin or the all-black schools like Spellman, Fisk, or Howard, black women
were socialized by these institutions to "throw off all shackles of egotism" and
to return to their hometowns and "be of as much service to all as possible."[75]
The historical educational tradition in black America, therefore, was toward
race service. The women who worked full-time jobs but still managed to
establish the kindergartens, libraries, hospitals, settlement houses, and
suffrage associations that served black America were trained to do so in the
name of the race, not themselves or their gender.

Reed was not alone in this kind of thinking, and his criticism suggests one
reason that many women opposed the Million Woman March, which was
held two years later in Philadelphia. In short, they did not want to appear to
be unsupportive of black men, who they believed were gathering on behalf of
the needs of the race. For example, a Maryland editorialist did not attend the
Million Woman March because she thought it the work of "uptight feminists"
avenging black women's exclusion from the 1995 Million Man March; women

who felt "jealous and left out," when they needed to be "proud, supportive and understanding" of "brothers who had some things they needed to do." Black women, she said, "should not be jealous or competitive when they [black men] finally decide to make a positive effort on behalf of the betterment of us all in the long run." Cleveland resident Paula Brazil thought the march held two years later for black women was a "Me Too" activity for which there was no need. "We need to be supportive of African-American men and their plight in this nation," she said. "We should spend time supporting what African-American men are trying to do instead of stepping out on our own."[76]

Although some women evoked feminism in their opposition to the Million Man March and support of the Million Woman March, most women who took these positions did so on the grounds of family salvation and racial unity. Like Promise Keeper wives, they thought that women had worked hard to keep the family together and they wanted black men and women to work *together* to save what they considered an endangered institution. For example, Alexis Nunley, a thirty-six-year-old mechanical engineer from Landover, Maryland, claimed that "in order to have the family unified, you need all of the elements there. . . . You can't have water without hydrogen and oxygen. If you want the message out, you can't have just guys delivering the message."[77] Ione Biggs, a Cleveland member of Women Speak Out for Peace and Justice, believed the exclusion of women was wrong. "I believe men and women need to work together. I think they could accomplish more."[78] Similarly, many women who supported the Million Woman March did so because they feared the demise of the black family. This was why Pittsburgh resident Linda Austin started organizing her trip to Philadelphia two months in advance; because, she said, the march is "trying to get us together as [a] people, especially the way the family is broken up." And Gloria Graves, a forty-four-year-old Detroit real estate broker, traveled to Philadelphia in hopes of bringing "back the family unit that has been lost."[79]

It is impossible to understand black women's enormous investment in the family, and their support of the Million Man March, without understanding the fact that black women understood the very real statistics that detailed the status of black men not just in the context of what these statistics said about the adult men in their lives, but also what they said, or might say, about their boys, male teenagers, and young-adult sons—their children. Black women internalized the high rates of drug abuse, homicide, incarceration, school dropouts, unemployment, and police harassment, and thought, not about their sons thriving, but whether their boys could survive. "I've got a six-year-old boy and I feel like I'm raising a target," said a contributor to writer Marita Golden's book *Saving Our Sons*. "Every time the telephone rings, my heart skips a beat," said a black woman interviewed by black *Washington Post* reporter Courtland Milloy.[80] Golden spoke for so many black mothers when she wrote, "As a mother of a black son, I have raised my child with a trembling hand that clutches and leads." Poignantly capturing the feelings of so many black mothers, she wrote, "I am no slave mother, my sleep plundered by images of the auction block. I dream instead of my son slaying the statistics that threaten to ensnare and cripple him, statistics that I know are a commentary on the odds for my son, who isn't dead or in jail." Golden knew what so many black mothers knew—even those who had the wherewithal to provide a middle-class lifestyle or better—that while they could do everything that was within their power to keep their sons on the straight and narrow, "always there is the fear that he will make a fatal detour, be seduced, or be hijacked by a white or a black cop, or a young black predator, or a Nazi skinhead, or his own bad judgment, or a weakness that I as his mother cannot love or punish or will out of him."[81]

This fear for their sons, the *next* generation of black men, was arguably the most important driving force behind black women's overwhelming support for the Million Man March. Take Professor Smitherman's objection to "feminist" opposition. Before cautioning black women to "beware the feminist trap," she described herself as a "mother of a son" who the school system labeled "hyperactive" and in need of medication and special classes. Had another black woman not intervened, her son, like so many other black males who, she claimed, were "disproportionately placed in special education and other kinds of slow-track classes in the educational systems of this nation," would have been someone who was not taught because he had been classified as someone unable to learn. Said Smitherman, "Yeah, we needed that March—and anything else that will highlight what is happening to our boys and men."[82]

This is apparently what led many women who were seen along the sidelines of the march to not only support the march but to attend it as well. Assistant prosecuting attorney Charlita Anderson, a single mother raising a seven-year-old son, thought it important to go because she wanted her son "to grow into a strong man."[83] She was joined in this sentiment by Sylvia White, a DC resident who had left her thirteen-year-old son home but intended to go back and get him because she wanted him to "see what was going on."[84] Vanessa Davis-Harper, a widow, stood holding each of her young sons by the hand. "I want them to understand what this means, this coming together of our black men, finally."[85] Another woman, from Manassas, Virginia, attended with her twenty-one-year-old son, Michael, in mind. "I want him to understand the importance of being black and liking it," she said.[86]

FIGURE 7. Although the Million Man March was explicitly for black men, women supporters were present and visible. These three women were among the many others who greeted the men as they gathered on the Day of Atonement. *Library of Congress, Prints and Photograph Division, CQ Roll Call Photograph Collection, LC-RC 1995-851 Frame 17.*

This kind of thinking from black women who supported the Million Man March was not unusual. They did not separate the family from the race; the strength of one presaged the strength of the other. If the family could be made whole—meaning if men could be brought back in as husbands and fathers— then the race would thrive and black people could survive postindustrialism and anything else. But their support was not just about the race; it was about themselves. It was self-interested realism. Frustrated with being both mother and father, both provider and nurturer, to the majority of black children, they reached out, almost desperately, to black men for help. From the numbers of men who showed up at the march, they were not disappointed. Indeed, they were heartened. For them the march translated into hope for the race because it meant that the next generation of men—their sons—would survive and make life easier for their daughters than it had been for them.

Promise Keeper and Million Man
March Women Compared

When we compare these two groups of women, the differences, at first, seem stark. Promise Keeper women clearly did not have the same sense of dread for their sons that black women across socioeconomic classes did. However we interpret the phenomenon of the "endangered black male," few black women did not know or have a black boy to be fearful for; hence, the overwhelming support for, and lack of organized opposition to, the Million Man March. Promise Keeper women also did not consciously attach their well-being, or their family's well-being, to their race. It is likely that like their husbands they felt that the fabric of America was only as strong as its families. But their interviews and testimonials do not speak directly to this. This reflects not only the nature of the sources, which mostly query PK wives about their husbands, but also reflects the fact that in America, racial minorities are "the other." Because whites represent the normalized presence, they are privileged to not think of themselves as raced. Most African American women, however, clearly linked their well-being to the family and, by proxy, to their race. This raises another important difference: the fact that these black and white women brought different histories to the family table. Race mattered in the 1990s. Because it had always mattered, it colored the different way that these women experienced familial relationships.

These are important differences but, as with the white and black men of the Promise Keepers, their significance depends in part on the depth of the similarities between Promise Keeper and Million Man March women. We should not, for example, lose sight of the fact that both these white and black women attached enormous significance to the family. It was their haven in the unfamiliar new America of the 1990s, an America where job security had disappeared, where women composed the majority of poorly paid workers, and where women were increasingly likely to raise children without the help of men. It was not that they felt the family to be free of oppression, an institution whose unequal distribution of familial labor and domestic abuse harmed women; it was that they wanted to transform the family to make it work for them. Neither group targeted the structural makeup of America that had made the family so unstable, nor did these black and white women look to the government for solutions. Instead, in keeping with an ethos that saw the family as part of the private domain, they felt that men and women could, with the help of the Promise Keepers and the Million Man March, work things out on their own. This made them quite similar.

The counternarrative that they offered to their critics was equally similar. Black and white feminists criticized Promise Keeper and Million Man March women for allowing men to control their lives, for being unequal marriage partners, and for diminishing their self-worth as wives and mothers. On the other hand, both black and white antifeminist critics painted an unpleasant picture of feminists as socialist, man-hating lesbians who were antifamily, out of touch with the mainstream, and, in the case of black women, race traitors. As noted earlier, equalitarian Christian women were considered destructive and dangerous. Their actions were thought to be "against no less than the Christian doctrine of God, man, and the Church."[87] Likewise, black women were warned not to sow "disunity" by opposing the march.[88] Caught between feminists who cried patriarchy and antifeminists who decried equalitarianism, both PK and Million Man March women carved out a precarious middle ground. They supported men without supporting male supremacy; endorsed families without endorsing gender hierarchy. They did not see themselves as conceding to patriarchy or women's inferiority. Rather, because they believed in the centrality of the two-parent heterosexual family, they believed their own self-interest was at stake. From their perspective, women who raised children alone, without emotional and/or financial support, were hardly liberated. In spite of their differences, therefore, Million Man March and Promise Keeper women had a lot in common.

In this they were like nineteenth- and early twentieth-century women who were in the forefront of the temperance, or antialcohol, movement. Temperance women were just as likely to be ardent supporters of equal rights for women and women's suffrage as well-known leaders of the latter movements like Susan B. Anthony, Elizabeth Cady Stanton, and Sojourner Truth. However, temperance women were more likely to couch their politics in the rhetoric of the family than to boldly tout the equality of men and women and women's right to vote. Since custom demanded that proper feminine women refrain from public speaking and participating in politics, temperance women advocated for divorce reform, gender equality, and women's need for power in the context of the injustice of leaving women and children at the mercy of abusive drunkards who bankrupted families. Though they were forceful public speakers, they feigned modesty and shyness while they insisted on a woman's right to legal equality. Their demure manner disarmed critics and enabled female temperance advocates to escape the epithets endured by suffragists and women's rights advocates who were disparagingly referred to as "unsexed" and "masculine."[89] As historian Carol Mattingly concludes: "By carefully presenting their cause as an unselfish effort on behalf of suffering women and children, and by scrupulously maintaining the cultural expectations that defined their sphere (except for their uncharacteristic public speaking), these women 'more than half convinced' powerful and influential newspaper editors to reconsider the legal position of their sex."[90]

Promise Keeper and Million Man March women functioned like temperance women. They were not the most radical in their personal politics but neither were they the most conservative. In fact, these terms fall short of describing them. Had they been ardent feminists they would have provoked even greater ire and malevolence from male supporters of patriarchy and been accused of sowing societal chaos. Already fundamentalists were prepared to excommunicate women who reinterpreted Ephesians 22 to mean mutual cooperation. Already black women, particularly academics, who objected to a men's-only march were ridiculed as being out of touch with the masses. Whether it was self-consciously political or not, it was easier to support woman's equality from the protective quarters of the family than to boldly come "out" as a feminist.

Useful here is the concept of *postfeminism* that was noted earlier. Researchers have found that while most women eschew activism on behalf of feminist precepts, most women "have semiconsciously incorporated feminist principles into their gender and kinship expectations and practices."[91] They take feminist accomplishments for granted, and yet, like Promise Keeper and Million Man March women, they are searching for a strategy to deal with America's new realities. In the '70s and '80s, feminists helped women understand themselves as sexually autonomous beings, helped them develop independent work lives and build self-esteem. But, as argued by Stacey, "neither feminism nor other progressive family reform movements have been useful in addressing the structural inequalities of postindustrial occupational structure or the individualistic, fast-track culture that makes all too difficult the formation of stable intimate relations on a democratic, or any other basis."[92] Feminism has also not been able to redress racial inequalities that subject black people to greater rates of homicide and put black men in prison in disproportionate numbers. Both PK and Million Man March women looked to the family, to themselves, and to their respective movements for solutions. This made them similar. Perhaps they should have sought help from the state, which has far more resources than they or their movements to redress the racial and gender discrimination that made their lives so precarious. But they did not, and this too made them similar.

This postfeminist outlook also allowed both Promise Keeper and Million Man March women to distance themselves from issues that their respective communities opposed. One of them was homosexuality. Although the interviews and testimonials of these women do not speak directly to this issue, in

America there has always been an association between women's rights and gender inversion. Historically, equal rights proponents were opposed because they upset proper gender roles and relations. Throughout the nineteenth and early twentieth centuries, the home was thought to be a woman's proper sphere and women who moved beyond it or who advocated for women's rights in the public sphere, the male domain, were criticized and mocked.[93]

Christian fundamentalists, in particular, held fast to the doctrine of separate spheres. To them, it preserved the integrity of the Christian family. They believed that as mothers and wives women were the guardians of societal morality, and if they forsook that role by either refusing to have children or straying toward politics or the pulpit, then they, like the devil, damned the world. As one contributor to a Christian journal noted after claiming that the scripture supported the essential difference between men and women: "When this difference is lost and man becomes womanish, or woman becomes mannish, then the proper balance is lost and harmony gives way to discord."[94] Until the 1930s, Christian fundamentalists believed that societal stability was founded on a world organized around families. The family, or divinized home, was ordained by God as a marriage between one man and one woman who were made to inhabit their separate spheres. "No nation or people can long survive in power, influence or greatness if the home is destroyed," wrote one fundamentalist teacher. One sure way for it to be destroyed was for women to step away from their "natural" roles. "Oh woman, stay a woman," said a popular evangelical minister. "Do not try to cross over."[95]

This thinking remained steadfast with many fundamentalist leaders of the 1990s who associated radical feminism with homosexuality. For example, in his critique of "Christian Women's Declaration," S. M. Hutchins, the senior editor of the Christian journal *Touchstone*, praised the signers for their opposition to homosexuality because, he said, "all reasonable citizens should join the attempt to curb the political and social influence of radical feminism and its attendant homosexualism, which are manifestly perverse and genocidal." However, he did not care for the equalitarianism endorsed in the declaration. He thought it as detrimental to the church as "sexual radicalism" was to society, "and the church's message to its crumbling society must include its traditional teachings about men and women if it is to be like the Church at all."[96] Those traditional teachings, according to Hutchins, had men and women in their proper roles as husband and wife, father and mother.

The point, however, is that by roundly denouncing radical feminism, signers of the declaration endorsed the fundamentalist condemnation of homosexuality, and thus escaped the most damning fundamentalist criticism, something that Promise Keeper wives were most likely doing by proxy when they insisted that they were not feminists. When they supported the complementarity and mutuality of men and women, PK wives, like supporters of the women's declaration, veered to the left of traditional fundamentalists who believed in gender hierarchy and women's obligation to obey men. They did not, however, place themselves entirely out of the Christian fold. They endorsed families, supported men, and held fast to the belief that a marriage was between a man and a woman. In this way, they put a lot of space between themselves and radical feminists who this Christian community defined as "perverse and genocidal."

African American women supporters of the Million Man March also secured their inclusion in black America by steering clear of feminism, which had many negatives attached to it. For example, because white women had not opposed slavery but had in fact benefited from it, and because they had historically used their white privilege to exclude black women from their organizations—in fact, from *any* white female orbit—many African Americans thought it treasonous for black women to align with them against black men, who were considered the natural allies of black women. Furthermore, because throughout American history women's rights advocates fought for rights that had been denied black men, many African Americans objected to black women fighting with white women for rights that white men had denied black men. The emasculation of the black male by white people was seen by many blacks as tantamount to the emasculation of the race. For these reasons, many black women steered clear of organized feminism.[97]

But like the wives of Promise Keepers they also steered clear of feminism because for many African Americans it was a code word for *lesbianism*, which, when added to the other inhibitors, put feminism off-limits. Historically, most, though by no means all, African Americans have steered clear of formal movements that associated them with gender inversion and "improper" sexual desire. Underlying this avoidance is the fact that throughout American history, black men were lynched for allegedly having abnormal sexual desire for white women, and black women were treated as though they were sexual hybrids.[98] Beginning with the importation of Africans as slaves, black women were worked in the fields and taxed as if they were men. By definition they were considered "mannish" women because they could, unlike native-born white women, be exploited for both their productive and reproductive labor. Like Sojourner Truth, who was made to bear her breast before an antislavery audience because male attendees did not believe that she was a woman, black women carried the burden of proving that they were not perversions of femaleness. One way free black women did this was to create a cult of respectability designed to show that they were just as maternal, sexually pure, and domestically inclined as white women. Necessarily coded heterosexual, the cult of respectability helped shore up the public character of black men as well as women, and it prevailed throughout the nineteenth and twentieth centuries among the black striving classes. It was utilitarian. It not only served as a defensive mechanism against the lynching of black men and the sexual assault of black women, but the cult of respectability also showed America that blacks, having embraced proper gender and sex roles, were worthy of equality with whites. "A race can rise no higher than its women" was a phrase heard among African Americans throughout the nineteenth and twentieth centuries. As long as women maintained proper feminine roles, men would be enabled to be properly masculine, and the race, it was thought, by leading men and women alike, would achieve equality.[99] As important as women's rights was to black women, the masses steered clear of formal movements because of the aspersions their participation might cast on black people's sexuality.

Black women who publicly supported feminism not only risked severe ridicule from whites, who throughout history mercilessly lampooned black women as unsexed emasculating behemoths but, as previously noted, they risked being called race traitors by African Americans.[100] Even though many men supported feminist causes, most African Americans did not believe that they could fight on two fronts at the same time, especially one that was dominated by women whose race and sex implicated them in the historical oppression of black people, including the lynching of black men and women. Moreover, because women's rights and feminist movements upset prevailing understandings of proper gender roles and sexual desire, and these under-girded African American claims to equality, most blacks prioritized race rather than gender in their fight for equality.[101] One need look no further than the previous comments of Ishmael Reed, Geneva Smitherman, and Abdul Allah Muhammad to get a sense of what Million Man March women were up against. By getting behind men and the family and by linking the hetero-sexual family to the future of the race, Million Man March women silently proved that they were not race traitors, not in league with white feminists, and not in any way sexually transgressive. In this they were like Promise Keeper women, who, while challenging their community from within, kept their insider status intact.

The Paradox of Postmodernity

At first glance the differences between the Promise Keeper and Million Man March women seem clearer than the commonalities. Their men gathered in separate arenas at different times. One was mostly white and the other overwhelmingly black. Race mattered, whether from a distant or up-close analysis. Black women did not consider the family apart from their race; for them it was *the* foundational institution, not of America, as Promise Keeper women would have it, but of black people. Their concern for their men, especially their sons, was predicated on the reality of peer and police inhumanity. Promise Keeper women worried about the males in their lives, their emotional well-being and their status as men, but they did not connect their whiteness to the family. Rather, their families were connected to their Christian faith and they tried to construct their families according to their interpretations of Christ's teachings.

Despite the difference that race made, however, there were paradoxical similarities in the ways and means used by each group to address the realities that beset them in the 1990s. Faced with high divorce rates, high rates of singleness, new formulations of the family, and the feminization of poverty, these black and white women supported their men's efforts to reconstitute the family as the central institution in their lives. They did not believe that the family would or could destroy them. Rather, it was a place for self-realization, an institution to be used to restore the familiar. They were lost in the USA, and in their search for security they were like other postfeminists who did not concede the fundamental feminist principles of women's autonomy and equality but still insisted that they were not feminist. Whether they knew it or not, both groups reached back to well-worn tactics of women like the members of the Women's Christian Temperance Union, who demurely fought for women's rights without appearing to do so and without alienating the power brokers of their respective communities. Because they felt lost, Promise Keeper and Million Man March women wanted to stay connected to their communities and did not step outside community boundaries on issues like homosexuality. Neither did either group endorse a public policy that might strengthen the family. Rather, these women, who differed in so many ways, took personal responsibility for regenerating the family, their foothold in an unfamiliar America.

Generally speaking, black and white women are usually perceived to be, if not on the opposite ends of the political spectrum, far apart on social issues. This comparison of female support for the Promise Keepers and Million Man March demonstrates otherwise. For better or worse (in sickness and health, and whether rich or poor), these black and white women thought husbands and wives, mothers and fathers could make the family work and anchor them in postmodern America. For that end, they gave overwhelming support to their men.

CHAPTER 4

The Fierce Urgency of Unity

The Advent of Post-Blackness

On Monday, October 16, 1995, many churches, mosques, and community centers in black neighborhoods opened to large crowds that gathered to pray for, and reflect with, the black men who were amassing on the Washington Mall for the Million Man March. Some who gathered were children who had been kept out of school in order to attend black history classes at church. Among those at the Advent Church of Christ in Columbus, Ohio, was nine-year-old Caroline Smith. When asked what she learned on that Day of Atonement, she replied, "We learned that the men in Washington know we're praying for them," and then she added, "we learned how to make more unity."[1]

Unity also emerged as a theme at the Million Woman March held two years later on October 25, 1997, on Benjamin Franklin Parkway in Philadelphia. Said Edith Cherry, a grandmother from Newark, New Jersey, "We've got to unite and this is a start." Philadelphian Barbara Smith thought likewise: "We are trying to unify ourselves as African-American women."[2] And Asia Coney, one of the two march organizers, showed that unity was a priority for her when she said, "Sisters needed and wanted to get together, just as men did, to show a force of unity and support for each other."[3]

As we have seen with the Million Man March, and now with little Caroline Smith and Million Woman marchers, *unity* was a catchall word: a noun, a verb, and an adjective. This chapter delves more deeply into the conceptualization of black unity and suggests that at the dawn of the twenty-first century, African Americans felt they were losing the indivisibility that had buffered racism and provided the necessary foundation for the fight for full citizenship rights. From a distance it seemed that the gathering of so many black men in Washington, DC, and then black women in Philadelphia, Pennsylvania, was evidence that black Americans were again mounting a freedom struggle by marching in the political tradition established long ago by the antilynching silent marchers of 1917 and 1922, returning black war heroes, Marcus Garvey's parades, and the historic 1963 March on Washington for Jobs and Freedom. But on the ground it was apparent that African Americans were fighting as much, if not more, to keep their community from falling apart than for any political agenda. This chapter argues that the marches in the 1990s reveal a people whose freedom movement had helped set in motion the undoing of black America as they knew it; a people who felt not only lost in the USA but lost in black America as well; a people who at the turn of the millennium found so many ways to be black as to negate the unifying force that brought them to Washington and Philadelphia in the first place.

Black Is a Country

Both the Million Man and Million Woman Marches were built on an understanding of black America as a community. What scholar Benedict Anderson says of nations as imagined communities is true of African America: "Regardless of the actual inequality and exploitation that may prevail in each, . . . [it] is . . . conceived as a deep, horizontal comradeship." This comradeship was welded by American racism that had at its core "one-drop" laws that made anyone who had a discernible black ancestor "negro"; laws that presumed a state of slavery for negroes for almost two hundred and fifty years; and Jim Crow laws and practices that undergirded the systematic terror tactics that created a uniquely different kind of citizenship for all African Americans. Forced to live and play together and forge a meaningful existence behind what W. E. B. Du Bois euphemistically called "the veil," black Americans developed their own institutions and neighborhoods, music, and culture— their own style, aesthetic, and food, their own ways of knowing. *Black Is a Country* is not only the title of Nikhil Pal Singh's book on the history of the long and unfinished black struggle, but for so many African Americans it also describes a reality. This is evident in the narratives of many who were born and raised in the segregated South. They portray the black community as one in which families did their best to shelter their young from white terror and in which black teachers put African American history at the center of American history. Black autobiography echoes these positive memories. Departing from the singular subject of unrelenting oppression, memoirs, beginning in 1969 with Maya Angelou's *I Know Why the Caged Bird Sings,* revision the past and punctuate it with a "life-sustaining community, rituals involving church gatherings, storytelling sessions, . . . cooperative work-projects, ... and poignant portraits of ... [the] family's orderly daily life."[4] Black memoir and autobiography so reify the notion that "black is a country" that what Anderson says of even a small nation has been true for African Americans: although they "will never know most of their fellow members, meet them, or even hear of them, ... in the minds of each lives the image of their communion."[5]

To understand the equation of race and nationhood is to understand what motivated so many African Americans to attend the marches, to watch them on television, or to attend a sympathy march in their hometown. Behind the call for unity that escaped the lips of many of the marchers was the feeling of loss. Facing a new century with some of the same systemic racial problems that had plagued blacks since slavery ended, many African Americans went to the national marches not only to voice their concern and opposition to racism, but, more important, they also went in search of unity, the tool they believed had brought them through the disasters and triumphs of the previous centuries, and the instrument that would restore the communalism needed to help them navigate the twenty-first century.

Vertical Sisterhood; or, Can't We All Just Get Along?

The dire social and economic indicators that have already been noted loomed large in the minds of the marchers. But just as important as the deepening poverty, the proliferation of drugs and violence, the rise in singleness and unwed parenthood, and the imprisonment of so many black men for nonviolent offenses was the perceived breakdown of interpersonal communication between black people. For some, this was both a cause and an effect of the difficult circumstances black people faced. The community—real and/or imagined—had been sustaining and its apparent collapse was troubling. While Million Man marchers acknowledged this by focusing on the violence that prevented the growth of what Anderson would call a "horizontal comradeship," Million Woman marchers focused on the acidity that characterized black female interactions with each other, an acidity that thwarted the development of a broad and deep sisterhood, leaving only vertical relationships in which black women regarded women outside their immediate personal orbit with suspicion.

As noted earlier, in 1997, the same year as the Million Woman March, the Centers for Disease Control found African American women to be the most unhappy of all Americans. Specifically, they reported that of white men, white women, black men, and black women, black females had the highest "negative mood" rate. The finding was consistent across all educational levels. While black educated women had three times a higher rate of "negative mood" than white men, the rate for less educated black women was four times higher. Living in a central city increased the probability of "negative mood," making inner-city black women the unhappiest and most depressed people in the country. The study did not pinpoint the primary causes of the "negative mood," but in rather convoluted language it concluded that those with mental health disorders and those susceptible to "negative moods as a result of normal stresses of everyday life" were most affected.[6]

While scholars and journalists like Ellis Cose[7] have addressed the issue of black women's "negative mood," Million Woman marchers add specificity to what we know generally. Aside from the reasons that Cose elaborated on in the *Rage of a Privileged Class*, marchers pinpointed their exclusion from high-paying jobs and the general limited opportunities available to them. For example, a young black woman from Northwestern University marched because she felt black women "are not equally represented in the work place in high positions."[8] Speaking about heading corporations and making policy decisions, Seattle state representative Dawn Mason said that black women "aren't there. So we don't have a chance and no one asks us. People think they can speak for us."[9]

Women marchers were particularly distressed over how America treated and stereotyped them, and this no doubt contributed to their "negative mood."[10] Said Howard University psychologist Audrey Chapman, "Black women have been assigned by society the role of 'universal mammy'—[we] suckle everybody and get sucked dry. When there's nothing left to feed ourselves, we get angry. . . . There are so many angry, overwhelmed, emotionally depleted sisters."[11] Phile Chionesu, the co-organizer with Asia Coney, agreed: "Black women have taken care of everyone else since the time we've been in this country. We've taken care of white women, white men, white children, . . . our own men, our own children."[12] She added, "We're saying we are hungry for a change."[13] Black women wanted to see themselves represented differently in media: "What I usually see in the media are black women being put down—as welfare cheats or sexually active teens," pined a former maid whose great-grandmother had wet-nursed white babies. "I feel betrayed when I see black women portrayed as lazy and no-account."[14] Another woman claimed that the women's march would "challenge stereotypes of black women as 'Sapphires,' matriarchs and welfare queens who make babies and little else."[15] It *could* challenge these stereotypes, said Minnie P. Allen, *if* the media discontinued its racial and gender-biased reporting. In a letter to the editor of the *Seattle Times*, Allen protested what she considered the limited to nonexistent coverage of the Million Woman March. She accused the media of sexism, claiming that it gave men's events like the Million Man March and the Promise Keepers far more attention than the Million Woman March. But she also accused the media of racism, saying that it preferred to show black women at their worst—as leeches of the welfare system and as angry black women who came together only to complain about white people. They weren't interested, she said, in black women "trying to unify, trying to heal from the past, trying to move forward in a world filled with obstacles and inequality." That, she said, didn't sell newspapers or boost television ratings.[16]

Allen's complaints suggest the catch-22 that bound all African Americans—particularly black women, who, as part of a multifamily group or as a single parent, had to address the racism *and* sexism that limited and suppressed their opportunities and those of their children. Black women and men were perceived as government parasites, as people who always wanted a hand-out. Comments from both the Million Man and Million Woman Marches about not asking the government or white people for help demonstrate black people's awareness of this perception, an awareness that prompted the inward turn toward self-help. And yet, blacks could not by themselves address the structural racism that made for higher rates of black unemployment, poverty, singleness, violence, and incarceration. One can imagine that if the marchers had made demands on the government they would have been perceived, yet again, as—to use Allen's phrase—leeches. But to not demand that the government and whites address systemic racism left marchers dependent on their own limited and inadequate resources, resources made that way by the systemic racism that marchers were reluctant to address. Black women, who historically have been more attached to children and the community, were positioned to see and feel this dilemma. No doubt it made for part of the "normal stresses of everyday life" that the CDC cited as a cause of black women's "negative mood." We can only imagine how individual women absorbed the paradox, and how it eroded their trust in individuals outside their immediate circle.

Million Woman marchers testified about this lack of trust, a component of what is here termed *vertical sisterhood*. "We can be so rude to each other," said one women, because too many think, "I can take stuff out on you because you're as low as I am."[17] Another claimed that "we are conditioned to build ourselves up by pushing others down."[18] "We don't even know how to talk to each other on our jobs," said a Chicago organizer who thought it would be a major accomplishment if different kinds of black women could just gather in one space for just one day.[19] A fifty-seven-year-old District of

Columbia resident targeted the generation gap as the problem. "Something is missing," she said. After an hour of conversation with a group of young university women, she distressingly concluded, "Something is not reaching them, I don't fully understand it."[20] Sixty-five-year-old Chicagoan Flora Humphries expressed feelings of loss and longing simultaneously when she confessed that she was "hopelessly stuck in the 60's." Articulating a kind of grief that black women across the generations felt, she pined: "I yearn for the days when every black woman was my sister. We readily acknowledged that our shared history of slavery, discrimination and racism created a common bond." It troubled her that in 1997 she could "pass black women in the street without making eye contact." In the '60s, she said, things were different:

> Our love for each other empowered our communities. It helped us look out for each other's children and watch each other's backs in the workplaces that were often unfriendly, if not outright hostile. Without it, we are a weak bunch. . . . Who will protect us, respect us, love us, if we don't first love each other? If we hold each other in contempt and low esteem, is it only because we do not love ourselves?"[21]

Realizing that Humphries's feelings of hurt and longing were pervasive among African American women, that they lacked the "horizontal comradeship" of which Benedict Anderson spoke, march organizers made a deeper and broader sisterhood an explicit goal of the march. According to Barbara Smith, the public-relations coordinator of the Million Woman March, for the year and a half that march organizers met before the march they agreed that repentance, restoration, and resurrection had to be the march's goals. Black women, said Smith, needed "repentance among ourselves—that we are not disrespecting or continuing negativity based on hue or our hair texture or class. We separate ourselves by class and academia. We have to deal with that." Black women, she continued, needed "restoration so we heal, we apologize, and we reach out to each other." After repentance and restoration had taken place, the entire black community could be resurrected as black women reached "out to our companion, our male counterpart, our family members, and then we move on into the millennium as a family."[22] In essence, although most Million Woman marchers did not believe that they had to atone for anything because they had stayed true to their families and communities, many accepted culpability for community disintegration. Asia Coney's directive to black women that they no longer "walk by your sister and not acknowledge her existence" evidenced organizers' belief that "horizontal comradeship" was very much a woman's responsibility and that they had let black America down by letting their differences, or what gender studies scholars would call intersectionality or multiple identities, supersede their common identity as black women.[23]

Apparent in their acceptance of this responsibility was an idealized understanding of the past as a time when African American women all got along. Indeed, just as black men found much in their past on which to model a contemporary masculinity, the past also presented black women with much to create a new femininity and a new sisterhood. Black women had, in fact, been the mainstay of black churches, the bedrock of African American communities. They had built schools, hospitals, settlement houses, libraries, and the book clubs out of which the black history movement grew.[24] During the midcentury freedom movement, women like Rosa Parks, Ella Baker, Fannie Lou Hamer, Angela Davis, and Johnnie Tillman, among so many others, had been moving forces that had advanced the cause of black civil and political rights. This was the history referred to in the mission statement's elegant prose that the march would "revive life as we once exemplified it."[25]

On October 25, 1997, many wondered whether the tradition that had positioned black women at the center of black struggle could be resurrected. Like fifty-five-year-old Mary Cleveland, many wondered whether black women would be "too jealous of each other, too bitchy, too disorganized."[26] DeNeen Brown, a staff writer for the *Washington Post*, wondered what effect the "competition among women over appearances, clothing and hairdos" would have on bonding that was supposed to take place.[27] Still others asked the question that *Chicago Sun-Times* journalist Mary Mitchell asked: "Can the sister toting a briefcase stand with the sister on welfare? Can the sister behind the desk stand with the sister pushing a mop and bucket? Can the sister who wears her hair in dreadlocks stand with the sister who has a blond perm? Can the church sister stand with the sister in the mosque?"[28] Too many black women did not know the answers to these questions, and it pained them that the questions had to be asked in the first place.

It should come as no surprise that the march could not entirely undo intrasororal suspicions or by itself broaden black sisterhood. Although the large turnout proved to Mary Cleveland that black women *could* get along—"We showed them," she triumphantly exclaimed[29]—and others found the march "spiritual,"[30] and still others went home, like DC resident Ella McCall Haygans, "apologizing for even thinking bad thoughts" about other black women, a significant number of women left the march without feeling renewed, rejuvenated, or even hopeful. On the whole, men emerged far more satisfied from the Million Man March than women from their march. There was almost no testimony from men that matched that of journalist Lorraine Kee, who said that "for me, there was no life-altering moment as a male

FIGURE 8. Many African American women gathered in Philadelphia to find or restore sisterhood. Some left with a feeling of buoyant wholesomeness, but many left without having found the sense of community they sought. The placard carried by this Ohioan captures the irony of seeking individual fulfillment in the company of millions, particularly among women identified as the unhappiest citizens in America. *Photo by Tom Mihalek/AFP/Getty Images.*

friend of mine experienced during the Million Man March two years ago. I can't recall any single moment when I was moved to commit to making my communities better."[31]

Whether the perennial suspicions were too much for a single march to overcome or whether the march itself spawned divisiveness, there was an unnamable chill in the air that had nothing to do with the rain that fell on march day. "I don't feel that warmth from the sisters. I saw that warmth at the Million Man March, and I watched it on television," said Philadelphian Christine Williams.[32] Edna Jones of Largo, Maryland, was equally disappointed. "I was really hoping to get a lot of inspiration and communication and fellowship with other women," but it "wasn't quite there," she lamented.[33] Veatrice Blue concurred. Unlike New Yorker Stanley Banks, who turned to a fellow marcher during the Million Man March and rejoiced in the warm reception he received, Blue told a reporter, "I actually felt some animosity out here. You can sense it from some women. It is a look that they give you."[34] That look, eyeing someone with resentment, was described by Tempi Satcher as "gritting." She said that she felt it a lot during the march. To Satcher, sisterhood meant "being able to talk to a strange lady about something you have in common, . . . being able to compliment another woman and say, 'you're looking good,' rather than gritting. It means lending an ear." She did not find this kind of sisterhood on the parkway. Satcher concluded, "I swear women can't be around each other too long."[35]

Others put the blame elsewhere. Many women faulted the vendors for interrupting the solemnity of the event. The sale of bean pies, T-shirts, tapes, and black art seemed to them to underscore the march's futility.[36] Others were like Earl Ofari Hutchinson, who opposed the Million Man March on the grounds that its rationale blamed the victim. These women wanted more concrete goals and action, and when they went to the march and did not find an agenda other than unity, they felt dissatisfied. Erika Peterman made this point in her commentary in the *St. Petersburg Times*. "All the chanting and hand-holding was nice. But where was the sense of purpose? Solidarity and affirmation are noble things, but to what end?" Like others, she felt she could have stayed home and achieved the same feeling.[37] "There was no public discourse that rallied the women or that mobilized them as a cohesive and purposeful, activist social collective," said a Howard University doctoral student explaining why so many women dispersed early into nearby restaurants.[38] The late poet and essayist June Jordan chastised black women on this very score. She thought it tragic that so many black women would gather under the odd organizing motto "Repentance, Resurrection, Restoration." Where, she asked, was the "outcry for rescue funds for public education, and rescue funds for public or subsidized housing, and rescue funds for job training and retraining, and rescue funds to establish acceptable, attainable, child care? . . . Not one petition," lamented Jordan. She commended black women for their ability to come together in love and "acts of committed, reliable, kindness." But she admonished black women for not using the Million Woman March for a tangible goal. Black women, she insisted, had to learn to harness and use their power to "come together for a specific, collective, political purpose, each and every time we convene a meeting of as many of us as we can persuade to stand or sit together united."[39]

When the commercialism and apoliticism is added to the unrealism of "reviving life as we once exemplified it," it is not difficult to see why so many women left the march unsatisfied and why "vertical sisterhood" seemed to prevail. After all, the black community *was* imagined. There had never been a time when the ties that bound—race and gender—were not corroded by those that divided: class, color, sexuality, faith, and political persuasion. To the extent that the men went to Washington to redefine and perform masculinity, and found healing in that process, they were bound to have more success than the women, whose purpose was to find spiritual healing in the reunification of a community whose unity had always been tenuous. *Washington Post* staff writer DeNeen Brown summed up the sentiment of many a Million Woman marcher when on leaving Philadelphia she expressed faith not in a broad horizontal sisterhood, but in her "little circle of sisters" with whom she communed when she felt the need. Said Brown, "They give me just enough faith to know that sisterhood—on a smaller scale—is something possible."[40]

Another Country

Shortly before the Million Man March, African American journalist Sam Fulwood III wrote a column for the *Los Angeles Times* under the headline "Blacks Not in Lock Step as Washington March Nears." Fulwood's article rehearsed the variety of opinions surrounding the gathering and concluded that the mixed opinions "mirror the mixed attitudes of black Americans as they grapple with their estrangement from themselves."[41] This estrangement, which was more visible at the women's march than at the Million Man March, is not visible from the aerial views of the marches or even from streamed recordings taken on the ground, but it does reflect the reality that sent African Americans to marches pleading with each other for unity.[42]

Before looking at what actually happened at each march, a look at black diversity is in order, if only to remind ourselves that the conflict black women confronted over sisterhood and that black men faced over violence had very deep roots in the historically based strategy of self-defense, which had always been fraught with tension. In short, there had never been a time when black Americans had been "just black." They had been light, brown, and dark-skinned blacks; elite, middle-, working-, and lower-class blacks; male and female blacks; and heterosexual, homosexual, bisexual, and transgender blacks. Take, for example, the Brown Fellowship Society, founded as early as 1740 in Charleston, South Carolina. Besides being restricted to free men with light skin, one had to have considerable means to pay the fifty-dollar membership fee plus monthly dues. Founded almost a hundred years later (1838) in the same city was the Humane Brotherhood, whose members were also wealthy but dark-skinned.[43] In the late nineteenth and twentieth centuries, some fraternities and sororities accepted only those who could pass the notorious "brown bag test," named thus because one's skin had to be lighter than that of a brown paper bag.[44] While working- and middle-class blacks without college degrees joined fraternal and sororal societies like the Masons, Elks, and Eastern Star, college-educated African Americans joined black Greek organizations. Blacks had also divided along lines of faith. African Methodist Episcopals (AME) did not take tea with Baptists, while black Episcopal, Presbyterians, and Catholics shunned both Baptist and AME for being overemotional.[45] Even when it came to politics, African Americans were never of one mind. Although the divide between the followers of Booker T. Washington and W. E. B. Du Bois was never as stark as it is often painted, African Americans divided over the best strategy to fight segregation and discrimination—whether it was better to accommodate racism by turning inward and focusing on community and individual development, or fight openly for civil and political rights. These divisions persisted through the midcentury freedom movements as a variety of organizations—NOI, CORE, SCLC, SNCC, NAACP, COFO, OAAU, MFDP, BPP, RAM, US, to name a few—that espoused either nonviolent direct action, legal action through the courts, grassroots political organizing, armed self-defense, nationalist economic community development, or a combination of tactics announced the diversity of black opinion.[46] Similarly, men and women had fought for black rights, but often in their separate organizations and often in conflict with each other. The founders of the 1896 National Association of Colored Women, for example, held fast to the idea expressed by Anna J. Cooper in 1892 that men could not represent the race, that women were its best representatives because they molded the home and community from which the black nation grew. And in 1972, the National Black Feminist Organization, and other women's associations, formed because its members did not think that the male-dominated black nationalist and civil rights groups represented black women's interests on issues like reproductive rights, workplace opportunity, or gender equality.[47] It has already been noted how the African American preoccupation with respectability exorcised homosexuals from visibility and the meaning of blackness. Their invisibility, however, did not translate into nonexistence, so on this score too, African Americans had been far more diverse, even oppositional with one another, than million mass marchers imagined.

And yet virulent white racism had demanded unity. At the end of the nineteenth century, W. E. B. Du Bois, one of the architects of black modernism, eloquently made the case for it. Unity was necessary, he insisted, not just for advancement but also for self-defense. Weighed down by economic competition from immigrants, the prejudice and hatred of native whites, and the pity of everyone else, Du Bois maintained that, for blacks, "our one haven of refuge is ourselves." If African Americans were to defend themselves and offer their genius to America on their own terms, terms that did not require that they lose their black culture, they had to be "inspired by one vast ideal," and black hearts had to "beat in one glad song of jubilee."[48] As much as black people strove for economic and political rights, they strove to make this ideal a reality; indeed, the former was believed to rest on the latter. Million Man and Woman marchers gathered in this tradition. They aspired to attain a life-sustaining union that could uplift the individual spirit, solidify the black nation, and act as a bulwark and buffer against racism. Unfortunately, marchers seemed unaware that Du Bois lived for almost a century (1868–1963) and did not see this ideal truly realized. At the end of the twentieth century, when black men and women ironically went to their separate malls to, as little Carolyn Smith put it, "make more unity," the ideal was even further away than the marchers realized. A closer look at what happened during the marches suggests that at the turn of the twentieth-first century, African Americans were not only grasping at an ideal that had yet to be realized, but also an imaginary one that was evaporating before their very eyes.

Although not always apparent on the days of the respective marches, divisiveness was spawned by the organization and leadership of each march. Take, for example, the Million Woman March. Phile Chionesu and Asia Coney, the march's organizers, reveled in their ordinariness. Unaffiliated with any major national organization, they were proud of their grassroots, outsider credentials. At the time of the march, Chionesu was the owner of a local African clothing and craft store and mother of a nine-year-old daughter. Coney, who had once lived in a one-bedroom apartment with her mother, stepfather, grandmother, and five siblings, had survived welfare and the murder of her twenty-three-year-old son and had organized her fellow tenants at the Tasker Homes housing project to save it from demolition.[49] Together, they seemed the most unlikely organizers of a march that, depending on who was counting, brought anywhere from 500,000 to 1.5 million women to Philadelphia on October 25, 1997.[50]

Ironically, the seeds of class division were embedded in the organizing strategy. Wanting nothing to get in the way of sisterhood, Coney and Chionesu eschewed everything that they felt could, which included corporate sponsors and mainstream media, local churches, and high-profile civil rights and traditional service organizations, including black women's sororities and organizations like 100 Black Women and the National Council of Negro Women. Said Coney, "We wanted this to be a grassroots operation and we wanted everyone included."[51]

Judging from the turnout, this approach worked not only for Coney and Chionesu but also for the many that lined Benjamin Franklin Parkway. That there was no dominating female counterpart to minister Louis Farrakhan, the organizer of the Million Man March, seemed to suit marchers as much as the absence of nationally recognized black women. C. Delores Tucker, the chair of the National Political Congress of Black Women, professed not to mind that her organization was not in on the organizing. "These community workers felt that they were not sometimes invited to the other marches and that the platforms of other marches didn't necessarily speak to their concerns. So I understand how they feel." Tucker, in fact, thought it refreshing "to see a march like this come up from the grass root."[52] So did Rita Wilson, who would not commit to the march's agenda even though she understood that it reflected "the reality of the sisters who put this together." "It is good," she said, "that this was not organized by the mainstream because that doesn't work. It does not trickle down."[53]

But some women clearly felt left out and put down. The Reverend Jeffrey Leath, pastor at one of Philadelphia's largest black churches, felt that many women in his congregation did not attend because churches had been left out of the planning.[54] Yvonne Dennis, a *Philadelphia Daily News* editor, did not attend because she had heard that "'professional women' weren't welcome at the march."[55] Although her friend told her that that was just a rumor, "part of the misinformation flying around," Frances Walker, a veteran civil rights worker in Philadelphia, and one of the original thirteen members of the march's organizing committee, confirmed what to some was the march's narrow pitch. In fact, she and eight others broke away from the organizing committee over what she called a "difference in philosophy and organizing styles." Walker said that organizers were "not as inclusive as we felt they should have been. Their focus was on grass roots; we felt they needed more women who were pioneers. I could not be a part of anything that was exclusive."[56]

This feeling only deepened when two pioneers, Rosa Parks and Coretta Scott King, declined invitations to speak, citing schedule conflicts. Although organizers were pleased that they had pulled hundreds of thousands to Philadelphia without the lure of these women or other high-profile mainstream personalities, some took their absence as an indication that middle-class women with mainstream ideas were not welcome. Others took the fact that the sound system was inadequate for a march of such proportions as proof that "untried activists had no business planning a march."[57] Still others were just happy grassroots women had proved the naysayers wrong. Said one marcher, "I didn't want the established Black women's groups who were rebuffed by march planners to be right . . . the sisters who privately felt snubbed, who had predicted that a national march put together by inexperienced organizers would be chaotic."[58]

The leadership and organizational divisiveness that emerged during the planning and execution of the Million Woman March paled in comparison to what had occurred two years earlier at the men's march. To say the least, Louis Farrakhan's leadership exposed deep divisions within black America. Public intellectuals, for example, were divided. Cornel West, Alice Walker, and Michael Eric Dyson were among those who supported the march. But Farrakhan's sexism, homophobia, anti-Semitism, and anti-Christianity led Angela Davis, Manning Marable, bell hooks, and Adolph Reed, among others, to oppose it.[59] The deepest division could be found in the religious community. Neither the National Baptist Convention nor the Progressive National Baptist Convention endorsed the march. The Reverend Bennett Smith, the leader of the latter group, understood that black Americans and some local pastors were "trying to look beyond Mr. Farrakhan and his views because of their need to do something about the plight of black men and the entire community," but, he said, "some of us have walked with Jesus too long to compromise that position now." The Reverend Henry J. Lyons, president of the National Baptist Convention, thought that since "Muslims do not believe that Jesus Christ is the answer for all of society's problems, marching with them would be both hypocritical and in violation of the word of God." There was, though, no consensus among Christian ministers about the march. Many supported it, but many were opposed. Those who opposed it did so for a variety of reasons. The Reverend Wyatt Tee Walker of New York felt he could not "in the name of unity" set aside twenty-five years of Farrakhan's "caustic criticism . . . leveled at black churches and black preachers." Referring to Farrakhan's anti-Semitism, Chandler Owens, the presiding bishop of the Church of God in Christ, said he did not "want anything to be said at a meeting that I am supporting to reflect unfavorably upon another nationality." The Reverend Eugene Rivers, pastor of the Azusa Christian Community in Dorchester, Massachusetts, was fearful that the "march was going to be the coronation of Minister Louis Farrakhan as the leader of Black America," and he did not want any part of it. The Missionary Baptist Ministers Conference agreed. They thought Farrakhan, with all his negativity, the wrong person to lead a "Holy Day of Atonement and Reconciliation."[60]

Those who went to the Million Man March despite their feelings about Farrakhan revealed an interesting new development in African America. The polls showed that most marchers were not anti-Semitic or anti-Catholic or anti-Christian or even sexist. They also showed that marchers found it neither unreasonable nor strange to "separate the message from the messenger."[61] The Reverend Joseph Lowery, president of the Southern Christian Leadership Conference, felt that conditions in black America demanded it. "The crisis is that great," he said. "Here's someone I often disagree with, someone I may not even like. But if the guy says let's put water on the fire, I'm going to help. The message obscures the messenger."[62] Forty-three-year-old Dupree Thornton of Baltimore felt the same way: "It doesn't make a difference to me if it's Farrakhan or Joseph Kahn, the idea is good."[63] "Some people confuse the issue of the messenger versus the message. For me, I tried to stay a little more focused on the message," said Major F. Riddick Jr., a Maryland resident.[64]

For many black people the issue came down to one of leadership, or, more properly, the lack of it. "You can count on two or three fingers the black leaders who would be seen as major national leaders," said Lu Palmer, a veteran civil rights leader. "Once you get by Jesse—and I insist Jesse has faded—who do you have?" Linda Greene, a Catholic and national fund-raiser for the Million Man March, agreed: "There's got to be someone to lead us, and he's [Farrakhan] the only person we have who can pull this together."[65] The findings of political scientists support Palmer and Greene. For example, political scientist Katherine Tate's data agree with Lu Palmer's assessment. Jesse Jackson had not been able to fill the void left by Martin Luther King and he had not been able to forge a viable movement. Tate documented and confirmed a "leadership problem." So did political scientist Robert C. Smith. His 1996 book on African Americans in the post–civil rights era is titled *We Have No Leaders*. After finding the influence of Farrakhan and the Nation of Islam "limited and marginalized in appeal," he concluded, "We are blind, and led by the blind."[66]

Smith's rather hyperbolic characterization of the state of black leadership makes a powerful suggestion about the era. Historically, African American leaders articulated and represented the political, economic, and social opinions of black people. Frederick Douglass, Martin Delaney, Booker T. Washington, Ida B. Wells, W. E. B. Du Bois, Marcus Garvey, Mary McLeod Bethune, and Martin Luther King Jr. are names associated with black leadership, people who were called race men and women because they dedicated their life's work to the progress of black people. Race men and women had their supporters and their detractors, and black people disputed their politics. Almost never, however, did African Americans perform the mental gymnastics necessary to separate race men and women from their message. Their constituents believed in them because they believed in their message. This separation act was not a recapitulation of historical divisions in African America but indicative of something new.

Also new was the unapologetic opposition of some black women. Although most supported the Million Man March, a new dynamic was revealed when significant numbers of women braved the race-traitor charge and publically pronounced their opposition to the march and to Farrakhan. Women like Julianne Malveaux, Jewel Jackson McCabe, and Rhonda Williams, cited at the beginning of the previous chapter—revealed a new dynamic. Novelist Toni Morrison and professor and activist Angela Davis identified it after the 1991 confirmation hearings of Supreme Court Justice Clarence Thomas when Anita Hill accused Thomas of sexual harassment and Thomas made himself the victim by claiming that he was the target of a high-tech lynching. At that time Morrison and Davis cautioned black women against aligning with black men against their own interests. For them, as for so many other women, the 1991 Hill/Thomas episode proved to be epiphanous. They could not excuse the multitudes of black men who dismissed law professor Anita Hill's allegations of sexual harassment against Supreme Court nominee Clarence Thomas. Like the 1,600 black women who signed the *New York Times* statement "African American Women in Defense of Ourselves," they believed that Thomas, and the men who supported him, manipulated the legacy of lynching and trivialized the historic sexual abuse of black women in order to protect Thomas against Hill's accusations. For Morrison and Davis, the testimony in that case shattered their unconditional race alliances. One thing is for sure, remarked Morrison about Hill/Thomas, "the time for undiscriminating racial unity has passed." "In matters of race and gender it is now possible and necessary, as it seemed never to have been before, to speak about these matters without the barriers, the silences, the embarrassing gaps in discourse."[67] For Angela Davis, Hill/Thomas "symbolically represented the passing of a conception of community with which many of us have lived." Said Davis, "I experienced it as a loss and as an emancipation." She could no longer talk about "my people" without understanding the "historical obsolescence of a particular sense of community we once found so necessary—a community that no matter what . . . was racially all-embracing."[68] The then chairperson of the U.S. Commission on Civil Rights, Mary Frances Berry, agreed. She felt no compunction about denouncing the march's directors, Farrakhan and Benjamin Chavis, the former executive director of the NAACP. While she understood how important it was for black men to affirm themselves, she was unequivocal in her distrust of these men. "I do not trust Louis Farrakhan or Benjamin Chavis to lead us to the Promised Land. I do not endorse the Million Man March."[69] Neither did seventeen-year-old Ameerah Pargo of San Diego, who thought it unfair to have a men's-only march. "Black women have come a long way too," said this high school student who had apparently not imbibed the notion of unity at any cost.[70]

Neither had sexual minorities. As we have seen, historically racist assumptions about black sexuality have made African Americans particularly cautious about conforming to proper gender conventions. Therefore, historically, the construction of black identity has been heterosexual, and black politics have generally been cloaked in a cult of respectability. For example, although Bayard Rustin drafted the original blueprint of the 1963 March on Washington, he had to keep his gay identity secret, and some, like NAACP head Roy Wilkins, objected to his leadership, thinking that it would be an embarrassment to the movement if homosexuality became an issue. At the 1963 march, therefore, it was all hush-hush in the name of racial solidarity.[71] Thirty years later, the issue of open black lesbians, gays, bisexuals, and transgenders (lgbts) came up again at the annual African American Bud Billiken Parade in Chicago. Then, the ad hoc committee of Proud Black Lesbians and Gays was at first denied a permit to march because, as the publisher of the *Chicago Defender* argued, they "would insight [*sic*] negative and confrontational behavior from the general public."[72] After much wrangling they did march in the August parade, but they were probably mindful of the report issued by the Chicago Horizons Community Services Anti-Violence Project, which reported that violence against lgbts was up 20 percent in 1992, with much of the increase coming on the predominantly black South side.[73]

As happened in the Billiken Parade, at the Million Man March black gays and lesbians would not be silenced. "Black gay men and lesbians really do exist," said Earnest E. Hite Jr. in an article entitled "Lift the Ban on Gay Men and Lesbians in the Black Community. "We are invisible and that invisibility promotes a pyscho-emotional diarrhea among our community and a profile cycle of shame and fear restricting the healthy development of Black gay men and lesbians."[74] Hite, a Chicago recipient of the Stonewall Award for his work with HIV/AIDS patients, joined the chorus of voices in the 1990s protesting black homophobia. When it came to the 1995 Million Man March, the chorus amped up the volume. "If we're not at the table," said Thomas Wilson, a lawyer for Prudential Insurance, " I have a fear these guys will be pegged as our leaders and then we won't have any voice at all."[75] "These guys" were men like Louis Farrakhan and William 3X of the Nation of Islam. During a speech in 1993, Farrakhan blasted lesbians: "I'm not knocking homosexuals; they are my family . . . but I know what God expects, and I know there's no future down that road. Don't tell me you're a woman trapped in a man's body. I'm telling you, if you ever get exposed to a real man, you would never go to a woman."[76] Although Farrakhan refrained from inflammatory homophobic remarks during the Million Man March, not all leaders of the Nation of Islam held their tongues. William 3X, a minister and organizer of the march, welcomed black gays to the march to atone for their sin of homosexuality, which he claimed "is an abomination in the eyes of God, just as fornication, abuse of women, and neglect of our children are sins."[77]

Remarks like these prompted an unprecedented open discussion and protest over the heterosexual construction of black identity. "Our presence as openly gay men and lesbians will counter the assumption that we do not exist or do not contribute to our community. Staying home or marching incognito colludes with those who wish to keep us invisible" was the message of the National Black Gay and Lesbian Leadership Forum.[78] For Darren Hutchinson there were several reasons that black gays and lesbians had to speak up about the march. It not only fed into the hands of those who felt that homosexuality was inherently abnormal, undesirable, and unblack, but because it allowed racist acts against black gays to go unrecognized and unpunished, it weakened the whole project of antiracist political activism. Hutchinson also felt that "the romantic embrace of patriarchal familial structures and intimate relationships . . . necessarily marginalizes lesbian (and gay) families and relationships because the latter do not directly perpetuate male domination over women."[79] Although many gays stayed at home, thinking, as did one, "I'm not sure that trying to force our way into it is the right thing,"[80] others, like Dennis Holmes, felt the march provided a "unique opportunity to empower black gay men and lesbians and black gay youth" by providing "positive images of open, courageous, proud and diverse black gay people."[81] Always on target, cultural critic Barbara Smith, who had previously cautioned black America not to blame gays for the perceived destruction of the black family, joined the chorus: "Homosexuality is not what's breaking up the black family," she wrote, "homophobia is."[82]

FIGURE 9. Black gays walked proudly at the Million Man March. Thirty-two years earlier, organizers of the March on Washington for Jobs and Freedom agreed to keep brilliant organizer Bayard Rustin in the background, lest his homosexual identity be used against black America. *Photo by Tim Sloan/AFP/Getty Images.*

As earnest as black lesbians, gays, bisexuals, and transgenders were about their inclusion, the marches nevertheless reflected black anxiety about redefining blackness. For example, at the marches no out lgbts were allowed to speak. Cleo Manago was supposed to speak at the Million Man March, and had prepared his speech about black diversity, but was pulled from the program at the last minute.[83] And at the Million Woman March, intolerance from the podium was pervasive enough for Sheila Alexander-Reid, executive director of the nonprofit association Women in the Life, to be fearful. Instead of instilling sisterhood "across shades and tones, attitudes and beliefs, sexuality and humanity," said Alexander-Reid, the unchecked intolerance "was scary to those of us considered outside of the mainstream." She thought it counterproductive to debate, as podium speakers seemed to be doing, "who was and was not a real African woman." Daunted, she was not sure which was more upsetting, "the statements or the cheers that followed them."[84]

Neither march even tried to reach out to black lgbts. Controversy arose early at the Million Woman March when word circulated that Angie and Debbie Winans, the youngest members of the popular gospel singing family, were going to sing their new song "Not Natural." A patently homophobic response to actress Ellen DeGeneres's coming out, the song preached that homosexuality was against God's principles. When an interviewer from the *Philadelphia Inquirer* asked Paula S. Peebles, the program committee chairwoman, about the controversy, Peebles replied that the march was an interdenominational event with no single religious perspective. She said that all women of African American descent were welcome but flatly added, with no intended irony, that the march was "not dealing" with issues relating to sexual orientation.[85] To Peebles's credit, the song was not sung, but there was a general silence on issues of homosexuality at the Million Woman March.[86]

The same was true two years earlier at the Million Man March. Given Louis Farrakhan's well-known homophobia, black lgbts did not expect him to be welcoming or to acknowledge this aspect of black diversity. Yet they probably expected more from Jesse Jackson, Benjamin Chavis, and Joseph Lowery—all of whom supported the 1993 March on Washington for Lesbian, Gay and Bi (LGB) Equal Rights and Liberation. In 1984 Jesse Jackson had welcomed gays and lesbians into his Rainbow Coalition and in 1993 he ac-knowledged that lgbts were "African American, Latino and white," and that they were of all religions and found in all socioeconomic strata. He noted that homophobes and racists were cut from the same cloth; that HIV/AIDS was ravaging African Americans and lgbts; and that it was a moral impera-tive and politically necessary for blacks and gays to fight for gay and black rights together.[87] From the podium, Benjamin Chavis, who had been recently elected president of the NAACP, promised sexual minorities that the oldest civil rights organization in the country "will stand with you" against all forms of discrimination and injustice, and asked lgbts to stand with blacks in their struggle against racism and South African apartheid and their fight for eco-nomic justice. In February of that year, the board of directors of the NAACP issued a resolution supporting the elimination of the ban on homosexuals in the military and supporting their rights to live free of discrimination.[88] The Reverend Joseph Lowery supported the '93 LGB march as well.[89]

But at the Million Man March, neither Jackson, nor Chavis, nor Lowery, nor anyone else acknowledged even the existence of homosexuality, let alone black lgbts. They talked about black manhood, the black family, violence in African America, and unity, but not black sexual diversity. The Nation of Islam's minister of health, Alim Muhammad, spoke of HIV/AIDS without so much as a mention of homosexuality.[90] Perhaps Lowery was referencing lgbts when he noted that black people had to free themselves from "the abuse of our sexuality," but his oblique reference was so sandwiched between his calls for freedom from addiction and freedom from economic impoverishment that it was unclear what he was talking about.[91] Interestingly enough, Jesse Jackson seemed conscious of the omission. His *published* four-page speech did contain *one* line wherein he directed black America to fight against "racism, sexism, anti-Semitism, anti-Arabism, Asian bashing, homophobia and xenophobia."[92] Yet standing before the men gathered on the Washington Mall on October 16, he did not speak the word *homophobia* and said only that black America had to stand against racism, sexism, anti-Semitism, anti-Arabism, and anti-immigrationism.[93] In sum, there was no homophobia at the Million Man March, as some black lgbts had feared, but there was no acknowledgment of black lgbts, period. The silence was truly deafening.

As we can see, therefore, a zoom-lens view of the 1990s gatherings is far more revealing than an aerial shot. From above, it seemed that African Americans were gathered in unity at the Million Man and Million Woman Marches to affirm their citizenship and demand equality of opportunity, demands that had been made many times before in national spaces. The closer look, however, reveals something more profound. Neither march was about demanding anything from anyone or entity but themselves. Besides insisting that every African American assume individual responsibility for her or his own shortcomings, blacks marched for community. This was new. Despite intraracial diversity, African Americans had always marched *in* unity, but the 1990s found them marching *for* unity. New too were separate male and female marches. In the twentieth century, even when black men and women saw issues differently, they had always marched together. The end of the century, though, found them marching apart. Also new were the separation of the leader's message from the leader and the very public debate on the utility of a heterosexual black identity. In short, the marches were a symptom of change. This was another country, not the black country African Americans imagined. Whether seen as the passing or the dawning of an era, the marches revealed the 1990s to be a watershed in African American history.

The Advent of Post-Blackness

If hindsight is twenty-twenty vision, then the debates over post-blackness that occurred in the early years of the twenty-first century shed light on what was unfolding during the marches.

Thelma Golden's 2001 *Freestyle* exhibition at the Studio Museum of Harlem signaled a new era. Featured in that exhibit were young African American artists whose work was not immediately or necessarily identifiable as "black art." Aside from the stark contrast with Golden's previous curatorial work at the Whitney Museum of American Art, and the fact that her new exhibit marked her debut at the Studio Museum, Golden's description of the *Freestyle* art as "post-black" ratcheted up interest and ignited a controversy. By 2005, when Valerie Cassel Oliver curated the *Double Consciousness: Black Conceptual Art since 1970* exhibit at the Contemporary Arts Museum in Houston, Texas, the debate about the role of race in black art raged at full pitch. At the center of that exhibit was Oliver's contention that "in the 21st century, we must acknowledge that we are not, nor have we ever been, monolithic. Today there is a push to acknowledge the complexity of the individual and his or her own experiences, thoughts, desires and ideals."[94]

This art-world debate over black identity was intense. The simplest implication of the term *post-black*—that black people were no longer black, or no longer identified as black, or no longer needed to acknowledge their blackness—was disturbing to many. "An African American artist needs a cultural rootedness as a foundation," said artist, curator, and art historian Michael Harris.[95] For John Bankston, a San Francisco–based artist whose work appeared in Golden's *Freestyle* show, black people could not be at a point of post-blackness because "work by black artists will always be interpreted in terms of race and work by white artists will always be characterized by the absence of race."[96] For Golden, "a conversation about 'black art' ultimately meant embracing and rejecting the notion of such a thing at the very same time." The term *post-black*, she said, "was characterized by artists who were adamant about not being labeled as 'black' artists though their work was steeped, in fact, deeply interested, in redefining complex notions of blackness."[97] So multifarious were the artists' ways of being black that in this exhibit, "blackness" did not act as a centripetal force. Ironically, the unifying force of this exhibit was "individuality," which gave birth to the title *Freestyle*. As explained by Golden, "Freestyle is the term which refers to the space where the musician (improvisation) or for the dancer (the break) finds the groove and goes all out in a relentless and unbridled expression of the self."[98] Golden's ideas were reiterated four years later by Oliver, who prudently noted that although "'post-black' . . . conjures a feeling of negation—a negation of blackness, . . . 'post-black' is not about negation of blackness, but what lies beyond the 1970's definition of blackness, a definition which at the time, sought to unify the community as monolithic." Art historian Horace Brockington reiterated Oliver's point. Black artists today, he argued in 2000, are "concerned with sexuality, gender and other identity issues as well as history and geopolitics." Said Brockington, black artists "suggest an unlimited individuality and variety. . . . They engage new strategies that allow the viewer to learn something altogether new about reality or self in unprecedented ways."[99]

Brockington agreed with Oliver that black art is not monolithic and that younger artists come to the term *blackness* differently than did their forebears. According to Oliver, new millennium black artists "are more open." "Blackness," she said, is "a sensibility" that grounds them but at the same time allows them "to show their own complexity." Willing to concede that the term *post-black* was problematic, Oliver averred that "while there is yet no language or term to define this movement, . . . there is a cogent sensibility which I see among these artists, one which I am extremely motivated by and grateful for."[100]

The post-black conversation did not stay in the art world; in fact, artists were only extending the dialogue that had been under way in the '90s, including that which surrounded the lobbying for unity over individualism at the Million Man March. The discourse among scholars, for example, centered on the gains made by the midcentury freedom movement and the difference class made. They found that as segregation declined and economic opportunity increased, more blacks than ever before attended to aspects of their lives other than race.[101]

This change in black America was the feature of a 1998 Public Broadcasting Service *Frontline* episode titled, aptly enough, "The Two Nations of Black America." Hosted by Harvard University professor Henry Louis Gates Jr., the show queried the emergence of a black America that was possibly divided more by class than it was united by race. One of the many points brought to light by "The Two Nations of Black America" was the fact that the last quarter of the twentieth century was marked by the substantial growth of the black middle class. In the years before the freedom movement, blacks who served black communities composed the black middle and upper classes. They were morticians, barbers, and beauticians. They owned the black restaurants, stores, and clubs that served African Americans. Black professionals, from teachers to doctors, also served a community that was almost exclusively black. This black middle class not only served blacks but usually lived in the black community that they served. The movement, however, changed the very nature of black America (and, by extension, America) by opening jobs that were previously closed. A Ford Motor Company list makes this clear. In 1963 Ford employed blacks as valets, porters, security guards, messengers, barbers, mail clerks, and telephone operators—a list that by its narrowness explained the urgency and militancy of the struggle for jobs and education.[102] By 1980 things had changed dramatically. Nationwide the number of professional and managerial workers had tripled, and the number of black sales and clerical workers, about half of whom were women, increased fivefold. Between 1970 and 1980 alone the number of black college students doubled, increasing from 522,000 to over a million. These gains were accompanied by an increase in earnings relative to whites. Though more likely than their white counterparts to depend on the income of both a husband and wife—a fact that reflected its fragility—the emergence of a substantial middle class was a hallmark of the movement for economic and political justice.[103]

The other point made by "Two Nations" was the growth of those called the underclass and the economic and cultural differences between it and the black middle class. As more than one-third of all blacks sunk into poverty, and as the unemployment rate for young black males reached 50 percent, group solidarity declined. Increasingly, the black middle class distanced itself from the urban poor by moving to the suburbs and by telegraphing their difference through dress, speech, and behavior. On the decline also was the sense of linked fate—the feeling that what happened to the race as a group affected all blacks as individuals. By the first decade of the twenty-first century, even race discrimination occupied a less central place on the "black" political agenda.[104] On "Two Nations," Gates, a distinguished African American scholar, put the question front and center: "How have we reached this point where we have both the largest middle class and the largest underclass in our history?"[105]

While "Two Nations" highlighted the class divisions in black America, it could just as well have pointed to the diversity in other aspects of African American life. As we have seen, not only class but also gender and sexual diversity marked African America. By the end of the century, black immigrants who came to America as a result of liberalized immigration policies were also changing the meaning of "black" culture. By 2007 in New York, Massachusetts, and Minnesota, one in every four black people was foreign-born; in Florida and Washington State, immigrants made up one-fifth of the black population. As they introduced their foods, music, traditional dress, and religion into their adopted American communities, they changed the meaning of blackness and tended to distance themselves from native-born African Americans.[106] Biracials further complicated black identity. Historically, one-drop laws passed during the colonial period and the nineteenth century made anyone with discernible black pigmentation or black heritage black. But the 2000 census let respondents self-identify as belonging to more than one race, and 11 percent of all respondents so identified. Like most black immigrants, many biracials want to be American more than they want to be black or white. Whether torn between two countries, two races, or two ethnicities, this ever-increasing group does not want to have to choose.[107]

While the post-black conversation did not surface until late in the 1990s and the first decade of the twenty-first century, it's obvious that Million Man and Woman marchers were not only feeling the effects of that which as yet had no name but were reacting to it as well. The two separate marches, the intersectionality made palpable by the Million Woman March, the feeling of estrangement both black men and women felt, the unclosetedness of lgbts, and the leadership issues were all symptoms of a new era in which the currency of racial unity was declining in the face of individual expression. Mass marchers sensed that the "community" was changing—if not disappearing—before their very eyes and their cries for unity revealed that they were unhinged by it. While it is ironic that marchers took personal responsibility for their failing communalism, it was totally predictable. On deck was the age of black individualism—an age ironically brought into being by the black communalism of the past.

Forty Million Ways to Be Black

In 2008, writer, novelist, and philosopher Charles Johnson gave a Martin Luther King address that subsequently was published as an essay called "The End of the Black American Narrative." In this essay Johnson argues that the African American narrative of slavery, Jim Crow, and lynching has dominated everything about black identity for centuries. "This unique black American narrative," he says, "which emphasizes the experience of victimization, is quietly in the background of every conversation we have about black people, even when it is not fully articulated or expressed. . . . It is our starting point, our agreed-upon premise, our most important presupposition for dialogues about black America," says Johnson. Basically, what Johnson argues in the essay is that African Americans need to bury this narrative because black people are too complex and multifaceted to be so easily categorized. "We challenge, culturally and politically, an old group narrative that fails at the beginning of this new century to capture even a fraction of our rich diversity and heterogeneity." In essence, Johnson calls on African Americans to develop a new story. "A new century calls for new stories grounded in the present, leaving behind the painful history of slavery and its consequences."[108]

Johnson's message was similar in substance to that put forth by *Washington Post* journalist Eugene Robinson. In October 2007, Robinson wrote an op-ed piece in which he proclaimed that "if there ever was a monolithic 'black

America'—absolutely and uniformly deprived and aggrieved, with invariant values and attitudes—there certainly isn't one now." Robinson, an African American, called for "a new language, a new vocabulary and syntax," because, he claimed "black America" is an "increasingly meaningless concept."[109]

And at the beginning of his 2011 book titled *Who's Afraid of Post-Blackness: What It Means to Be Black Now*, writer, news correspondent, and social critic Touré recounted an interview with scholar Henry Louis Gates Jr. in which Gates said that there is no authentic blackness, that the possibilities for black identity are infinite. Said Gates, "If there are forty million Black Americans then there are forty million ways to be Black."[110]

Scholars, particularly historians, have always known that there never was one way to be black. But they have also known that black solidarity was not only an effective strategy of self-defense necessitated by a white majority in the days of slavery, Jim Crow, pogroms, lynching, state-sanctioned murders, and disfranchisement, but it was also a means of cultural, psychological, and economic survival. Black unity, tenuous though it was, was a necessary prerequisite to the kind of black independence touted by the likes of Johnson and Touré. Without the unity of the mid-twentieth-century freedom movement, black people would not be able to even think about leaving behind their painful history.

Although black laypersons do not usually experience the world the way historians do, it should come as no surprise that faced with the new and uncomfortable realities of postmodern existence, African Americans would reach back to the familiar—gatherings, marches—to go forward into the unfamiliar realities of twenty-first-century black life. Different groups did the same thing at the turn of the twentieth century when industrialization, corporatization, and urbanization made daily life unfamiliar. Ordinary black Americans, like white Promise Keeper families, knew that change was in the air, felt that change in the 1990s, and tried to deal with it at the Million Man and Million Woman Marches. They felt the loss of community and this left them without secure footing in an America that could be, had been, and was hostile to nonwhite Americans. Surely deindustrialization, globalization, feminism, and multiculturalism were causes of their distress, but their testimony reveals sadness about intraracial and interpersonal black relationships—relationships that seemed to mediate against a unified "black country." A sign of the times, of postmodernity, was that in taking personal responsibility for changing community relationships, they reified individuality—the very thing that was diminishing the communalism they sought.

CHAPTER 5

Things Fall Apart;
the LGBT Center Holds

Shortly before the 1993 March on Washington for Lesbian, Gay and Bi Equal Rights and Liberation, sociologist Margaret Cerullo wrote an article summarizing what she saw as the promise and perils of the era. Befittingly titled "Hope and Terror: The Paradox of Gay and Lesbian Politics in the 90s," Cerullo characterized the recent Clinton victory as bittersweet. Sweet, because unlike Ronald Reagan or George H. W. Bush, Clinton had treated lesbians, gays, bisexuals, and transgenders (lgbts) as American citizens and given them reason to believe that the White House would stand with them in their fight against the relentless assault on their rights. But it was bittersweet because since the November election Clinton had waffled on his promise to end discrimination against lgbts in the military, reminding them of how hard it was to hold liberals accountable to their rhetoric. Cerullo also saw hope and terror in the choices that confronted sexual minorities. Clinton's election was a welcome foot in the door, but how would they represent themselves as they pressed forward? Would they go forth with a politics of respectability, a politics that "won't frighten the powerful . . . understanding that emphasizing the fringe might only feed stereotypes and help justify or rationalize or give focus to the hatred that exists against us?" Or would they unite at the grass roots and "not leave one another isolated when we face attacks that are going to have implications for all of us"? For Cerullo, this was the pressing concern. She wondered, "How much are they going to extract from us in exchange for laws that promise us a measure of safety and redress? How much are they going to extract from us in conformity, obedience, and internal policing?"[1]

Lesbian feminist civil rights activist Loree Cook-Daniels was equally fretful, though she expressed it a bit differently. In an article titled "We Need Every Tool in the Box," Cook-Daniels likened the lgbt community to the variety of nuts and bolts, hammers, and screwdrivers in her toolbox. Some of them were well used but others gathered dust. "But when I have a job that can only be done by a teeny, tiny hammer that I've never used before, I am grateful that I once invested in the full assortment." Cook-Daniels went on to say that sexual minorities only strengthened themselves when they embraced everyone in the community. Exclusionary practices only weakened them. "Don't insist that the drag queen give up his skirts, or the political appointees be outspoken on the job, or the street activist 'grow up,' or the bisexual advocate choose one side or the other," she cautioned. "These folks make up our toolbox, and I want to be sure that when the time comes, we won't find that we've trashed the perfect tool for getting the job done."[2]

Lgbts marched on Washington in 1993 and again in 2000 for the same reason other groups marched: to end their isolation by gathering with people perceived to be like themselves, to express their unhappiness with American culture, and to try to change the culture so they could live more satisfying lives. Like the other marches, the process of bringing people together exposed not only the unifying elements but the divisions as well. Cerullo's and Cook-Daniels's writings capture the major dilemma that confronted the lgbt community in the 1990s. In the decade that saw average heterosexual Americans become more accepting of sexual minorities, the challenge for this diverse group was how to maintain solidarity and also embrace difference; how to achieve and wield power within the establishment and not be co-opted by that power or establishment; and how to be respectful of their multiple identities. These were issues that had preoccupied sexual minorities since the birth of their first formal organizations in the 1950s, but as the community became more visible, something the marches helped make possible, resolving them became more crucial. Who belonged to the "community," how it defined itself, where it would find strength, and how strength was understood were questions that became more urgent as the 1990s wore on and sexual minorities became visible and vocal. The 1993 and 2000 gatherings were the third and fourth national marches staged by lgbts, and while both marches demonstrated their desire and attempt to stretch the community's boundaries in order to work across identities, the marches also demonstrated how complicated and nearly impossible such stretching was.

From afar or above, the 1993 and 2000 marches looked like other national marches. With the exception of the super-large quilt representing the many lives lost to the AIDS epidemic, there were the familiar crowds, banners, and speeches. Much can be learned from this angle, but a ground-level view reveals more about the impact of multiculturalism, feminism, and the global economy. This chapter argues that, much like what happened to African Americans at the end of the century, the forces of postmodernism acted as a centrifugal force pulling sexual minorities in multiple directions, stretching them to an almost breaking point.

The Personal Is Political; or, "Visibilizing" the Despised

"There are as many reasons to march next April as there are queer people in this country," said organizers Roger Doughty, a former president of the Gay and Lesbian Activists Alliance in Washington, DC, and Rebecca LePere, the former managing director of the NAMES Project Foundation—AIDS Memorial Quilt. In a newspaper established for the sole purpose of publicizing the 1993 March on Washington for Lesbian, Gay and Bi Equal Rights and Liberation, Doughty and LePere answered the questions "Why March? Why Now? Why 1993?" The answers they gave did not separate the personal from the political. As much as they felt that lgbts needed to "declare to our elected officials and to the nation that we, as human beings and as citizens, demand our rights," they also argued that they needed to "celebrate ourselves and the incredible community of which we are a part." For Doughty and LePere, celebration and protest went hand in hand. They urged people to attend the march to "celebrate each person's story" and merge their individual stories into a powerful whole. A closeted, self-hating people would be ineffective freedom fighters, they argued, but together millions of lgbts could effect change at the grassroots level.[3] Both the 1993 and 2000 marches effectively blended the personal and the political. In doing so they made Doughty and LePere's observations about the many reasons to march a truism that was at once both heartening and foreboding.

At the top of the list of things to celebrate were the numbers who attended. Like all of the marches during the 1990s these marches generated conflicting reports about attendance. Opponents generally downsized the crowd and proponents usually inflated it.[4] For march organizers it was enough that several hundred thousand attended both marches and that, unlike the 1987 national march, it was not ignored by the press.[5] "What difference does it make if there were 100,000, 500,000 or 1 million," asked one editorialist. "There were more than enough people on the Mall to send a message that the gay rights movement is a force to be reckoned with."[6] In fact, the 1993 and 2000 marches were covered on network news programs and cable news channels. C-SPAN broadcasted both events in their entirety.

This had more significance for sexual minorities than other groups because as a matter of course they were encouraged to keep their "peculiar" sexual proclivities to themselves and to hide their different sexual preferences and gender identities from public view. The march was a particularly effective political tool for just this reason. Said one editorialist, the march "will get massive media coverage . . . putting us in the living rooms of America and even the world."[7] National marches also allowed those who were closeted to see and actually count the hundreds of thousands who were like themselves. Marches were membership invitations to join a vibrant, nurturing community whose power was revealed in its visibility and whose clout grew in proportion to the numbers of people who "came out" or refused to hide what many perceived to be sexual deviance. Doughty and LePere thought this was especially important for teenagers. In pitching the march they asked readers if they could remember what it was like to grow up queer "alone in some homo-hostile place." The '93 march would "show Gay, Lesbian and Bisexual teens they're not alone."[8] Black lesbian feminist Jewelle Gomez also understood the value of "outing" the entire community. Having marched in African American and lgbt marches, she had given up on changing the minds of bigots or the votes of legislators. Gomez's focus had shifted to the lone person who "flips through all the channels to watch the news like I used to do and sees me, or thousands like me, and understands that none of us is ever really alone."[9]

The need to feel nurtured stands out as the most frequently cited reason for marching in 1993 or 2000. For sure, marchers listed political, economic, and social concerns, including the need to find treatment and a cure for HIV/AIDS, but because so many lived secret lives, fearful of discovery, the need to feel that they were a part of a compassionate community was a prerequisite to organizing locally and nationally to fight for the different facets of equal rights. "Everyone came to DC and had a taste of the kind of freedom that lets you hold your lover's hand in public," said Caroline Appleby of Greensboro, North Carolina.[10] "I've spent most of my life on the other side," said thirty-two-year-old Shelly Spector, speaking of being always in the minority. "It's exciting to walk around proud, not like something's wrong with you."[11] Forty-one-year-old Alabamian Alice Dilbeck and her partner Betsey Applegate likened their experience at the 2000 Millennium March as akin to "breathing." "It's really something to be somewhere where you can be yourself," Dilbeck said. Her girlfriend piped in, "And where you can be in the majority."[12]

Ed Cedar's experience is instructive. He went to the 1993 march from Charlotte, North Carolina, but wanted to preserve the feeling of freedom he had at the march. He had a "renewed enthusiasm for loving," and he wanted to sustain it. And he did. The march, he testified, gave him "the courage/pride/ fortitude to come out to about six people at work and about ten neighbors at my condo meeting." When coworkers and neighbors asked where he got his tan, he unhesitatingly answered, "At the March on Sunday." When they gave him a puzzled look, he added, "AT THE GAY RIGHTS MARCH ON SUNDAY!" Cedar wrote that he knew he could not maintain the complete "high" he had felt at the march, but, he insisted, "I am determined to keep the feeling with me. And the only way to do that is to experience, and force yourself to experience that freedom everyday. And you do it by . . . being OUT!"[13]

Doughty's and LePere's concern about teenagers was shared by most organizers and they wanted them to have an experience like Cedar's. Young people were more vulnerable to bullying and self-hatred, and, although suicide statistics did not disaggregate sexual orientation in cause-of-death reports, experts estimate that lgbts from fifteen to twenty-four years old made up a significant number of those who killed themselves.[14] Speaking for then Wisconsin congresswoman Tammy Baldwin, Jerilyn Goodwin, her press secretary, said, "It can be very frightening as a teenager to think that you may be gay and you don't know anybody else who is feeling like you. Being able to participate in something like this, or just see it happening, can give you a sense that you are not alone."[15] One seasoned marcher who reported that he saw more young people at the 2000 march than at the three previous national marches thought that teenagers benefited from the march. "They come out so much earlier now," and the march, he thought, helped young people find a supportive community to join.[16] It did just this for eighteen-year-old Joshua Burton of Virginia Beach. At the 2000 march he felt he had finally found his "people." A reporter noted that the politics and mission of the gathering practically eluded Burton as he spoke of finally gaining "the right to live, the right to love." "This march," he affirmed, "lets me know I'm not alone."[17] Among the speakers Burton heard at the march was Corey Johnson, cocaptain of a Massachusetts high school football team. He told marchers how supportive his teammates had been when he came out. Johnson counseled the likes of Burton to "live our lives truthfully" and "be brave."[18]

March organizers also paid special attention to those like Burton who lived in small towns or rural communities. It was especially hard to be a sexual minority in isolated areas where everyone knew and cared about everyone else's business; where being out exposed one to daily rebuke, ridicule, and violence. College student Luis Quintero, for example, described Laredo, Texas, his hometown, as "a very closed community when it comes to lesbians and gays." Another student at the University of Texas at San Antonio, Caryl Cunningham, found it hard to be gay even in San Antonio. "Living here in Texas, you feel kind of isolated as a community," she said.[19] The march made her and Quintero feel part of something larger than their Lambda Student Alliance, an lgbt campus organization. Speaking of the importance of national marches to those from small towns in Georgia, Harry Knox, of the Georgia Equality Project, reminded his interviewer that "the battle for full equality in Atlanta is very different than it is in Cordele and Statesboro and Rome."[20] An editorial written by two Taylorsville, Utah, marchers underscored Knox's point. Kathy Worthington and Sara Hamlin noted that most of the 300 people from Utah who attended the 2000 march had not been able to go to a previous event of that kind. They found the march "an empowering and unforgettable experience" and "they came away with new courage and determination to fight for equality.[21] Said singer Melissa Etheridge, who came out as a lesbian shortly before the '93 march at which she performed, "I grew up in Kansas and I didn't even know the word [lesbian]." A march, whether you go or see it on television, "brings it home . . . brings it to the small town, the small place."[22]

Marches also let lgbts in small places know what the big issues were. At the top of Doughty and LePere's list was the underfunded Ryan White CARE act to combat HIV/AIDS. Discrimination in employment, housing, medical benefits, marriage rights, and the military were added to the hate crimes endured daily. Marching on the nation's capital, it was argued, helped marshal lgbt voting strength. Said Doughty and LePere, marching "loudly shouts to America our numbers, our demands, our strength, our diversity, and our absolute determination to accept nothing less than equal rights." Activist David Mixner argued that gay voters could be the margin of victory in a tight race for control of Congress. "The Millennium March" he argued, will "serve notice to those in political power that gay, lesbian, bisexual and transgender people . . . are serious about participating in our democracy."[23] By and large, marchers and their supporters endorsed these views. The official demands at both marches also included repeal of sodomy laws and all laws that criminalized private sexual expression between consenting adults; access to health care; an end to discrimination in areas of family diversity, adoption, custody, and foster care; the inclusion of lgbt studies in educational curricula; the right to reproductive freedom and choice; and an end to sexism and racism.

If there was one demand most marchers could agree on, it was for more government spending on HIV/AIDS research and health-care programs for victims of the disease. In both 1993 and 2000, when many lgbts and their supporters said they went to Washington "to march for those who can't," many were alluding to friends and family who were sick or dying from HIV/ AIDS, which had been ravaging the gay community since the early '80s. The fight against the callously indifferent Reagan administration had been the centerpiece of the 1987 march, a year that saw 40,000 die from the epidemic.[24] Still three years away from the anti-HIV therapy that drastically lowered AIDS deaths among gay men, funding for more AIDS research was one of the signature issues in 1993.[25] Speaking of the Reagan and H. W. Bush years, poet and author Paul Monette, who died of an AIDS-related illness two years later, said, "With all my heart, I don't want to die of AIDS, and its gonna happen to me because of these 12 years of neglect."[26] Organizers of the '93 march wanted to send a message to newly elected Bill Clinton, who, during the '92 campaign, had promised to stand with the grief-stricken, but who had not yet appointed the promised AIDS czar nor put an AIDS expert on Hillary Clinton's health-care overhaul committee.

In 1993, the HIV/AIDS epidemic still made the pilgrimage to Washington a particularly emotional undertaking. Men like Los Angeles lawyer Michael Nava, whose partner had died the previous August, were rageful. He had not marched since the anti-Vietnam peace movement, had not even joined the 1987 lgbt march because HIV/AIDS had not yet touched him. But 1993 was different. "I flip to the obituaries where row after row of men are pictured, most of them born the same decade as me. I think about their faces every time I see Hollywood airheads wearing a red ribbon where their hearts should be. I'm marching . . . because Chris can't," he wrote. "I'm going to Washington because I can't sit back anymore and let someone else take the risks for me when it's my rights that are on the line."[27] Many who agreed with Nava carried placards that read "Silence = Death"; others demonstrated outside of the U.S. Department of Health and Human Services the weekend of the march. While some marchers attempted to storm the offices of the Pharmaceutical Manufacturer's Association, others laid down in front of the White House in a "die-in" demonstration.[28]

Lifting the ban on gays in the military was another signature issue of the marches, though more in 1993 than 2000. Clinton had promised that if elected he would immediately issue an executive order that would allow open gays to serve. But when both Congress and military brass balked, he delayed the order for six months, ostensibly to give the Pentagon and his defense secretary time to draft a new policy. In the meantime, marchers used the March on Washington to push their position that countless thousands of gays and lesbians had served and continued to serve well and honorably in the nation's military, and that there was no evidence that their presence had been harmful.[29] "In Vietnam, sexuality was not the issue," said Tom Norton, who had flown a medical helicopter. "We were over there to do a job, and some of us died doing it."[30] World War II army veteran Herb King urged gay and lesbian vets to march with the Gay, Lesbian and Bisexual Veterans of America contingent wearing uniform parts, service ribbons, and other military identifications. Vets needed to show their support for Clinton's proposal to lift the ban, and the march was the perfect vehicle. The media, he argued, would be out in full force, looking for highlights for their stories. "A huge turnout of veterans and servicemembers would be the top story and it can have a great impact on the attitude of our legislators and the general public."[31] The media did cover veterans but that was not what was most important to lesbian journalist Karen Ocamb. The march, reported Ocamb, "enabled a number of lesbians and gays in the military to shore up their courage, step out of the closet." Their pride, she contended, served to remind their communities, as well as stubbornly homophobic Senator Sam Nunn, the leader of the opposition to lifting the ban, that "lesbians and gays are also proud Americans."[32]

In sum, most marchers at the 1993 and 2000 marches had very personal reasons for marching. They needed affirmation; they needed to be around people who were like themselves; they needed to feel "normal," if only for a day. They and most organizers understood how important it was for this despised minority to celebrate themselves through "visibilization." Visibility built self-esteem, encouraged self-awareness, melded and broadened the community, and helped lgbts deal with loss and feel less lost. And marches were a perfect visibilization tool. They brought individuals together in community before the entire world, broadcast the potential political power of the group, and let lgbts in small places know what issues took priority. Herein, though, was a problem. If the multiple personal stories did not cohere but gave way to multiple political stances, it could be difficult, if not impossible, to march together, much less build a unified political movement.

Marching to Different Drummers

Shortly after the 2000 Millennium March, Donald I. Hammonds, an openly gay African American, wrote an editorial in the *Pittsburgh Post-Gazette* arguing that the 1993 march was "the beginning of a time of fragmentation for the gay and lesbian movement." "It was most clear in 1993, and especially now [in 2000], that we, as gays, lesbians, transgendered persons and other sexual minorities are moving in different directions," he wrote. Hammonds did not think it was a bad thing. "Social movements need to make room for different expressions and ways of 'being' to remain healthy, fluid organisms. Change is good, change is necessary," he maintained.[33] What Hammonds recognized was that the gay and lesbian movement for equal rights was becoming a victim of its own success. It had welcomed people of all races, creeds, and socioeconomic groups. It had expanded its definition of sexual minority, and march demands demonstrated that the movement had broadened its platform to address the concerns of its diverse constituencies. Throughout the 1990s the movement celebrated its diversity and tried to heed Cook-Daniels's advice to appreciate "every tool in the box." Diversity, though, became the very thing that almost tore the movement apart.

At both the 1993 and 2000 marches, diversity was celebrated as a good thing. There was a "we are the world" ambiance that marchers were proud of. For example, when *Lesbian News* columnist Vicki Torres described the 1993 march, she joyously noted that "we were everyone and everything." "We were military service veterans. . . . We were Latinos. . . . We were African-Americans. . . . We were Asian Americans, parents of small children and teachers," she wrote. "If one image could capture the March, it would be a shot of all of us, all together, all different."[34] Significantly, unlike the 1987 march, the 1993 March on Washington for Lesbian, Gay and Bi Equal Rights and Liberation included bisexuals in the march name, itself an indication of the expansiveness of the movement. Including bisexuals, said Victor Raymond and Laura Perez, March on Washington organizers for the New England region, made the movement stronger. Including them allowed "bisexuals from all over the world, from all sorts of different communities, old and young, working-class and monetarily wealthy, African, Latina/o, Asian, indigenous, and the unending rainbow of people of all colors, people with disabilities and able-bodied people, monogamous and non-monogamous, celibate and promiscuous, religious and atheist, womyn and men," to march for freedom.[35] At the Millennium March in 2000, organizer Dianne Hardy-Garcia also hyped the diversity of the marchers: "Every kind of group is represented—from the leather community to the parents."[36]

As important as inclusiveness was to getting people to attend the marches and be "loud and proud," and as essential as it was to the "majority for a day" feeling that made marchers feel so whole, diversity was a hindrance to setting movement goals and prioritizing them. What historian Joanne Meyerowitz said of transgenders held for all lgbts:

> They differed from one another in gender, class, race, religion, and ethnicity. They had different personalities, and they held diverse political views. They did not necessarily agree on whether biological forces or early childhood experience had shaped their gender identities or on the versions of masculinity and femininity they expressed. They had different sexual preferences and varying

degrees of participation in, comfort with, and tolerance for other forms of gender and sexual transgressions.[37]

In sum, not everyone belonged to the "community" the same way, and national marches exposed not just the diversity of the movement but the divisions as well. Take, for example, the belated recognition of bisexuals in the liberation movement. Raymond and Perez's call for bisexuals to march was as much a protest against past exclusion as it was a celebration of inclusion. In their article they referenced the tension between bisexuals and gays and lesbians who wanted them to choose between being gay or straight. In the same breath that they argued that they had always been in the movement though not always out and not always valued, they ranted, "As bisexuals, we do not get half-bashed or only partly discriminated against, we don't lose half our children or half our jobs."[38]

Transgenders also stood on the periphery of the movement, which until the 1990s privileged issues of sexual orientation over gender identification. Transgendered people, "an umbrella term used for those with various forms or degrees of crossgender practices and identifications," includes, among others, "some people who identify as 'butch' or masculine lesbians, as 'fairies,' 'queens,' or feminine gay men, and as heterosexual crossdressers as well as those who identify as transsexual—those who hope to change the bodily characteristics of sex."[39] Historically, transgenders clashed over what determined one's gender, self-definition or biology. Some lesbians thought that transsexual women appropriated the female body in order to exploit women.[40] Others objected to female impersonators and cross-dressers because they seemed to perpetuate sex-role stereotypes: "Here is a man dressing up as a woman and wearing all the things that we are trying to break free of—high heels, girdles, corsets, stockings—all the things that were literally binding women," said lesbian feminist activist Jean O'Leary on why she had stood against transvestites in the 1970s.[41] Still others were fearful that media coverage of "the fringe" would hurt the overall quest for civil rights.

Transgenders who called on their cohort to join the marches shared with bisexuals the need to educate lesbians and gays as much as heterosexuals. Phyllis Randolph Frye, for example, was angry that transgendered people were "given a short shrift" in the '79 and '87 marches, and equally angry that lesbians and gays were still so myopic as to not include transgenders in the 1993 march name. Transgenders had to march, not necessarily to show solidarity with gays and lesbians, but to teach them that sexual orientation and gender identification were not the same thing and that they had to make the distinction clear to legislators codifying lgbt rights. Wrote Frye: "Insist that the term 'transgender' is included. They used to say gay. Then they learned to say lesbian and gay. Now they are learning to say lesbian, gay and bisexual. Insist that they learn to say lesbian, gay, bisexual and transgender."[42]

Differences between white and black lgbts also surfaced at the marches. The perennial complaint of the latter was that white lgbts were insensitive to African American issues. When Thom Bean reflected on the 1993 San Francisco Pride Parade, he described his experience as akin to being a "raisin in a sea of sour cream." Even though he had lived in San Francisco for over fifteen years, for the one and a half hours that he stood watching the parade he saw no familiar face. White gays, he concluded, were "willing to accept black invisibility," second-class black citizenship, the racism of gay skinheads, the National Socialist Gay League, and gay white Republicans.[43] "The white gay community is built around just that—white gay men," complained Timothy Benson, manager of a black gay men's health center.[44] White men failed to realize, said one black gay man, that "they were born with a sense of entitlement that our skin color will never allow us."[45] While some gay black men complained about the tendency of white men to objectify the black male body, turning black men into "mythic black sexual monsters,"[46] others pointed to the privilege of those white gays whose economic wherewithal allowed them to gentrify black neighborhoods and displace poor African Americans. When white gays praised the diversity of the committees that organized the 1993 and 2000 Washington, DC, marches, black gays responded that they were excluded from the myriad of local organizations that impacted the lives of lgbts. "There are still gross inequities in the racial make-up within the mainstream," said Don Thomas, editor of *BLK*, a national news magazine for black gays and lesbians.[47] Black gays and lesbians also faulted white lgbts for their glib equation of black and gay civil rights. Whereas whites were more likely to see black and gay oppression as the same, blacks emphasized similarities in the means of social control while pointing to the subtle and glaring differences between black and gay oppression.[48]

Apart from lgbt racism, some black sexual minorities just felt distant from whites in the movement. Some believed that associating with them only further estranged them from black America. "The issue of sexual equality for them is primary, for us it is secondary," said the same black gay who noted that white skin imparted entitlement.[49] Bashir Shakur was as turned off by the white males "who seemed to define how a lot of homosexuals or lesbians see themselves" as she was by the terminology they used. "Queer? I'm not feeling that. I can't embrace lesbian either. I hate the way the word sounds; it's not an attractive word. It's hard being bisexual, omnisexual, multisexual, whatever you want to call it, when people have their [white] agenda and expect you to just represent their agenda."[50] People like Shakur embraced the concept and term *same gender loving* (SGL) people.[51] They preferred to think of themselves as women who love women or men who love men because unlike the terms *lesbian* or *gay* it was not associated with "whiteness," it connoted more than just sex or sexual orientation, and the term defined SGLs as loving people, which was self-affirming. Self-defining themselves as same gender loving people gave black SGLs a black context in which to build self-esteem. Twenty-year-old Malaka Sanders identified with the term immediately. To her it acknowledged "that we are of African descent and have a different history that shapes our living and loving, and thus, different interests than white lesbians and gays."[52] Ayuko Babu, founder of the Pan African Film Festival, embraced SGL for a different reason. Since it was black-inspired and expressed black emotional longing, it brought black SGLs closer to black people. "If you define yourself within a Black context," he wrote, "it's harder for more reactionary elements within the Black Liberation Movement to exclude you." In other words, putting distance between themselves and white lgbts had the potential to reduce their marginalization within black America.[53]

Still, with all of these reservations, some African Americans went to the lgbt national marches for the same reasons they went to the Million Man and Woman Marches—to visibilize themselves, to educate those who would exclude them, and to feel whole with people like themselves. Activist Gabriel Gomez urged blacks to attend the 1993 march if only to give blacks equal representation: "White gay men have brought their concerns based in their realities to this movement. It's only fair that everyone else get equal time." Gomez added, "No matter how we see ourselves as different, I suspect the leaders of this country will still consider us all one big perversion."[54] "For too long," argued Michael Crawford, who marched in the 1993 and 2000 marches, "the gay organizations that are predominantly white have not adequately addressed people of color issues. With the Millennium March we have the opportunity to be present and make sure that all colors of the rainbow are visible."[55] The Reverend Irene Monroe felt similarly. About the Millennium March, she said she could "condemn the march or attend it." She chose "to be in it and to make sure there's some sort of change that takes place" and to make sure that the movement "addresses a multitude of oppressions."[56]

Monroe's comment pointed to other fault lines within the lgbt community—that between its left and right wings, radicals and conservatives, and gay males and lesbians. Tension between gay males and lesbians, for example, had existed ever since the 1950s and '60s homophile movement. Billye Talmadge, an early member of the Daughters of Bilitis (DOB), a lesbian organization established in

1955, remembered that male gays and lesbians hardly communicated with each other then "because the gay male feared women, and a lesbian was a woman. And the same thing existed on the other side." She also cited lesbian animosity toward gay guys who lesbians blamed for the trouble the entire community had with the police. It was their "indiscriminate sex, their bathroom habits and everything else" that invited police scrutiny and brutality.[57] Del Martin, one of the founders of the DOB, had to constantly remind members of the Mattachine Society, a predominantly gay male organization established in 1951, that lesbians were not an afterthought. Fed up with their condescending and patronizing attitudes, Martin, at a Mattachine convention in 1959, fumed, "What do you men know about Lesbians? . . . Lesbians are *women* and . . . this 20th century is the era of emancipation of women. Lesbians are not satisfied to be auxiliary members or second-class homosexuals."[58] Like blacks and other minorities whose racial identity influenced how they experienced homosexuality, gay men and lesbians experienced their homosexuality differently. Lesbians experienced oppression because of their gender *and* because of their sexuality. Many were raising children alone, were victims of domestic violence, had fewer job opportunities than men, and were paid less than men for doing the same work.

The feminist movement of the 1960s and '70s provided lesbians with an alternative identity and political movement. Though there existed as many tensions between lesbians and feminists as between gay males and lesbians, the many lesbians who joined the feminist movement gained a female consciousness about sex and sex roles through which they critiqued their male counterparts. As Rita Laporte put it in 1968 after becoming president of the DOB: "When you've accomplished your aims in the homophile movement, you can proudly point to the fact that now lesbians have *full* second class citizenship, along with all women. That's nowhere near enough for me. I was not only born a lesbian, but a feminist as well!"[59] Lesbian feminists felt that gay men had been socialized just as badly as straight males and had the same chauvinistic expectation of females. Meanwhile, the feminist lens allowed many lesbians to critique gay male sexual behavior as similarly promiscuous and self-destructive as that of all males, and lesbian relationships as more committed and settled.[60]

The AIDS epidemic structured a reconciliation of sorts. Although many lesbians took note of gay men's lack of concern for female health issues, and although many blamed gay men's promiscuity for the spread of the disease, many nevertheless became AIDS activists and caregivers.[61] So many AIDS victims were being abandoned by their families and losing their jobs and insurance that many lesbians, over the objections of those who opposed diverting lesbian energy to male gay causes,[62] felt they couldn't abandon gay men. Feminism notwithstanding, the AIDS epidemic exposed all homosexuals to heterosexual contempt. "It occurred to me," said Alaskan Sara Boesser, "that if the men lost their rights, I'd lose mine as well." She added, "If these people were being discriminated against on the same grounds of who I was—a homosexual—then I needed to stand up with them."[63] Boesser understood that AIDS cast a pejorative net over lesbians because they were homosexuals, and homophobes did not differentiate gay men from lesbians when they opposed antidiscrimination ordinances and civil rights and domestic-partner legislation.[64] By the time of the marches, AIDS organizing had brought lesbians and gay men together in a variety of organizations and centers.

Nevertheless, although many lesbians had leadership roles in the 1987, 1993, and 2000 marches, a subcurrent of enmity was apparent. Some women, like Venetia Porter of the New York Division of the Office of AIDS Discrimination, described themselves as "pissed off" because, despite all the work done by women, only men were recognized as experts on the AIDS crisis and no one noticed that people other than white men were dying of the disease.[65] On the other hand, some men were wary of the leadership roles women were playing in the movement for lgbt rights. Said a North Carolina man, who expressed his concerns in an editorial letter following the 1993 march, "If I were straight and I saw that broadcast [of the march] I would think the women were in charge and the men cowered before them. . . . From my vantage point it looked like not only a disproportionate number of lesbians running the March from the podenum [sic] but a disproportionate number of hostile lesbians."[66] Conservative Stephen Miller agreed with him. When the organizers of the 1993 march established the march leadership committee with a stipulation that there be 50 percent gender and 25 percent racial parity, Miller complained. He argued that the void left by the death of gay male leaders from AIDS was the impetus behind the takeover of the gay liberation movement. Lesbian feminists, he argued, "moved in and fundamentally altered the nature of gay politics" such that male solidarity was "now anathema."[67]

There were other fissures that usually overlapped each other. The Reverend Irene Monroe, the black feminist leftist cited earlier, wanted lgbts to fight not only against racism and sexism but also against anti-Semitism, homophobia, sexism, and classism. All of the "isms" were tools of oppression, and unless they were all tackled together, they would fracture the multicultural society that had to be the goal of the movement. In a multicultural society, she reiterated, "no one is left behind, and every voice is lifted up."[68] Most leftist people of color, therefore, felt that they had to fight on multiple fronts because they were oppressed on multiple fronts. "It would be as difficult to separate my racial identity from my sexual identity as it would be to separate the left side of my brain from the right," said Michal Crawford.[69] Others, like activist cross-dresser Nicole Murray-Ramirez, thought gays and lesbians had to merge their fight for equality with other civil rights groups in order to create coalitions. "As we want other civil rights organizations to embrace our cause and to support us, we must also embrace and support other communities," Ramirez said.[70] Like Ramirez, many lgbts, whether racial minorities or not, thought their fight was for human rights and as such could not be separated from all such struggles. "By linking gay and lesbian liberation to the question of human rights, we are saying that our identity, our sexuality—our very being—is at its core a question of our humanity and must be respected and defended in the same way that societies look upon other questions of human rights," said an editorial in *Breakthrough* magazine.[71]

When left-wing gays looked at the issue of gays in the military from a human rights perspective, they objected to making the military ban on open gays a priority. "The essence of our liberation must be about life—not oppression and killing," said this same *Breakthrough* editorial. For those who thought that the American military was America's imperialist arm oppressing people the world over, the fight for equality in the military was misdirected. They pointed to American atrocities in Vietnam, the American invasion of Panama, and the first Iraq war as examples of American imperialist exploits. Why fight for lgbts to be able to kill and intervene in the name of the United States, when at home the highest court in the country would not uphold their rights, they asked. Why not fight at home for AIDS funding and civil rights? "You want the right to serve in the military of a country that has decided not to protect the civil rights of dykes and faggots? You want your queer friends to kill and die for a country which ignores our relationships, which has dragged its feet and allowed tens of thousands of faggots of every color to die from AIDS, which sees dykes and fags as the largest threat to family and nation?" wrote an anonymous editorialist who went on to decry the 1993 march leaders as short-sighted for making equality in the military a goal.[72]

As suggested by this editorialist's language, many on the Left were unapologetically queer, an identity adopted in the 1990s to denote prideful sexual deviance. Queers are unashamed of their sexual dissonance; they celebrate what the media call the fringe—the drag queens and cross-dressers, fairies, leather people, dykes, and sadomasochists. They applaud practices condemned as immoral, such as public sex or prostitution. As queer theorist Michael Warner said, in queer culture "there is no truck with bourgeois propriety."[73] At the 1990s marches, queers refused to act straight and denounced politics they deemed assimilationist. To act like everyone else would be to capitulate to the shaming tactics used by heterosexuals. It would be even worse to divorce the movement from the very thing that made lgbts different—the way they loved and had sex. Said the anonymous editorialist quoted in the previous paragraph, instead of marching in 1993 to join the U.S. military, lgbts should join the "queer liberation army, an army of lovers and ex-lovers to fight for our right to love." Unabashedly, the writer called on lgbts to march for real freedom:

> Fight for the right to take your lover's aching and wet pussy into your hungry mouth, to twirl her pearl and taste her deep inside. Fight for the right of your lover to slide his hard cock into your waiting asshole and to pump you full of his passion and desire. Fight for homo liberation, not assimilation.[74]

For a good many lgbts, this queer's thinking was way too radical. Said lesbian novelist Lee Lynch upon returning from the 1993 march: "As we return from the nation's capital to our communities, can we look squarely at the fact that we do scare our neighbors?" She continued, "We can thrash about in self-righteous anger and spew forth high moral platitudes till we're blue in the face, but those Americans we call our enemies are just like us inside." Lynch called on lgbts to find common ground. The march, she believed, was empowering. People from remote places like Shickshinny, Pennsylvania, and Wagon Mound, New Mexico, would return to their communities as clarions of energy and ambassadors for lgbts. By showing up in great numbers, they had demonstrated their political strength and their ubiquity. But, said Lynch, sexual minorities would be most effective if they learned "to help the frightened let go of a fear that no longer serves anyone well."[75]

Lynch's position was not atypical and people like her became more vocal as the '90s wore on. For example, Matt Nannery from Brentwood, New York, wrote a letter to *Newsday* complaining of a picture the newspaper ran in its coverage of the '93 march. The picture, of two tattooed, bare-chested men embracing, was "a wrong picture" of the march because it fueled the fantasies of those who would like to deny them their rights. "I'll bet your photographer had to look long and hard for a photo with the shock value like that one," wrote Nannery, who thought a self-serving press played up the differences between gays and straights in order to create conflict that they could report.[76] No doubt Nannery was pleased with the *New York Times*'s characterization of the march as "Ozzie and Harriet." Quoting a *Los Angeles Times* article by Bettina Boxall, the *New York Times*'s editorial noted that "for the most part, the demonstrators were conventional, orderly, and well-behaved."[77]

People like Lynch and Nannery chose to focus on the similarities of gays and straights rather than the differences. Dawn Strecker of Maryland, for example, thought that the '93 March on Washington was responsible for

FIGURE 10. Pictures like this one taken at the 1993 March on Washington for Lesbian, Gay and Bi Equal Rights and Liberation were thought by many lgbts to be hurtful to the movement. Critics complained that journalists used provocative pictures like this to take advantage of the sentiments they stirred. *Photo by Robert Gitrous/AFP/Getty Images.*

the greater acceptance she found in Baltimore, so much so that she thought that it was "becoming less necessary to have parades to say you're gay."[78] For Strecker, the operative issue was family togetherness, a concern of all people regardless of sexualities. Jay Zander attended the 2000 march with his partner, Wichita resident Steve Wheeler. An AIDS patient, Zander thought it important to march to show people how "normal" gays were. "These are just regular people," he said. "They live their lives, they hurt, they love, they cry, they laugh."[79] Lynn Robinson of the Vero Beach, Florida, chapter of Parents, Family and Friends of Lesbians and Gays wanted the mundane elements of the 2000 march emphasized. "We're not some fringe element," she said. "I'm the most mainstream girl you know."[80]

While Robinson marched to demonstrate her mainstream credentials, others soured on marches because they felt their more conservative positions were silenced. Stephen Miller, cited earlier, was one such person. A former board member for the Gay and Lesbian Alliance Against Defamation in New York, Miller broke with the organization over what he described as "the rise of political correctness and its censorship ways." He felt that in the left-wing-dominated movement, "race and gender were given precedence over individual merit."[81] It was wrong to give more attention to the multiple oppressions of racism, sexism, and classism than to core lesbian and gay issues, and he deplored the national march organizations for trying to get equal representation by setting race and gender quotas on its membership board.[82] This white gay male described himself as a victim: of blacks who, he claimed, ranted about racism in the lgbt movement but ignored homophobia in black America; of male-bashing lesbian feminists who seemed to him to have stepped into the void left by male AIDS victims; of queers who fed the appetites of the malicious right by opposing faith and family; of left-wing lgbts who insisted on government health-care programs and ending workplace discrimination, which, to his mind, would lead to extensive government regulation and interference with individual rights. A conservative, Miller thought the movement should jettison its multicultural feminist agenda. He felt that gays suffered as much, if not more than, women and minorities, and that when march platforms called "for a broad left-wing alliance to overthrow capitalism [and] establish socialism," their effectiveness was diluted. Lgbts, argued Miller, should march for an end to discrimination that made them second-class citizens, an end to sodomy laws and the ban on gays in the military. They should also fight the antigay Defense of Marriage Act and perhaps workplace discrimination laws. "But," he added emphatically, "that's it. Period."[83]

But clearly, what made sense to Miller was outlandish to others. For lgbts who resisted choosing between their multiple identities, Miller's position would only uphold racial and ethnic hierarchies. For lesbian feminists who felt as oppressed by their gender as by their sexual orientation, Miller's position would do nothing to establish equality between men and women. For queers who prioritized sexual liberation, Miller seemed to be headed backward, not forward. For transgenders and bisexuals, Miller's strategy was far too limiting. Given the many different directions of lgbt thought, Miller believed his position reasonable and rational. But for millions, he represented the status quo—a white male trying to consolidate his privilege with a strategy that was far too proscriptive. And yet, some kind of united front had to be established if sexual minorities were to fight collectively for their rights and survive the homophobes who in the 1990s organized against them. As challenging as were the divisions within the movement, they were not as threatening as the challenges from without.

Special Rights

The 1990s were remarkable for America's intolerance *but* growing tolerance for sexual minorities. In many ways the decade-long struggle between the forces of acceptance and rejection determined the nature, structure, and platform of the turn-of-century 2000 Millennium March.

The election of Democrat Bill Clinton in 1992 seemed to be the dawn of a new era. Under the leadership of Ronald Reagan and then George H. W. Bush (1980–88; 1988–92), Republicans had at first ignored, and then underfunded, HIV/AIDS research. Their traditional-values platforms demonized sexual minorities along with racial and ethnic minorities and feminists. Clinton was a breath of fresh air. Unlike his predecessors, he seemed comfortable with lgbts, held public discussions with them, and could talk about their issues without flinching or seeming embarrassed. The fact that he made gays in the military, an AIDS czar, lifting the travel ban on people with HIV, and appointing sexual minorities to high-level offices campaign issues was a remarkable shift that suggested that lgbts would have a friend in the White House.

But Clinton was a disappointment. His "Don't Ask, Don't Tell" compromise, as opposed to an outright end to the ban on gays in the military, was seen by most sexual minorities as "institutionalized bigotry."[84] He never lifted the travel ban on people with HIV but rather signed a bill into law that instituted stricter provisions on travel. Additionally, he did not break with the H. W. Bush policy of keeping Haitians infected with HIV detained at Guantanamo Bay until a federal judge ruled that the detention was unconstitutional. No one with HIV/AIDS expertise was appointed to Hillary Clinton's health-care panel, and the person he belatedly appointed as AIDS czar, Kristine Gebbie, was considered by many to be inexperienced. His failure to even be in Washington, DC, the weekend of the 1993 march was seen by some as evidence of his abandonment. Said former San Francisco supervisor Harry Britt, "Our success in the 90s will not depend on Bill Clinton but on how assertive we are."[85]

Two anti-lgbt state referendums, Measure 9 in Oregon and Amendment 2 in Colorado, made Britt's prediction more than just rhetoric. Removed from federal jurisdiction, these state referendums were intended to prevent sexual minorities from being considered a protected class of citizens, a status that would have given them legal protection against discrimination and hate crimes. The Oregon measure failed with 56.4 percent voting against to the 53.5 percent who voted for it. But the Colorado Amendment 2 passed by a margin of six percentage votes, with 47 percent of voters voting against and 53 percent voting for the amendment. The language used by the respective states was very different and suggests the two-pronged approach of lgbt enemies.

The measure in Oregon represented the tactic intended to provoke moral outrage. It prevented all governments and school boards from using their money or property to promote homosexuality, pedophilia, sadism, or masochism. All levels of government, including public-education systems, had to set a standard that recognized those behaviors as "abnormal, wrong, unnatural and perverse" and that were to be "discouraged and avoided." These ideas were exemplary of those put forth by the evangelical Right. Take, for example, the teachings of Minneapolis trial attorney Roger Magnuson. At a 1992 gathering of the conservative organization Concerned Women for America (CWA), he spoke authoritatively about homosexuals who "testify to the regular consumption of human waste and fecal matter." When his audience shuddered he reassured them that their reaction was proper: "Homophobia is the natural revulsion normal people feel in the face of sexual perversion," he said.[86] Beverly LaHaye, founder and president of CWA, thought likewise. She believed that "homosexuals want their depraved 'values' to become our children's values." Because she thought that "homosexuals expect society to embrace their immoral way of life" and "are looking for new recruits,"[87] she gave proponents of the Oregon proposal free airtime on her syndicated radio show *Beverly LaHaye Live,* a Christian talk show that reached hundreds of thousands of listeners. In the case of the Colorado amendment, she flew to Denver and actively campaigned for its passage. In Colorado, the Local Prayer/Action chapters of CWA distributed hundreds of thousands of tabloid-style newsletters citing "facts" like "Lesbians are now having babies, conceived by homosexual semen," and "Fact: Homosexuals are 12 times as likely as heterosexual teachers to molest children."[88]

As effective as was the morality-based campaign against homosexuals, another tactic proved more powerful in its ability to sway voter opinion. In 1991 LaHaye authored a document entitled "The Hidden Homosexual Agenda." In it she documented her version of the history of the "Homosexual Movement" from 1948 to the 1990s. By her account there "appeared to be an explosion from the closets" between 1968 and 1970, and from then on the gay movement assumed an unprecedented militancy. According to LaHaye, "homosexuals may differ" on many issues but "they have agreed on a specific agenda for the movement" by which they hope to obtain the ultimate goal of "total acceptance." That demand, said LaHaye, was that "Americans accept the homosexual community as a legitimate minority having the same legal status as married couples in society." Homosexuals are demanding, wrote LaHaye, total acceptance, not just tolerance. They have, she said, manipulated America's traditional values so that their values appear to be rights that the government and society must affirm. For LaHaye, and the many that she spoke for, sexual minorities were fighting for the *special* right to have their *values* accepted as rights. "This concept of sexual deviants being given special rights and privileges because of their sexual orientation, challenges, if not subverts the entire fabric of America's foundation," she declared. If homosexuals were designated a special class of people—like racial minorities had been—then their values, argued LaHaye, would be protected by law. Once that happened, the Judeo-Christian values at the core of American society would disintegrate; promiscuity, AIDS, and prejudice against heterosexuals would ensue; and classrooms across the nation would be inundated with homoerotic curricula that would ultimately recruit American youth into homosexual lifestyles. "The Hidden Homosexual Agenda" reviewed all of the legislative victories scored by lgbts and argued for the mobilization against a politics that enabled these special rights. Homosexuals, LaHaye's report maintained, already had "the same rights as heterosexuals." What they actually want, she said, "is to be granted special privileges to carry out their illicit practices to receive affirmation of being that legitimate minority."[89]

As argued by LaHaye and others, the "special rights" strategy became the linchpin in the Christian Right 1990s antigay campaign. Its effectiveness was demonstrated when Colorado's Amendment 2 passed. In contrast to Measure 9's highly moralistic language, Amendment 2 implicitly represented gays as people who wanted more rights than heterosexuals and the same rights as racial and ethnic minorities. The amendment stated that no homosexual, lesbian, or bisexual could lay claim to "minority status, quota preferences, protected status or claim of discrimination." Though proponents believed the language of Oregon's law—that homosexuality was abnormal, wrong, and perverse—the focus of Amendment 2 was on denying lgbts the same *civil rights* that had been given to minorities to redress previous discrimination.

Coming at a time when polls showed growing tolerance, even acceptance, of gays and lesbians, the "special rights" campaign was especially lethal. For example, a *USA Today* telephone poll of 1,065 adults taken on the eve of the '93 march showed that people polled were evenly split on giving gays the same coverage under civil rights laws as blacks and women, with 48 percent both opposed and in favor. Women were more supportive than men (56 percent to 35 percent) as were younger respondents between eighteen and twenty-nine (56 percent). There was also an increase in the number of people who believed that being gay was not a chosen lifestyle—the idea hawked by the Christian Right—but something one was born with. While only 31 percent thought homosexuality was genetic, this was up from 16 percent in 1983. Meanwhile, fewer people in 1993 than in 1983 thought that homosexuality was something that developed over time. In 1983, 25 percent of those polled thought that it developed over time, but this was down by eleven percentage points, to 14 percent, in 1993.[90]

No doubt the greater acceptance of lgbts was helped along by television. According to communications scholar Ron Becker, in the early 1990s competition from cable television forced the networks to seek edgier, more hip programing in order to appeal to the eighteen-to-forty-nine-year-old audience. "By 1995 there seemed to be little room on network TV for sentimentality, wholesomeness, or heartwarming narratives about the American family living in the heartland. Domestic dramas and family sitcoms were out of fashion and squeezed to the margins," argues Becker.[91] However, there *was* room for gay characters and gay-themed episodes, and as the 1990s progressed they increased exponentially, as did the subplots, jokes, and innuendos dependent on homosexuality. According to Becker, by the 1996–97 viewing season, thirty-three different queer characters were scattered across twenty-four different prime-time network programs.[92] The new programming reflected the changing taste of consumers who, being more exposed to a variety of cultures, drove an economy thirsty for a variety of new goods, information, and entertainments. It appealed to a new cohort that some would define as neoliberal—people who considered themselves fiscal conservative social liberals; people who appreciated or were at least open to cultural, racial, and gender differences; people who considered themselves cosmopolitan; people whose politics were centrist or left of center; people who were likely supporters of Bill Clinton.[93]

With the polls showing less repugnance toward sexual minorities and television programming normalizing them, the special rights tactic was timed to derail tolerance and acceptance. By pairing morality and civil rights in such a way as to make affirmation of lgbt civil rights look like approval of an immoral lifestyle, the strategy targeted all who were uncomfortable with unconventional sexual desire and gender identification. By arguing that homosexuals did not want the same civil rights as heterosexuals, but in fact wanted exceptional rights, the strategy made lgbts look extreme. For example, people like twenty-three-year-old Steven Doering from Toledo, Ohio, could not isolate the issue of civil rights from concerns about immorality. From Doering's perspective, the immoral gay lifestyle had nothing to do with civil rights: "It is just a lifestyle and it doesn't go along at all with normal morals. . . . I don't think they should have separate rights just because they're gay." On the other hand, those like forty-three-year-old Patricia Strausbaugh of Bowling Green, Ohio, were not swayed by the special rights argument. For her, individual civil rights existed independent of lifestyle. Comparing gays to women and African Americans, who similarly had demanded equal rights, Strausbaugh maintained: "I don't think they're asking for anything special just like the women's movement and the black movement didn't ask for anything special."[94] The special rights campaign was targeted at the Doerings of America, and there were many like him.

It was also geared to build a coalition between the Christian Right and minorities, especially African Americans.[95] Unlike the Promise Keepers, whose racial reconciliation did not evidence a political angle, Christian Right organizations like the Traditional Values Coalition and the Christian Coalition enlisted African American social conservatism and sensitivities about civil rights in their antigay political crusade. One needed only to hear the heterosexist rant of the Reverend James D. Sykes, pastor of the St. James African Methodist Episcopal Church of Tampa, Florida, to realize that the special rights campaign touched a nerve in black America. When the Ku Klux Klan marched against gays in 1991 in a town near Tampa, Florida, Sykes declared that "if I knew that was the only reason the Klan was marching, I'd march with them." Sykes's qualifying remark showed not only how clearly he understood the ironic implications of his philosophical alignment with this historically racist organization, but also how deep the lgbt rights issue cut in African America. Sykes vehemently opposed the NAACP's endorsement of the 1993 March on Washington for Lesbian, Gay and Bi Equal Rights and Liberation on two grounds. First, as we have seen, many African Americans, including many black lgbts, resented the parallels being drawn between the oppression endured by blacks and that endured by sexual minorities. Sykes's notion of the latter was of affluent, self-indulgent whites who were indifferent to racism. He claimed he was not against gays, only against "them trying to coattail on our civil rights movement." He resented even their use of the title "March on Washington," which for him evoked the iconic image of Martin Luther King framed by the columns of the Lincoln Memorial. But Sykes opposed lgbts on another level as well. Discarding the NAACP's political coalition-building, Sykes contended that "the National Association for the Advancement of *Colored* People" (Sykes's emphasis) has no business "jumping on the bandwagon with people who are immoral." Sykes thought it unfortunate that blacks did not have the clout to effect political change without lgbts, but he likened joining with them to making a deal with Satan. Said Sykes: "Martin Luther King and the others did not march down in Selma, Alabama, for no gays to be walking naked in the streets of Washington, D.C."[96]

If Sykes's opinion was the minority view in black America, the majority did not speak up. As previously explained, historically, African Americans have put distance between them and anything associated with sexual deviance. In 1993, when march organizers solicited marchers and supporters for their Washington demonstration, clergy from twelve predominantly African American denominations met in Cleveland, Ohio, and drafted a position paper opposing the march and a pending bill in Congress, the Civil Rights Act of 1993 (H.R. 431 of the One-Hundred-Third Congress), which proposed giving lgbts the status of a protected minority. The series of meetings began in March. The clergy, who met every week for about two months, represented approximately 28,000 active members. When they finished "The Black Church Position Statement on Homosexuality," they took it back to their respective congregations for opinion and input, whereupon 2,500 congregants signed a petition against the proposed civil rights legislation.[97] Basically, the fifteen-paragraph statement cited biblical teachings that explained homosexuality as immoral; cited psychological evidence that homosexuality was a chosen lifestyle that could, with therapy, be changed; and expressed opposition to the proposed civil rights legislation on the grounds that homosexuality was a choice but "race, ethnicity, and gender may be denied or discounted but they represent a reality that does not change." The report further stated that "homosexuality is an identity orientation that develops over time and is expressed through behavior and/or lifestyle. . . . Therefore it would be inconsistent, illogical, and immoral to equate an ontological issue (referring to what one is) with a behavior issue (what one does)."[98] The interdenominational Ohio group then shared "The Black Church Position Statement on Homosexuality" with African American clergy groups in Omaha; Pittsburgh; Kansas City, Missouri; and with black pastors of congregations affiliated with white denominations. Though this last group was asked not to sign off on the declaration because their congregations might not agree with the pastor's personal opinion, the overwhelming support for this manifesto affirmed white Christian Right organizations' perception that they had as much, if not more, to offer African Americans than the lgbt Left.

The 1993 video *Gay Rights, Special Rights: Inside the Homosexual Agenda* produced by the Traditional Values Coalition followed up on this assertion. While television coverage of the 1993 march contributed to the growing visibilization of lgbts, simultaneously inviting closeted gays to "out" themselves and join a vocal beloved community, *Gay Rights, Special Rights: Inside the Homosexual Agenda* took march footage and used it to demonstrate the Christian Right's perception of a perverted community. The forty-minute film not only recounts the evils that will befall America if lgbts are given minority status, but it employs a zero-sum game argument to convince minorities, especially blacks, that gains made by lgbts would diminish those won during the civil rights movements.[99]

This is done effectively by contrasting the African American 1963 March on Washington for Jobs and Freedom and the 1993 March on Washington for Lesbian, Gay and Bi Equal Rights and Liberation. Images of Martin Luther King and other dignitaries are contraposed with transvestite striptease scenes and same-sex kissing and dancing couples. Voice-overs and on-screen comments by Edwin Meese, Pat Robertson, and Trent Lott—who were known to feminists and civil rights advocates for their misogyny and racism—juxtapose "legitimate" minorities with "illegitimate" sexual minorities, who are cast as wealthy, educated, white professionals who had never been discriminated against, or denied the vote, or segregated from the rest of society. Lou Lopez, identified as a member of the Anaheim, California, school district, appears on screen to say that the "Hispanic community does not want to be compared to homosexuals," and Raymond Kwong, identified as president of the Chinese Family Alliance, says that "the government has no business putting its stamp of approval on a behavior-based group, let alone elevated to full minority status."

African Americans are featured more than other minorities and they echo Sykes in their outrage at the prospect of lgbts being granted minority status. Flanked by other African American women, Jan Rice, who is identified as being from the Committee of Public Affairs, says "there's just no comparison" between lgbts and minorities. Although lgbts never proposed taking rights away from blacks, Rice maintains that "for them to want protection under this law and to try to further beat down the minorities and further lessen their [minorities'] chances of equal protection and equal chances at jobs, I just think is ludicrous." The women surrounding her agree. So does African American Lester James of the Traditional Values Coalition. For him, the "high-handed" attempts of gays to gain minority status are "an offense to black America" and an attempt to "undermine and belittle the entire civil rights efforts of the 1960s." Cheryl Coleman, another African American, repeated the idea that lgbt rights threatened black rights. Identified as a public affairs representative, she claims that granting lgbts minority status would "completely neutralize the Civil Rights Act of 1964" because amending the civil rights bill would give anyone "with any type of central preference, which would include everyone," protection under the law. Seemingly oblivious of minority lgbts, and the fact that white conservatives used the same rationale to oppose affirmative action for minorities and women—that it would give the undeserving an unfair advantage over whites—Coleman presses her argument that special rights for lgbts would mean that "there would be no protection for minorities specifically."[100]

In sum, as the 1990s progressed, the special rights strategy gained currency across the nation. Not long after the 1993 march, the liberal advocacy group People for the American Way (PFAW) issued a statement about the religious Right proclaiming that "no argument in their rhetorical arsenal has yielded more mileage for their voter mobilization and fundraising than the 'special rights' message." So effective was this tactic that the PFAW thought it necessary to distribute a flyer listing pro-gay counterarguments to be used in debates with special rights advocates, debates pro-gays had to win if they were to prevail in 1994 when citizens in nine states would decide on ballot initiatives like those in Colorado and Oregon.[101] Meanwhile, around the same time, Ralph Reed, executive director of the Christian Coalition, proclaimed that "we are not going to concede the minority community to the political left anymore."[102] Citing polls that showed that on social and economic issues African Americans and Hispanics held opinions similar to his white constituency, Reed concluded that his and other Christian conservative groups found blacks and Hispanics fertile ground for recruitment. As outlined by Reed, the Christian Coalition planned to start with ballot initiatives in California, and if successful expand their recruitment. They planned to end the policy of renting their membership list only to white churches. Now they would expand their constituency by sending voter guides to "every black and Hispanic church that we can get on a list."[103]

Reed's comments and those of the People for the American Way illustrate the battle lines that were drawn in the early 1990s. The polls reflected more acceptance of sexual minorities, but the Colorado victory and the success of the special rights strategy showed that acceptance to be tenuous. Clearly, the latter two-thirds of the 1990s would be crucial for sexual minorities. They would have to convince straight Americans that they did not seek anything beyond what they were entitled to by virtue of their humanity and American citizenship. This was easier said than done because as external pressure mounted, internal divisions deepened.

The Millennium March of 2000

Writing in the *Nation*, sociologist Joshua Gamson described the Millennium March as "the first of its kind." The fourth mass lgbt march to be held in the nation's capital, Gamson was obviously not referring to the event's placement in the sequence of national marches. Rather, the march was a first because of the way it was organized and the acrimony it sparked. The "strangest and most revealing first," said Gamson, was the fact that "bands of lesbian, gay, bisexual and transgender activists are working as hard as they can to convince other lesbian, gay, bisexual and transgender people not to attend a national lesbian, gay, bisexual and transgender march on Washington."[104] The sparks that flew before, during, and after the march were a direct result of external pressure put on lgbts who were already splintering from within.

Those who protested the march and discouraged others from going were, generally speaking, queers, sex radicals, leftists, and people of color—people who put a premium on cultural, racial, and ethnic diversity. They were angry about a lot of things that mostly came under the heading of assimilationist politics. At the top of their long list of grievances was the top-down organizing by the Human Rights Campaign (HRC), the wealthiest gay lobby organization in the nation, and the similarly wealthy Universal Fellowship of Metropolitan Community Churches (UFMCC), a Christian denomination founded to minister to sexual minorities. Queer radical Tristan Taormino described the HRC as "one of the richest, most conservative, most powerful, and (among many activists) most despised gay and lesbian organizations in the country."[105] Sounding a similar note, historian John D'Emilio described the HRC's organizational culture as "a culture of arrogance."[106] "This was such a dramatic shift in how the other marches had been organized," said New Yorker Leslie Cagan, a coordinator of the 1987 March on Washington.[107] Previous marches had been organized by grassroots organizations that met locally and discussed whether a march was a good idea and then, collectively, set the march's purpose and agenda. By contrast, said black activist Barbara Smith, this march "was called by a few self-appointed white 'leaders' sitting in the Human Rights Campaign Office."[108]

Some protested the closed process by establishing the Ad Hoc Committee for an Open Process (AHC), whose members led the very public opposition to the march. Besides the secretive process, they objected to a national march that could potentially drain resources and energy away from the local and statewide ballot referendums where lgbt rights were on the line. They were also offended by the Christian-oriented name of the march, which carried no mention of gays, lesbians, transgenders, or bisexuals. Though no doubt influenced by the Reverend Troy Perry, founder of the UFMCC, who was apparently one of the "self-appointed white 'leaders' in the room" alluded to by Smith, for AHC member Bill Dobbs, the absence of a signifier was an affront. "It's a way to hide the identities," said Dobbs. "They are trying to water it down."[109] The Ad Hoc Committee for an Open Process also thought that the white-led HRC and the UFMCC were trying to expand their base at the expense of people of color and the overall heterogeneity of the movement. Said AHC member Diana Onley-Campbell, "A small group of people made the decision to have it, and those of us who are people of color, transgender and part of the leather community were excluded from that process." Accordingly, the AHC demanded that racial and ethnic minorities and labor activists have representatives from their organizations be put on the board.[110]

Another thorn was the crass commercialism. The complaints ranged from the preponderance of celebrities to too many corporate sponsors. Advertisements, including those of United Airlines, the Showtime network, and PlanetOut, a media and entertainment company catering to lgbts, were so prominent that Bill Dobbs thought the march was less a civil rights demonstration than "a marketing event"[111] For Billy Hileman, a cochair of the 1993 march, the fact that the United Airlines logo was above the stage of the march proved it belonged to United, and "is not obligated to the constituency it intends to speak for."[112] While Rick Garcia, a representative of a gay rights group called Equity Illinois, thought the Millennium March an apolitical "tchotchke sale on the Mall," a critic describing himself as a white Latin American said it amounted to "a fairly standard street festival with gay people in it."[113]

This critic also lamented the homogenized culture that was projected. There were no "leather daddies, trannies, drag queens and hard-core dykes, shirtless lesbians and people of color from all origins."[114] The crowd, he wrote, "consisted of mostly men, mostly white and mostly shirtless, mostly looking like every other mostly shirtless white man in the group, drinking expensive lemonade and having a fabulous time."[115] Seattle resident Christopher Smith, founder of Bigot Busters, an organization dedicated to defeating antigay initiatives, similarly opposed the erasure of lesbians and gays of color, queer radicals, and labor organizers. Speaking to ensure that "grassroots activists, glitter-haired drag queens, and leather-clad dykes" did not get shoved aside by "uptight Wall Street homo-brokers, ultra-cool lipstick lesbians, and overpriced political consultants," Smith protested the seeming new direction of the movement. "Supposedly, our issues now are forming stable relationships, supporting gays raising children, satisfying the desire to legally wed, and returning to the churches of our youth!," he claimed. Though he understood the politics behind the agenda—the need to defeat the special rights advocates—he nevertheless objected to an lgbt agenda that "screams the need for acceptance from Küche, Kirche und Kinder fundamentalists" (emphasis added).[116]

An ad published by the AHC and signed by 300 prominent activists summed up the concerns and objections of those troubled by the Millennium March. Much more was at stake, the ad claimed, than just the process of calling the march. The very soul of the movement was on the line, signers insisted. The fight was about the direction of the movement and whether it would be about freedom, justice, and equality for all: "This is about power and how it is wielded, manipulated and abused. Who sits at the table and who decides how the table is set." Arguing against the "normal" or assimilationist agenda of the HRC, the ad proclaimed:

> We want a movement that fights for the rights of each of us. Even if we do not fit into the corporate image of an "American family." That these national

organizations project white Christian middle-class representations and set the agenda accordingly is nothing less than institutionalized racism. Claims to diversity mean nothing if the sexual is sanitized and no genuine effort is made to include the perspectives and leadership of lgbts from different races, classes, sexualities and genders.[117]

Despite the uproar from march opponents, including the AHC, the march proceeded and drew record numbers to the Washington Mall on April 30. San Francisco state assemblywoman Carole Migden was probably right when she opined that most marchers were unconcerned about the power struggle among the leadership—the "inside baseball," as she put it—and that what determined attendance was whether supporters could afford to go, could get off work, and whether their friends were going.[118] In 2000 there were more "out" lgbts than ever before—a measure of the success of the visibilization tactic—and they were, like marchers before them, eager to demonstrate their existence, to quell feelings of isolation by being in a majority, and to be among those who were hopeful about the future. Evidence that marchers were aware of the damage done by the special rights strategy come from people like Pam Lessard of Melbourne, Florida, who proclaimed "we are the same," or like Adam May of Atlanta, who insisted that "we're only asking for the same rights as everyone else. . . . Depriving one person puts everyone at risk of losing."[119] If organizer Dianne Hardy-Garcia was right, there were more people from small- and medium-sized towns than at any previous national march, which to her signaled a truly national movement.[120]

Ironically, while march opponents feared the loss of the movement's heterogeneity, marchers touted their own brand of diversity. One of the most interesting facts about the marchers was their celebration of a newfound freedom to be more than their sexuality, to be an individual who could project any number of identities. Tennis great Martina Navratilova, for example, said that being gay was an important part of who she was but it was not all of who she was. "That's just one part of me. I'm many, many things." This was part of her argument against special rights. If she became a spouse or a parent, she needed the legal rights to take care of her family. "This is not about special rights, it's only about equality," she maintained.[121] Like so many others, marcher Bruno Manning identified not just as gay but as a father. He wanted no more rights than any other family man because, he claimed, "we are a family at the same level as any . . . straight family and we deserve respect and recognition."[122] For some gays, region was the signifying identity. Jim McCarthy of Dayton, Ohio, proclaimed, "We're not just leather boys and drag queens. . . . A lot more of us are plain ol' boring Midwesterners."[123]

As suggested by McCarthy, at the 2000 Millennium March, "boring" emerged as a badge of victory. Although many would hardly identify Dan Savage of Seattle, a writer of racy tales of homosexual life, as boring, he identified himself as such: "What's wrong with being boring?" he asked. "The vast majority of people are boring and stupid and cheap."[124] Savage was clearly mainstreaming himself and the movement, as was Jennifer Vanasco in a provocative piece titled "Boring Is Beautiful." Vanasco turned the argument against mainstreaming on its head by claiming it to be a radical response to anti-lgbts. Mainstreaming was radical because "it's unexpected by homophobics, many of whom seem to think we hide pointed tails under our Gap jeans." What was radical about being boring, reasoned Vanasco, was the unprecedented ability to be so "when and where we want to . . . be our full awkward selves, instead of the selves pigeonholed by our sexual identities." Vanasco clearly understood the limitations of boring when she said that "it will get us our rights faster than outrageous—at least will get us white, middle-class rights." But Vanasco was willing to sacrifice others because, to her, boring was, as she put it, "comfortable." Once white, middle-class lgbts got the freedom to marry, adopt, and the legal ability to keep their jobs and apartments, they could, she said, perhaps "focus on other rights vital to our community, like equal pay for women, racial justice, protection against gender bias and education and job training for the poor." Sounding very much like post-black devotees who relished the freedom to express more than their racial identity, Vanasco claimed that "boring is rebellion" because for so long lgbts had fought fiercely for the right to be ordinary. In Vanasco's mind, the boring white middle class had finally emerged victorious.[125]

This was galling to nonassimilationists. Vanasco was obviously unaware of the role that "outrageous" had played in lgbt history. Many of those considered outrageous—the fairies, butches, cross-dressers, transvestites—had courageously carved out the lgbt rights and spaces that normals were now appropriating. Historically, the outrageous were the clarions. For decades they had brazenly announced lgbt existence while others hid their identity and secretly watched where and how the outrageous gathered.[126] The media's fascination with them had actually worked to the movement's advantage because the coverage of them exposed the community, an exposure that the closeted secretly took advantage of. The marches only heightened this exposure and visibilized this world that was legally bondaged and socially circumscribed. Now that the outrageous had successfully led the way in visibilizing the movement, assimilationists were stepping in and taking it over, leaving behind those who could not or would not blend in.

In short, the Millennium March was like an earthquake, sending the tools in the toolbox in different directions. The takeover of the march by the assimilationists was reminiscent of the kind of political expediency that captured the woman's suffrage, labor, and civil rights movements. Early in the century, Northern white suffragists argued against granting African American women the vote in order to win favor from Southern congressmen; at midcentury, labor and black civil rights organizations sacrificed leftists in order to appease anti-Communists. In each case, movement leaders sacrificed crucial constituencies in order to dilute opposition to their cause and win political favor. Now, under pressure from special rights proponents, assimilationists deemed it beneficial to showcase lgbt *sameness*—to show how un-American it was to deny white Americans who were willing to serve and die for America, who were gainfully employed, monogamous, consuming parents, the basic rights of citizenship. By emphasizing lgbt ordinariness and whiteness, assimilationists like Vanasco hoped to negate the charges of lgbt immorality and exceptionalness, and thereby dismantle the grounding arguments of fundamentalist homophobic thought. In doing so, they also alienated a substantial minority of their community.

The Center Holds

When the *New York Times* opinion piece that characterized the 1993 march as Ozzie and Harriet was published, an important caveat was added. The writer noted how understandable it was for gay Americans to fixate on "normalcy" given how they had been so demonized. But, said the writer, "it's a dangerous idea" to base full citizenship rights on how conventional or orderly or well-behaved people are. The measure of a just society is not how the Ozzie and Harriets are treated but whether the same full citizenship rights are given to those who don't look like the people next door.[127] Margaret Cerullo and Loree Cook-Daniels, quoted at the beginning of this chapter, obviously agreed. Their concerns were similar to those of the editorialist. They wanted freedom for the entire community, not just those who could be identified as respectable. In 1993, this seemed an open question; by the 2000 Millennium March, the question seemed to have been answered.

As had happened at all of the other marches/gatherings, multiple identities proved a stumbling block. This of course was profound since like Promise Keepers and African Americans, sexual minorities gathered on the basis of their identities. Being with others like themselves made them feel whole, happy, and fulfilled. National and local marches visibilized them in unimaginable ways and increased exponentially the numbers who lived open, unapologetic lives. But as Loree Cook-Daniels noted in 1993, the community itself was multicultured, economically layered, and racially and sexually diverse. All did not experience or serve the community the same way. It was ironic and yet predictable that the success of visibilization would divide and exclude rather than unite and harmonize. And it was tragic that sexual minorities could not offer the entire community to America and be accepted, and that their opponents used their multiple identities as a divide-and-conquer strategy.

The first years of the new century did in fact mark the expansion of lgbt rights. In June 2015, the Supreme Court made same-sex marriage legal across America, and same-sex couples gained all of the benefits of that status. In the first fifteen years of the new millennium, sexual minorities gained the right to adopt children, serve openly in the military, use antidiscrimination laws to work and live freely, and have the same rights to privacy as other Americans. These rights have made the lives of lgbts remarkably better. The community, such as it was and is, did fall apart, but clearly it did not disintegrate.

CHAPTER 6

Guns and Motherhood

A Millennial Maternalism

On the first Mother's Day of the new millennium, a Connecticut mother told hundreds of thousands gathered for the Million Mom March the story of her son. He had survived a head shot by a gunman who took a .380 semiautomatic Beretta handgun to the top of the Empire State Building and opened fire. "I received a phone call that changed my life forever," she recalled. Another mother, a Californian, told a similar story with a familiar refrain: "I received the phone call that every parent dreads," she began. Her daughter, a camp counselor at a California community center, had survived a shooting that sent five-year-olds running for their lives. Most women spoke of loss, not survivors. A Washington, DC, mother described her son and daughter, who had been murdered before they could go to their proms or high school graduations. "I will live with a broken heart for the rest of my life," pined a New Orleans woman whose child also fell victim to gun violence. A Michigan mother said that she daily mourned her six-year-old: "There is not a day that goes by that I do not cry as I go on with my life without my daughter. A part of my heart went with her. It is so hard for me to think that I will never see her smile, laugh or play again. I can never hold her and kiss her again. Or see her grow up, get married, and have a happy life."[1]

The mass of mothers who gathered on May 14 looked not only for peace and healing, but also for action. Those who knew the gut-wrenching pain of losing a child to gun violence came to share their pain with strangers. "My heart hurts," said Petra Zavala as she gathered with the Million Moms who marched in Westwood, California.[2] At the Washington march, some, like a Brooklyn shooting victim's mother, found strength through song and prayer: "Father God, we're asking for joy where there is sadness. . . . We are asking for your healing power for those who have lost loved ones to this disease, gun violence. . . . We are also asking for your protection over those who have not lost a loved one to this disease . . . that you cover them and their loved ones from the heartache and pain." Others came to give support and to make a stand against senseless loss. A Columbine (Colorado) High School teacher came with her husband, son, and two daughters. "Enough is enough!" she cried. "The safety of our students, our children must come first." In addition to hearing and participating in prayer, witness, testimony, song, and poetry, everyone who attended expressed a desire for action. "The mothers of the world are angry," said the mother of a Columbine victim, "and you never never tick off a Mother! Politicians take heed, we are watching you. The hand that rocks the cradle rules the world. We are united and we are here to protect our children."[3]

Though the Million Mom March seemed unique, motherhood and activism have been wedded ever since mid-nineteenth-century women organized against slavery, alcohol, and prostitution on the grounds that such social evils made America an unhealthy place for their children. Throughout the twentieth century, mothers mobilized for peace to ensure their children's futures. While some women transformed motherhood into a weapon against environmental pollution so that their children could have clean air and water, others have fought for racial purity and heterosexual norms. The Million Mom March, hardly the first effort to change the world by cradle-rocking hands, was a first in other ways.[4]

It was the first time that American mothers took aim at gun violence and gun control. In 2000, America had the highest rate of gun violence in the developed world, and in 1998 the Centers for Disease Control and Prevention reported that ten children and adolescents every day were killed by firearms. Though down from a high of sixteen deaths per day in 1994, it was, for those concerned, ten too many.[5] In calling for gun licensing and registration, child-safety locks, and waiting periods, the Million Moms hoped to begin decreasing the number of deaths.

The Million Mom March also represented the first coalition between mostly white suburban mothers and urban mothers who were mostly of color. Politicians, commentators, seasoned activists, and even historians saw the potential of such an alliance: "Different women, different backgrounds, different neighborhoods, same cause," as one reporter put it.[6] "It's a new group that's coming out," said a march organizer, excited about the diversity of the grassroots movement she had helped to organize.[7] When asked by a *New York Times* reporter about the alliance's significance, Annelise Orleck, a historian of working-class women's organizing, spoke of the potential power of the movement: "It's a good way to bridge differences of ideology. . . . It makes possible at least a temporary coalition of a wider range of people than might have been drawn out by a march that was billed strictly as a gun control march."[8] Emory history professor Mary Odem agreed. "When you use the word 'mother' it cuts across ideology, class, racial divisions. It goes beyond all that."[9]

Historically, black, brown, and white women have had a hard time coming together on anything. As we have seen in chapter 3, black and white women often wanted the same things but because their desires had different historical roots, race and circumstance dictated their separation. In the 1960s and 1970s, African American women and Chicanas organized feminist movements separate from white women for this very reason. When they worked in small groups, white women had not always been receptive to tackling race issues and women's issues at the same time—something black and Hispanic women have had to do. Seldom did white women understand the inclination of black women to put race first, even in the face of rampant sexism.[10] On the other hand, black women pointed to white women's history as enslavers, racial purists, and segregationists.[11] Since most women of color were more likely to work for, or be the housekeepers of, those they were now paired with politically, the Million Mom alliance that brought all women together to pray and mourn and protest and organize was as exceptional as it was promising. Could it be that their children had not died in vain? Could black, brown, and white mothers unite over their dead children and build a coalition strong enough to effectively challenge one of the most powerful lobbies this country has ever seen—the National Rifle Association (NRA)? Could these mothers do what the Promise Keepers pledged to do—bridge the chasm of race? From a distance, on May 14, it appeared to be so.

Like all the other marches and gatherings, an aerial shot of the Million Mom March reveals less than does a close-up view. From above we see maternalist politics alive and well, in harmony with feminism and congealed around a unitary idea of what a mother is and the kind of citizenship she represents. But this picture does not reveal the heated debate over the meaning of, and relationship between, feminism, motherhood, and citizenship, a debate that impacted the cross-race alliance the Million Mom March tried to build. It also does not reveal the way multiculturalism and feminism worked in real life when women of different races and classes had to build a political coalition. Historically, maternalism has sparked controversy from left to right, and the Million Mom March held true to this tradition. While building on a rich history of maternalist activism, the march also triggered age-old conflicts about the definition of good and bad domesticity, proving that at the turn of the new millennium, postmodernity had not changed things. Maternalism was still as perilous as ever.

The Hand That Rocks the Cradle

Emotions matter, say sociologists, and this was never truer than in the case of the Million Mom March.[12] Though they came from different backgrounds, the marchers shared common feelings and a common frame of reference. When Donna Dees-Thomases, the founder of this gun-control movement, first heard, in August 1999, that a gunman had stormed the North Valley Jewish Community Center in Granada Hills, California, she described herself as "immobilized with shock." As she listened to television reports of the incident and the history of gun violence in America, she was "stunned," and then she was "mad." When she went online and typed in the words *gun control*, fear overwhelmed her. When Dees-Thomases asked herself why the issue had not troubled her before Granada Hills, she speculated that unlike other reports of gun horror, even of Columbine, this one "happened to children similar to my own." It was this realization that brought out her shame. This series of emotions transformed her from someone who, by her own admission, read the newspapers only for the gossip pages into a leading activist for gun control. Something else, however, drove her to lead hundreds of thousands of people to the National Mall on Mother's Day, 2000. As she describes it, she was driven by a "latent, fierce, maternal instinct." It was this "unleashed" instinct that drove her to organize the Million Mom March, which in 2002 became the Million Mom March United with the Brady Campaign to Prevent Gun Violence.[13]

Dees-Thomases's calling to antigun activism was not unlike that of countless others. Columbine was the impetus for Janet Mills, Karen Segal, and Renae Popkin, all of Marietta, Georgia, to march for gun control in Atlanta, Georgia, on Mother's Day, 2000. Mills said that when Columbine happened, "I was on the phone with Karen for hours just crying. Neither of us could hang up." April Rayborn went to the same march. As she held up a sign that said "Republican Mom for Gun Control," she explained that it was the killing of her daughter's classmate and mother that motivated her.[14] Another mother, Shikha Hamilton, was sitting in a hospital, at her sick daughter's bedside, when she heard of the murder of a six-year-old girl by her six-year-old classmate right in the schoolroom. Infuriated by the killing, she then and there resolved to do something, and subsequently became the president of the Michigan Million Mom March.[15]

Joining mothers like these were those who had been moved to action by immeasurable grief. Mary Leigh Blek, a staunch conservative from Orange

County, California, got involved in gun control shortly after her son Matthew was shot down in New York by three fifteen-year-old boys who attempted to rob him. She became president of the Bell Campaign, a grassroots gun-control organization that preceded the Million Mom March and that subsequently provided the financial oversight for Dees-Thomases's organization.[16] Carole Price took over the Maryland chapter of the Million Mom March after her thirteen-year-old son, John, was shot and killed by his friend's nine-year-old brother, who was showing off a gun. After her son's death, Price dedicated her life to encouraging parents to ask about the presence of guns when children visited their friends. She became honorary chairperson of Asking Saves Kids (ASK).[17] After her son was murdered, Brenda Muhammad of Atlanta organized the group Mothers Against Murdered Sons and Daughters. Loss also pushed Frances Davis into the fight for gun control. In separate incidents, all three of her sons—Rahlake, Andrew, and Frankie—were shot and killed.[18]

More than grief and anger, however, brought these women together. Whether it was forged before gun violence wreaked havoc in their lives or after, these women shared a critique of America that could be found at Promise Keeper rallies or the Million Man and Woman Marches—that something had gone terribly wrong with the country. Million Mom marchers wanted to send a message regarding the "bigger picture about guns and society." "Things cannot go on as they are," wrote an editorialist from Buffalo, New York.[19] "It's the violence, stupid," was the way a Chicago editorialist put it.[20] As in the prayer quoted earlier, the metaphor of disease was widely adopted. "America is really sick," said Anne Van Prooyen of the Atlanta area. Guns were a major symptom of the problem, but violence was the disease.[21]

As with any disease, an antidote was needed, and Million Mom marchers believed that mothers were that antidote. Theirs was an essentialist understanding of motherhood. Mothers were protective; mothers kept children safe; mothers were peaceful; mothers were nurturers; mothers put health, education, and welfare issues first; mothers knew best. It was a mother's duty to protect her children, to keep them safe. "The gun lobby may be powerful, but a mother's love is more powerful," said Carol Kingsley, whose husband was shot to death in San Francisco in 1993.[22] "Nobody feels the issue more strongly than mothers. We're the experts when it comes to protecting our children," declared Brookline, Massachusetts, philanthropist Barbara Lee.[23] And no one was more powerful than an angry mom. "I think angry moms are the strongest force on the face of this planet," said Lisa Amspaugh, a thirty-eight-year-old mother of two. "A mother is someone whose anger is good," said Millie Webb, the then president of Mothers Against Drunk Driving (MADD). "Mothers are there to nurture and care for the world."[24]

Mothers, they argued, were multitaskers who combined good citizenship with motherhood. Like their forebears, who since the American Revolution had rendered themselves, as historian Mary Beth Norton tells us, "keepers of the nation's conscience, the only citizens specifically charged with maintaining the traditional republican commitment to the good of the entire community,"[25] Million Mom marchers pledged themselves to crusade in the name of morality, to march to redeem a country stained by violence, to organize locally to enact antigun laws and unseat gun advocates, and to "make our tears a raging river of votes." "WE VOTE!" said Rosie O'Donnell to the hundreds of thousands gathered on the National Mall on May 14, 2000. "Are you listening Congress, Senators? We vote and we will be watching you!"[26]

All of this does not surprise historians who know that history really does repeat itself. This mothers' movement for gun control followed a pattern first established in America in the late eighteenth century and continued during the nineteenth and twentieth centuries. As explained by historian Linda Kerber, in the early years of the republic, politics and intellectual activity were thought to be the province of men. Women who addressed political issues were thought to threaten the sanctity of marriage and were ridiculed as masculine and insulted with impunity. Only the republican mother was spared criticism because her life and her intellect were dedicated to the service of civic virtue. As Kerber put it, her "domestic behavior had a direct political function in the republic." Since republics were thought to be fragile, the republican mother was theorized (mostly by women) as the family member who was the bulwark against autocracy. As mothers socialized their sons and daughters to be moral and virtuous citizens, they strengthened the nation and simultaneously "justified women's absorption and participation in the civic culture." Republican motherhood redefined women as more than helpmates to their husbands, and the formulation became the foundation of the argument for women's education. Throughout the nineteenth and into the twentieth century, women, in the name of moral motherhood, fought not only for their educational advancement but also against slavery, alcohol, and prostitution. They justified their fight for the vote on the grounds that as mothers and wives they were guardians of the family and nation. Facing less restrictions in the home than elsewhere, women, says historian Carl Degler, expanded their influence and power by transforming the world into one large home.[27]

The Opposition

Just as mothers' movements have a long tradition, so too does opposition to them, and the opposition has always been as passionate as the mothers' movements. This time around was no different. Coming as it did during this period of extreme anxiety about the meaning of American manhood, the issue of guns and mothers intersected with negative ideas about feminism and multiculturalism in an explosive way. Put differently, the Million Mom March deepened anxiety about masculinity while it simultaneously helped fuel a backlash against minorities and women that was already well under way.

The catch-22 of mothers' movements has always been that when mothers take responsibility for the moral fiber of the nation or community, they leave themselves open to the charge that their failings as mothers have exposed the family, community, and nation to the ills that their movements address. If they had been better mothers, there would be no need for their movement. American history is full of this kind of rebuttal. For example, at the turn of the twentieth century, when America entered the imperial scramble and mothers staked their claim for temperance and the vote, they were chided for abandoning the home, for fostering an effeminate manhood, for being too masculine—indeed, for emasculating men by usurping men's authority at home and in public.[28] Mother-blaming reached new heights during the World War II crisis, when American manhood and patriotism were again put under a microscope. No one did more to institutionalize mother-blaming than Philip Wylie, whose 1942 book *Generation of Vipers* virtually institutionalized what he called "momism." "Mom is a jerk," said Wylie before he went on to disparage "Mom's" consumption habits as trifling, her child-rearing methods as doting and smothering, and her physical person as overweight and sexually unattractive. Mom, said Wylie in his 1955 edition, is "ridiculous, vain, vicious, a little mad. She is her own fault first of all and she is dangerous."[29] While Wylie let loose on white middle-class mothers, E. Franklin Frazier confirmed centuries of white commentary on black motherhood by proving that black mothers were the quintessential bad mothers. In his 1939 book, *The Negro Family in the United States*, Frazier described rural black mothers as "dominant," without morals, and possessive of only "elemental maternal sympathy." Frazier documented out-of-control illegitimacy, unwed urban mothers who, he claimed, were known to throw their babies in the garbage can, and working-class mothers who were either neglectful of children or overly focused on them. Over twenty-five years later, in 1965, Daniel Patrick Moynihan used Frazier's study as the basis for his description of black matriarchy, which was cited as the root cause of emasculated men, family and community disorganization, and even the early 1960s urban riots.[30] With this kind of history, the opposition to the Million Mom March promised to be fervent, if not fanatical.

Feminists were among the first to object. Many were hopeful that the Million Moms might succeed where other lobbying efforts had failed, and agreed that the "image of the bereaved and angry mother is the only one weighty enough to counterbalance that of the male hunter and patriot deployed so successfully by the NRA."[31] Nevertheless, they were dismayed that the Million Moms did not address the issue of guns more expansively. "When will our culture have moved far enough beyond the view that women exist only to birth and care for [male] babies, that we witness the spectacle of huge numbers of women organizing to protect *themselves*?" wrote a male editorialist from Kalamazoo, Michigan.[32] Another feminist critic complained about the equation of womanhood and motherhood. She winced when she thought of the number of times she heard "well-meaning people say that the most important job a woman can do is be a mother." Non-moms, she said, "have found tons of ways to nurture the globe and create productive lives. We babysit, teach, counsel other people's children; we heal, work in public policy, lead community groups, create art and have lives that are caring, conscientious, inventive and meaningful." Like June Jordan, who in 1997 objected to the nebulous objectives of the Million Woman March, this Oakland, California, editorialist wanted a more focused agenda. To her, the Million Moms' "pregnancy metaphors" were "tiresome," their agenda too limiting ("Where's the Million Mom March to support public schools?"), and their constituency too exclusionary ("the issue of gun control is too big, too deadly serious to be addressed by mothers alone").[33]

These feminist critiques of maternalism were by no means new.[34] Maternalism and feminism have always had an uncomfortable relationship. Much like the seeming contradiction between affirmative action and equal opportunity for all, it has proved difficult and controversial for women to argue for equal rights and equal pay for equal or comparable work in the same breath as they justify maternity leave and tax-supported child care. The suffrage coalition divided on this point after the Twenty-First Amendment was passed. The National Women's Party supported the Equal Rights Amendment, which recognized no differences between men and women, while organizations like the Women's Trade Union League, the League of Women Voters, the General Federation of Women's Clubs, and the Young Women's Christian Association fought for legislation that gave women rights that recognized the differences between men and women.[35] As we have seen, this difference in the meaning of equality separated feminists from women of the Promise Keepers. Recent critics of maternalism not only lament the linking of women's politics and fate to biology—a potentially dangerous association in a period dominated by political conservatives whose political agenda includes limiting women's reproductive choices in the name of family values—but many feminists also argue for their reproductive right not to have children, or to have alternative families composed of a same-sex couple. The 1990s were also marked by feminist critiques that bemoaned the child-centeredness of American society. In the context of the Million Mom March, they not only took issue with the lack of attention to the number of *women* who were victims of gun violence, but they also wondered why mothers had to take responsibility for a problem perpetrated mainly by men. As Katha Pollitt wrote in the *Nation*: "The gun culture is a highly masculine preserve, and so is most gun violence—drive-by shootings, mass murders by school kids, racist killing sprees, domestic murder-suicides. Who leaves those loaded guns around for kids to play with, anyway? Shouldn't it have been a Million Dad March?"[36]

As powerful as the feminist critique was, it was drowned out by pro-gun advocates. They made all their standard arguments: guns don't kill people, people kill people; gun control will not stop criminals; new laws are not needed if current laws are enforced. Moreover, it did not help that Donna Dees-Thomases's sister-in-law was a friend of Hillary Clinton. Even though there were many Republican women who were leaders and marchers, conservatives alleged that gun control was a liberal preserve, and support from Bill Clinton, who had by May 2000 been disgraced for sexual indiscretions, did not bolster the argument being made in the name of moral motherhood.

But against the Million Moms, pro-gun advocates went beyond the standard anti-gun-control arguments. They adopted the time-honored tactic of attacking the moms themselves, confirming feminists' fears that mothers who took responsibility for gun control would be blamed for all of society's ills. Education, not regulation, was their answer. If moms stayed home and took time to teach their children right from wrong, respect for human life, and the difference between a real gun and a toy gun, the crime rate would be lower.[37] "Where were the moms when the six-year-old stole the gun from his home? Where were the moms when the Columbine kids were plotting their expedition? Where was the mom in Oregon when Kip Kinkel put together his arsenal?" asked Washington State resident Charles Sanborn.[38] Steve Kruse, from North Platte, Nebraska, blamed moms for everything from errant children to lack of prayer in schools: "Where were they when their children got home from school, latchkey in hand, to find only an empty house? Where were the million moms when it was time for a daily family dinner? When it was time for a mother-to-child chat? . . . Where were the million moms when it came to keeping a family together rather than divorce? And most important . . . where were the million moms when they banned my Lord and blessed Savior from school?"[39] An editorialist in the *Atlanta Journal-Constitution* had an answer: "They should tear themselves away from the TV, shopping and marching up and down the street waving banners and spend more quality time with their children."[40] While some pro-gun advocates pointed a finger at parents in general, most took direct aim at moms: moms who "wished the government to raise their children," moms who "turned their 'oven mittens' in too early for a career," and "lazy moms, who are trying to shirk their own responsibilities."[41]

With Wylie-like precision, pro-gun advocates hit their mark. The Million Mom March use of the term *mom* was unfortunate because, as we have seen, momism in America has negative connotations. The media's use of the term *soccer mom* made the choice even more unfortunate since it implied a particular kind of consumption and style of mothering, and not a caring, thoughtful person. In twenty-first-century America, soccer moms are known for overscheduling, suffocating, and doting on their children; for cowing their husbands; and for driving their SUVs from kids' events to kids' events.[42]

When pro-gun advocates were not ridiculing mom for the way she mothered, they caricatured her as overemotional, a familiar put-down of women who have from time immemorial been thought to be governed by their wombs. Rather than evoking compassion and concern about the death of so many children, the sight of mourning mothers evoked disgust, even rage, in pro-gun advocates. Suzanne Fields of the Cleveland area called the Million Moms "naive and emotional, short on facts and long on sentiment."[43] Sonja Monsen of Tampa, Florida, complained that the Million Moms were "misguided" women who believed that "simply because they are moms their irrational, emotionally-driven beliefs should trump logical, fact-based reasoning."[44] Not surprisingly, conservative Camille Paglia weighed in. With her usual blistering, sharpshooter aim, she zeroed in on the Million Moms' emotionalism: "It doesn't take a weatherman to figure out that the average citizen doesn't want national policy determined by packs of weeping women."[45]

Emotionalism, then, proved a double-edged sword. While effective in bringing mothers together, it nevertheless left them vulnerable. Even though sociologists warn against the false dualisms of emotionalism versus rationality and instrumental versus expressive social movements, activists work hard to be perceived as rational and pragmatic because social movements can be rendered ineffective if they can be dismissed as softhearted.[46] Too much emotionalism can be detrimental. Image is important, says sociologist Maurice Halbwachs. Loaded with emotional content, images inform ideas about which people discern truth. Historian Temma Kaplan demonstrated how mothers acting in their capacity as caretakers challenged the authoritarian governments of Chile, Argentina, and Spain by using photos, paintings, and slogans and by participating in mass spectacles to shame government officials. In Kaplan's cases, emotionalism met with some successes.[47] Emotionalism also worked for Promise Keepers and Million Man marchers. In trying out a new, softer kind of manhood in same-sex gatherings, they were able to restructure their priorities and find peace and happiness. However, it proved less effective for the Million Moms because in addition to healing themselves they were making explicit demands on the government. Unfortunately, their opponents were able to counter the powerful image of mourning mothers and dead children by caricaturing mothers as weak and spineless.

Opponents also offered up some effective images of their own, images that revealed how they were handling postmodern issues of masculinity, feminism, and multiculturalism. One was the patriot. Because it was untenable to claim that guns and children were a good mix, they subtly linked guns to freedom, masculinity, patriotism, and God, and then, while dressed in Revolutionary War attire, contrasted themselves to crying females.[48] Moms, they argued, threatened traditional liberties, especially the right of self-defense, which, they argued, was the principle that led to the severing of the colonies from Britain. Repeating a Thomas Jefferson dictum, they proclaimed, "What country can preserve its liberties if its rulers are not warned from time to time that its people preserve the right of resistance? Let them take arms."[49] Mike Ingle, from the Charlotte area of North Carolina, linked his Second Amendment rights to the First Amendment when he argued that "if that [right to bear arms] is taken away, then I don't understand how you'll defend your right to worship the way you want to."[50] Charlton Heston, the spokesperson for the National Rifle Association and its multiple-term president, struck the perfect patriotic pose. The actor, who as Moses liberated the Israelites, often talked about the Ten Commandments and the Bill of Rights in the same breath. "As an American and as a man who believes in God's almighty power, I treasure both," he said. He usually ended NRA meetings by holding a Minuteman-like musket high over his head and vowing that his enemies would have to pry the musket from "my cold dead hands."[51]

It was not just that moms were espousing tyranny by government regulation and thereby leaving the nation exposed, but also that their gun control would leave families defenseless and men without means to protect them. However they perceived the new demands of manhood, whether they bought into the softer, kinder persona or not, gun advocates did not concede the male's role as protector. Indiana resident Jeff Erycole, for example, asked a familiar question when he queried a reporter: "Do you think I should remain passive when there are criminals out there with guns?"[52] Maria Heil, a pro-gun proponent, seconded Erycole's emotion. She was against gun control, in part because "criminals will not target men who appear to be strong."[53] The *National Review*'s Andrew Stuttaford likewise made a pitch for strong men when he wondered where dads stood in the whole equation, and if American society was to be run first and foremost in the interest of its children by particular kinds of moms. He, for one, did not like being treated like a child. "The American people are not all children," he warned.[54] Scott Mize agreed. His editorial ridiculed "plucky moms scolding the big boys." He thought that since American women were not encouraged to be strong, the Million Moms had unwisely "bought into the nanny state's prescription for safety."[55]

Ironically, at the same time that gun advocates painted the Million Moms as consuming, sobbing, and unpatriotic, they offered a different image of womanhood to Americans: a pistol-packing mama who was strong, self-assured, and, they claimed, feminist.[56] Even though the "pistol-packin' mama" seemed to contradict NRA fears of emasculating women, they claimed that these women would stand strong for liberty and defend the family against criminals. Good mothers embraced guns, argued Maria Heil: "If you care about your children, you should make sure you have the ability to defend them." Heil also made the case for feminism. Criminals, she said, target the weak and since women "overall are seen as the weaker sex," criminals target women. Owning and knowing how to use a gun was "empowering," she said. "I don't like to use the word 'feminist' but when a woman can carry a gun for self-defense the woman has equality, and if the so-called feminist movement is about equality then I guess I would be a feminist."[57]

The Second Amendment Sisters felt justified in making the claim for maternalism *and* feminism because, unlike the Million Moms, they argued not just for children but for women. Suzanne Fields argued that while the pistol-packin' mama was not the most feminine image for a woman, "packing heat is beginning to make sense in a world where a woman is often defenseless without a man at her side." "When a gun is the only thing that stands between a woman and an attacker, that gun gives the woman a fighting chance to come out alive."[58] A few argued against gun control because they wanted women to be able to protect themselves against husbands and other male relatives. Said one woman, "If Nicole [Brown Simpson] had [had] a gun, her kids [would] still have a mom. . . . I will not be a Nicole."[59]

Finally, playing perhaps their most powerful card, pro-gun advocates zeroed in on the issue of rape. They often carried signs reading "A Gunlock Is Safe Sex for a Rapist" or "Rapists Love Gun Laws." The picture of a blonde carrying a gun read: "As seen by would-be rapist, for about 0.2 seconds."[60] "Rapists," said Dave Kopel, conservative research director of the Independence Institute, "are afraid of armed victims."[61] Conservative *Boston Globe* columnist Jeff Jacoby told readers: "Make no mistake: Those who prevent law-abiding women from arming themselves with guns make it easier for rapists to attack

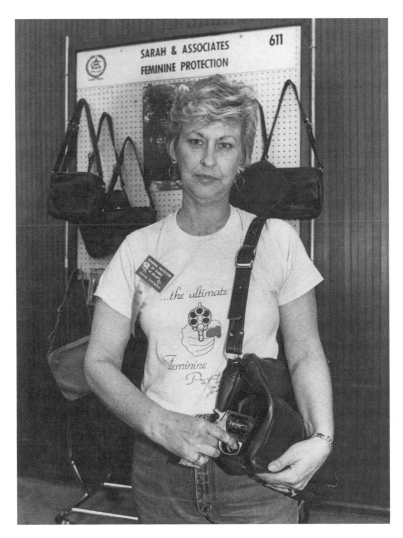

FIGURE 11. Critics of the Million Moms argued that women who carried guns were feminists because they did not need to depend on a man for protection. Here, a saleswoman models a handbag explicitly designed for carrying a handgun. *Photo by Barbara Alper/Getty Images.*

them with impunity."[62] Another conservative, blogger J. H. Huebert, likened gun control to putting a "Rape Me" sign on all unarmed women.[63]

Women are subject to many kinds of violence, so the preoccupation with rape should have raised antennas. Why was there so little concern over domestic violence, a traditional feminist concern? Pro-gun advocates who focused on rape, an act that has a dramatic raced and gendered history, not only cast doubt on their feminist credentials, but unveiled their coded message.

Historically, when white women proclaimed their need for protection from rape they usually meant, both explicitly and implicitly, that they needed protection from black men. As noted in chapter 1, it was a measure of white men's manhood and masculinity to provide that protection.[64] This had been the case during the years of African American enslavement. It reached new heights after the Civil War, and near hysterical proportions from 1882 to 1901, when more than a hundred people, most of them black men, were lynched every year. The pretext for the murder of black men was the same as that used to keep white women in their proper domestic place: black men, it was argued, were primordially driven to rape white women, who in turn needed to stay out of the public sphere, safely ensconced in the home where white men could protect them. From the slaughter of Robert Moss, a Tennessee entrepreneur; to the 1923 pogrom in Rosewood, Florida; to the 1930s Alabama Scottsboro case; to the execution of fifteen-year-old Emmett Till in 1955, the murder of black men in the name of white womanhood served to maintain the traditional racial and sexual hierarchy that kept whites over blacks, and men over women.[65]

Ironically, it was the Million Moms who breathed new life into this ancient American race/sex dynamic. When they made the case that Americans were not safe, that violence was spreading like a disease, they unwittingly helped resurrect the template on which so much of America's racist and sexist practices were built. Said Cathy Kopecky, western Pennsylvania coordinator for the Million Mom March, "I think people are really getting that it's not only happening to other people."[66] "No one—and I mean no one—is immune from gun violence," warned Orange County Republican marcher Mary Leigh Blek.[67] When gun advocates like former NRA president Marion Hammer said, "I'll tell you what women want more than gun control. They want to be safe in their homes," they were only reiterating what the Million Moms had been preaching.[68]

But gun advocates and Million Moms did differ significantly in their approach to safety. The Million Moms took a fairly benign, color-blind approach to gun violence, a subject we examine shortly. Gun advocates, however, put a race on the face of violence and thereby delivered a not-so-subtle race-coded message. For them, violence was not just spreading; criminals disrupted the peace and made the public unsafe. When the Million Moms bolstered their argument for gun control with the claim that twelve children a day were killed by guns, gun advocates disputed their assertion on the basis that *children* weren't dying; *criminals* were. "You have to delve into how they define children," said Maria Heil. "Yes, there are twelve a day, but that's for twenty and under. That includes the highest crime group there is—the fifteen to twenty year olds. So most of that twelve children a day is including criminals, gang members who kill other gang members, police who kill criminals, citizens, ordinary citizens who defend themselves and kill a criminal."[69] While Suzanne Fields argued that careless people and schizophrenics were part of the problem, she too identified the "bad people who shoot people" as "adolescent gangsters who kill each other over drug turfs."[70] Without the rabid racism that no longer accompanied late twentieth-century right-wing rhetoric, this argument effectively racialized Fields's fear of crime by redirecting attention onto black men who since the 1830s had been constructed by the mainstream media as demons, and who in the 1990s emerged in news reporting and prime-time police dramas as America's quintessential villains and predators.[71] Though hardly the perpetrators of most of America's crimes, in 2000, young black males between fifteen and nineteen years old did have the highest imprisonment rate for criminal activity and did have the highest rate of death caused by firearms than any group in the country. Ever so aware of the public's association of black men and violence, Million Man marchers had performed a softer, kinder masculinity five years earlier. Still, in 2005 even the 1980s former secretary of education, William Bennett, linked African Americans to criminal behavior when he said: "I do know that it's true that if you wanted to reduce crime, you could—if that were your sole purpose—you could abort every black baby in this country, and your crime rate would go down."[72]

Gun advocates' argument about negligent moms also subtly evoked another familiar raced trope: the bad black mother. This image took hold during the slavery era. Though perceived to be capable of mothering white children as mammies, black women were accused of carelessly smothering, starving, and neglecting their own children while they pursued sexual activity with abandon. After slavery, the image of the black woman as promiscuous merged with one that maintained her sloth. Together they came to represent the negative image hurtful to so many Million Woman marchers. She was a single-parent welfare queen, devoid of moral worth. With her libido out of control, she made babies so that she could live off the public dole. She was, as critic Wahneema Lubiano writes, thought to be "a moral aberration, and an economic drain," who was given responsibility for the destruction of the "American way of life."[73]

In short, at the turn of the millennium, gun advocates reached back into America's premodern and modern history and drew on familiar tropes—the black male rapist, the helpless white woman, the white male protector, the negligent emasculating mom, and the promiscuous black mother—to advance their argument against gun control. They challenged the maternalism of the Million Moms by urging them to retreat to the domestic realm and raise their children more responsibly. They redefined feminism with the argument that mothers could do more from the home to affect the contagion of violence that beset the nation. If they learned to use a gun, they could protect not only themselves but also their children from the criminal/rapist who plagued the land. Without ever identifying that criminal by race, they fingered him as the black male rapist who had for centuries roamed the land. Very effectively they put a face on the images of the children the Million Moms said were dying at a rate of twelve a day. That face did not draw a sympathetic response from gun advocates who, unlike the mothers they opposed, were not interested in advancing the cause of multiculturalism, something the Million Moms were trying to do.

Race and the Million Moms

The demonization of black children and mothers came as no surprise to African American women. Many had supported the Million Man March precisely because they feared for their sons and they needed black men's help to protect them. Those who joined the Million Mom March had no illusions about the uphill struggle the maternalist gun-control movement faced. Along with their allies in the movement they tried to educate the Million Moms. Ultimately, the Million Mom March took a "color-blind," race-neutral approach to the problem of gun violence and gun control.

Black Million Moms knew what Million Man March women knew, that, historically, dead black children and especially dead black boys pulled no compassionate emotional strings. Therefore, their first order of business was to educate.[74] Accordingly, Adrienne Young, the mother of Javon Thompson, a Carnegie Mellon art student killed in 1994, told a group of Pittsburgh Million Mom March organizers that they needed to acknowledge the gun violence ravaging black America: "I said whenever they hear about our children dying, it's always gang violence. When their children die, it's gun violence. If that angry boy did not have a gun, my son would not be dead. When I stood up and said this to these ladies at the meeting, they looked at me in astonishment, as if it had never dawned on them that it's the same thing."[75] The same black female reporter who reported Young's story told one of her own, about her nephew Antonio Rykard Jr., who was shot in the back of the head and dragged to a wooded area. "His death didn't rate more than a newspaper brief," she grieved. As a reporter, a black female one at that, Monica Haynes probably knew better than most that "no one seems to care whether there is one little black man-child killed or a thousand."[76]

By all reports—from marchers, reporters, and commentators—black and Hispanic women made up a very small minority of the participants of the May 14 march and the movement as a whole, but those who did participate had a distinctive point of view.[77] On the one hand, they were bitter that white women came to the issue of gun violence only after white children became victims and only after gun violence seemed to be spreading to white American communities; on the other hand, they were grateful for help against a problem they knew they could not defeat alone. "We have lost the most children proportionately than any ethnic group. . . . Our voices need to be heard, our faces need to be seen and our pain needs to be known," said Adrienne Young.[78]

Young called for inclusion. Like Haynes, she understood that minority children were perceived as the "other" and devalued as children. On some level the black mothers, like Million Woman marchers, probably also understood that the nation saw them as bad mothers. Still, they fought along with other minority mothers for their children's rights. They spoke of "our children." Said Frances Davis of Philadelphia, "We have to start thinking not just my child but our children." Carol Ann Taylor agreed: "We must begin to look at each child like he or she belongs to us—no matter what color, what geographic area or economic background. . . . We must respond, because, if we don't save our children, who will?" Los Angeles participant Carolyn Macias said, "We are marching for all the children, whether we know them or not." Lillian Ileto, the mother of the Filipino American postal worker who was killed by the same white supremacist who shot up the Granada Hills Jewish Community Center, echoed Taylor's remarks. "I am asking you to reach out and to let your children know that we are all equal. Help our children to be tolerant of each other . . . and let them know that gun violence has no place."[79]

Like other Million Moms, minority mothers argued that gun violence was a cancer spreading across America, but they also gently chastised the Million Moms for thinking that its spread was limited to minority neighborhoods. "You just don't know," said Frances Davis, who had three sons gunned down. "So you can't say not my child, it's not in my community. . . . It can happen to anybody at any time, as long as there are so many guns available on the street and there's so much anger out there." Davis did not say it from a scholar's lectern, or from a pulpit, or from a campaign stump, but from her heart. Her message was clear: "Unfortunately the tragedies that happen in the schools, especially in suburban schools, it's like a wake-up call."[80]

Many white women in the movement agreed. As gun violence came to their town, they abandoned previous notions of safety. For example, Melinda Lee of Longmeadow, Massachusetts, saw the shooting of a Michigan six-year-old by another six-year-old as a "wake-up call that said, 'You can't sit around in your safe, little suburban town anymore.'"[81] When the local headlines broadcast the murder of a college student whose boyfriend killed her with a gun, Diana Bock, a resident of Clark, New York, took heed. "People say to me, 'It wouldn't happen here. Not in Clark.'" Bock, who decided to go to the Mother's Day march, thought, "But that's what Columbine people thought."[82] It took the shooting of her child at the Granada Hills Jewish Community Center to transform Loren Lieb into an activist. According to Lieb, "Before the shooting, my approach to gun control was, 'Yes, it's a problem, but what can I do about it? I live in a safe community.' Then I found out that was very false thinking."[83]

White women's newfound perspective included mea culpas. "For too long we have ignored the gun violence epidemic because it was always in somebody else's back yard," said Donna Dees-Thomases, the founder of the movement, who credited New York lieutenant Eric Adams of 100 Blacks in Law Enforcement with "bringing a sense of realism to our cause, because kids in his community were dying every day."[84] On the other side of the country, in the Los Angeles area, Kathy Friedman wrote an e-mail message that was read and circulated at black church services in Los Angeles. "We will no longer stand silently on the sidelines as you walk through the shadows of darkness in your neighborhoods. We will instead walk side by side."[85]

And, like Promise Keepers who pledged to bridge the racial divide, many tried. In some areas of the country, interracial maternalism seemed to succeed. Cathy Kopecky must have heard Adrienne Young speak of the different way that black and white death was perceived. As the western Pennsylvania coordinator for the Million Mom March, she filled five buses for the march and thought she would have to add two more. "So much of the black violence stuff was always talked about as gangs and we could reason it was gang stuff," she said. "I think people are realizing that that's not true, and shame on us for not acting sooner." Not only Kopecky but another Pittsburgh-area woman, who was in the room when Young made her appeal, got the message and anonymously sent Young $1,000 to help her rent buses to bring African American women to the march.[86] An editorial in the *San Francisco Chronicle* likewise suggested interracial cooperation. While most commentators noted the mostly white marchers at the Washington and local-area marches, this editorialist was buoyed by the diversity of the Oakland, California, march, reflecting the "rich racial and cultural makeup of the Bay Area."[87]

If Oakland was the exception, and by all accounts it seems that it was, we need to know why. The Pittsburgh incident is revealing. Many minority women lacked the resources to travel to Washington. Claudette Perry, a DC organizer, reasoned that black women did not get involved because much of the recruiting was done on the Internet and "there are a lot of inner-city folks who don't have computers."[88] When Brenda Muhammad, a black woman from Atlanta, Georgia, wondered why there was not more involvement of African American women, "the most affected by it all," as she put it, she reasoned that black mothers often had another child at home to care for. "Some aren't able to volunteer the time," she said. "Some don't have time to mourn."[89] Mary Dejevsky, a reporter, gave yet another reason. She was told by some of the black women who did attend that their friends and neighbors resented the fact that gun violence only became a national issue after white children were killed at Columbine.[90]

The Los Angeles march provides a laboratory for exploring other reasons that minority women's participation was low. Although the Million Mom March was held in Washington, smaller marches were held throughout the country for those who could not travel to the nation's capital. Los Angeles was the only city to hold two marches, one in the predominantly white, affluent suburb of Westwood, and the other in downtown Los Angeles, on Olvera Street, close to minority neighborhoods. The march was originally planned as one big event but participants could not agree on where to hold the march. Minority women wanted to hold the event in their neighborhood where gun violence wreaked the most havoc. But many, though not all, of the white women opted for Westwood. The sparks flew as the mothers tried to decide. Victoria Ballesteros, one of the organizers of the downtown march, fumed as she told a reporter: "I don't know how any organization that wants to make a difference on this issue can at the same time say: We don't want to work with communities of color. . . . And that's essentially what they are saying when they say they don't want to go east." Ballesteros got active in the gun-control movement after attending Million Mom meetings at which Latinas were not well represented. She immediately started faxing Spanish-language radio and television stations and visiting churches and grandmothers' groups. Ballesteros's activities seem to have upset the march organizers, or so Joy Turner, an African American woman, surmised. Dawn Sinko, a mother from the predominantly white Westside area and cochairman of the Southern California Regional Million Mom March, said she thought that the vote to hold the march downtown should stand. "We are really aware that this issue has been going on in communities of color for a really long time. . . . We chose Olvera Street because it serves people from five different counties of Southern California and it's the birthplace of L.A., and that's very much in keeping with our theme of birth and motherhood."[91]

But Ann Reiss Lane, the head of Women Against Gun Violence, planned a separate march because participants from San Fernando Valley and Westside were unfamiliar with the downtown area and were afraid to venture there. Lane admitted that "there are some women who think that everything east of La Cienega is as crime-ridden as the Rampart Division." She added that for other women it was too much trouble to make the long trip downtown and that the Federal Building in Westwood, at the busiest intersection in the city, was a traditional site of protests and therefore the perfect venue. When Ballesteros and others charged this group with racism, Lane said she was "deeply hurt" by the accusation and denied it. The city, she said, had a lot of problems and the gun-control movement could not solve all of them. "We live," she said, "in a vast area of 10 million people . . . a city divided, where people live in enclaves. I see this as an opportunity for as many people as possible to participate, by giving them two locations at two different times." Ballesteros, on the other hand, saw having two marches as "sad and ridiculous." Joyce Black, an African American woman who cofounded the group One Voice to mobilize mothers across racial lines, thought that having two separate marches was "insanity." "You cannot solve a problem with people marching off in different directions. If we do not march unitedly, we do not achieve a good end. It's just that simple." Joy Turner tried to spin the conflict positively: "It's not the Westside march, or the downtown march. It's the Million Moms March. . . . It's just like a wedding. Everyone's mad now, but this is about preventing our babies from dying."[92]

Fabian Nunez's optimism was a bit more tempered. The political director of the Los Angeles County Federation of Labor, Nunez thought that the attempt to bring these women together was clearly a breakthrough. "How often do you have concerned parents, mothers in particular, from different social classes coming together to tackle a common problem?" Still, Nunez understood that their effectiveness would depend on their ability to get along: "People always look at how do you deal with this from the perspective of the community where they reside, not how to deal with it from a broader, more holistic way." Joyce Black agreed with Nunez. Reflecting on the split, she said: "We have to understand that in order to solve this problem of gun violence, women have to unite with harmony. Our children are watching." What they saw on May 14 was one rally that began at 9:30 a.m. in Westwood, followed by an 11:00 a.m. march, and another rally that began in downtown Los Angeles at 12:30 p.m., followed by a march that started at 1:00 p.m.[93]

This incident speaks volumes about the dearth of black and minority women in the Million Mom March. Although there were many white women who crossed racial boundaries to work with minority women, it was usually minority women who had to cross over to work with white women. *They* had to educate white women, tell them that gang violence was gun violence, that gun violence in their communities was not always gang violence, that their children *were* children and deserved to be treated as such.[94]

Most white women, including Donna Dees-Thomases, came to the issue of gun control with little understanding of race. Her own account of the Million Mom March, *Looking for a Few Good Moms: How One Mother Rallied a Million Others against the Gun Lobby*, published in 2004, shows her commitment to universalism and demonstrates no structural analysis of American racial hierarchy. One searches in vain for a reference to race or even a suggestion that racial issues are involved in the gun-control fight. Race or ethnicity emerges only when Dees-Thomases describes Dana Quist, a Florida organizer, as pleading with a "singsong Puerto Rican accent"; when she describes a meeting with the man she credits with teaching her about violence in African American neighborhoods, Lieutenant Eric Adams of 100 Blacks in Law Enforcement; and when she identifies Jacquee Algee, of Atlanta, as an African American.[95]

The incident that forced Dees-Thomases to identify Algee's race proved the rule of the color-blind approach of the Million Mom March. It involved *The Oprah Winfrey Show* and a call made to the show threatening to boycott it and the Million Mom March because the African American community was not properly represented. According to Dees-Thomases, this created a mini-crisis because, as she put it, Oprah was "sensitive to any charges—founded or not—of being in any way unfair to African-Americans." When Dees-Thomases told the producer that Algee was black, the crisis passed. But the events surrounding this episode tell us a great deal more. According to Dees-Thomases, the woman who called the show belonged to a group of Million Mom March workers that Dees-Thomases identified as "a small band of malcontents." They stirred up conflict and a lot of anxiety, particularly when it came to the purpose of the Million Mom March. Originally, the march used the slogan "Mobilizing for Commonsense Gun Control." This slogan was subsequently changed by Dees-Thomases to "Mobilizing for Commonsense Gun Laws." The "malcontents" railed against this change and wrote an e-mail to the entire Million Mom database, an e-mail described by Dees-Thomases as "militant and uncompromising." According to Dees-Thomases, the e-mail caused her to lose two Connecticut organizers, one of whom was "an editorial writer for a conservative newspaper." Apparently, the "malcontents" thought Dees-Thomases conceded too much to conservatives because the change was made to appease Southern women who were for gun safety but not for gun control. Like the decision made by suffragists to accept the disenfranchisement of black women in return for Southern support of woman's suffrage, this compromise had expediency written all over it.[96] And Dees-Thomases compromised without a second thought. When the Violence Policy Center offered the Million Moms a grant if they would adopt their goal of the outright banning of handguns, Dees-Thomases refused it: "I said I couldn't do it. The Southern moms already made it abundantly clear: They would bolt faster than a bullet if we changed our stance from regulating to banning handguns. One Southern mom had even told me that she'd have to start shopping at her Piggly Wiggly in disguise if our mission became to ban guns entirely."[97]

Whatever the race of the "malcontents" (Dees-Thomases is careful not to reveal it), when it came to the difference between commonsense gun laws and gun control, and gun control and a ban on handguns, clearly the latter choice in each case was the more radical option, and minority women, particularly black women, would have been better served by it, most obviously because they suffered the most from gun violence.[98] Not only were their children, especially their male children, more likely to die by a gunshot, but also because they themselves were likely to be murdered by someone wielding a firearm. The disproportionate number of black male deaths and nonfatal gunshot wounds has overshadowed the fact that black women have a murder rate that is much higher than white women. Throughout the 1990s, black women, most of them in their mid-thirties, were murdered at a rate more than three times higher than white women. Also, black women had a pregnancy homicide risk about seven times that of white women, and black women between the ages of twenty-five and twenty-nine were about eleven times as likely as white women in that age group to be killed when pregnant or in the year after childbirth. Most of these murders were committed with handguns. Since most of the handguns were stolen, registration laws and waiting periods—solutions offered by the Million Moms—would not have made much difference. Although statistics are vague on the type of guns used in suicides—which is highest for white males—all available data suggest that registration, waiting periods, and even gun locks would not bring down the suicide rate. Given these facts, clearly the more radical approach to gun violence would have made more sense to minority women.[99]

The Perils of a Color-Blind Maternalism

In 2002, Nancy Hwa, a spokeswoman for the Brady Campaign, said of mothers: "The moms are an early warning system. They let us know when something is happening in their communities."[100] If Hwa is right, then they are like the miner's canary that Lani Guinier and Gerald Torres use metaphorically to talk about race in America.[101] If, once in the mines, the canary died, miners knew that their lives were in peril. Guinier and Torres use the canary to warn that the disabilities suffered by America's minorities foreshadow coming trouble for all Americans. This story of millennium maternalism should be our canary. The Million Mom March was unable to sustain the momentum it gained from the initial May 14, 2000, event. By 2004, when political scientist Robert Spitzer wrote about it, identifiable membership had shrunk, offices were closed, thirty out of thirty-five employees had been laid off, and it had folded into the Brady Campaign.[102] If we follow Hwa's lead and take the Million Mom March as an early-warning system, or Guinier and Torres's lead and take it as a canary, there is indeed much to be troubled about.

The good news is that, like maternalist movements past and present, the Million Mom March allowed mothers to transform the maternal experience into political work and to reconceptualize their unpaid, often devalued labor. Million Mom mothers whose children had been victims of gun violence had felt not only grief but helplessness before they joined the march movement. Their anguish had made them sour on America. Through the Million Mom March they transformed personal pain into civic action and did it comfortably among people who understood their pain and nurtured them. Women who had little or no experience speaking before large audiences or organizing groups found their voices and mobilized hundreds of thousands of mothers. For a time they scared the National Rifle Association because they gave the nation a powerful counterimage to the masculine patriot: a dutiful, sorrowful, maternal citizen come to rescue the nation. The movement also brought women of different backgrounds together. Those who were willing to reach across America's racial and cultural divides learned that guns were indeed the great equalizer. They felled rich and poor, black and white, urban and suburban Americans.

But unfortunately, what philosopher and feminist Sara Ruddick theorized about maternalist movements—that like any politics they are always "limited by context, incomplete and imperfect"—held sway in the Million Mom March.[103] Emotionalism has its uses in social movements, but here, as is often the case, it proved to be a double-edged sword. The visible suffering of mothers was a powerful mobilizer of both people and sentiment, but their public display of grief also evoked fear and disgust—fear that this maternalist movement would be successful in eliminating guns, a literal and figurative symbol of American masculinity that, despite the efforts of the Promise Keepers, was still very alive and well; and disgust at the weeping mothers whom gun owners felt were made powerless and weak by their failure to own a gun.

The Million Mom March also faltered on what was meant to be its pillar of strength: its diversity. Race mattered in this gun-control movement. Just as the Promise Keepers had underestimated the difference that race made in the way black and white men experienced America, the Million Moms underestimated the impact of the different perceptions of black and white death. From the Revolutionary War patriot to the black beast rapist, the opposition delivered race-coded messages that had resonance among all Americans, not just NRA sympathizers. Since the historic and contemporary face of American criminality is a black male, the Million Moms' color-blind approach proved just as much a double-edged sword as their public displays of suffering. On the one hand, it might, as Dees-Thomases suggested, have increased the membership and contributed to *political* diversity—bringing both liberals and conservatives into the fold—but it also inhibited the development of an effective rebuttal to the race-coded pro-gun arguments, thus decreasing the likelihood of *racial* diversity. The Million Moms had no answer when their opponents evoked race and claimed that criminals and not children were dying. To address the argument they would have had to address systemic racism and would have had to argue forcefully enough to arouse sympathy for black male children who did, and still do, die disproportionately from gun violence. They would have had to become advocates for the many poor black mothers who, through what political scientist Ange-Marie Hancock perceptively identifies as the "politics of disgust," have been devalued and stigmatized as unworthy bad mothers.[104] In short, they would have had to tackle, head on, the logic behind William Bennett's assumption that black Americans were to blame for crime in America and are the real and legitimate source of white fear, a fear that the Million Moms themselves believed in and tried to capitalize on.[105]

In short, to come together successfully, black and white Million Moms would have had to do the same thing Promise Keepers and the Million Man and Woman marchers would have had to do—overcome their history.[106] That they could not speaks to the connection between the overwhelming support black women gave to the Million Man March and the historically tense relations black and white women have had with each other. Although the Million Mom March took place almost five years after the men's march, the Million Moms' failure to even mount a defense of black children as children and not criminals clarifies the faith that black women put in black men to nourish black children. In hindsight they could say that their fear for their children, especially their boys, was not misplaced and that as contentious as black male/female relations could be, black men were better allies than white women. The Million Mom March agenda, like those of the Promise Keepers and Million Man and Woman marchers, was not very broad. One wonders whether the Million Moms themselves could have overcome their own fears and prejudices and led a sustained movement against the historically rooted racial tropes of the bad black mother and the black criminal rapist. Although it is doubtful that turn-of-the-century maternalism would have survived any better than it did had white suburban mothers chosen to do so, the fact is that even without taking the more challenging tack, it did not survive and had limited success.

Epilogue
Reflections on Marches, Identity, Intersectionality, and Postmodernity

In 2013, on the fiftieth anniversary of the March on Washington for Jobs and Freedom, President Barack Obama hailed the courage and vision of those who had marched for change a half century before. Though he made note of the march leaders, especially the Reverend Dr. Martin Luther King Jr. and John Lewis, the current Georgia congressman, mostly his speech commemorated the ordinary people—the janitors; maids; blue-, pink-, and white-collar workers; veterans; immigrants; mothers; and fathers—who drove, hitchhiked, walked, or took a bus or train to stand with each other on that historic occasion. These courageous Americans, Obama said, believed that America could change and they believed in their power to bring about change. He praised the march, not just because of the legislative measures the march helped bring about but also because of what the march did for its participants, the ultimate agents of change. It helped them to dream differently. People dare to dream differently when they march, said Obama. The faint of heart get courage from those they march with, the president said. Speaking of what the individual gained from marches, Obama maintained: "When we turn not from each other or on each other, but towards one another, . . . we find that we do not walk alone." To his mind, the '63 march was transformative because it changed the marchers as much as it changed America. "America became more free and more fair" because of it. Describing the youthful marchers of the 1960s and like-minded citizens of 2013 as people who had a "hunger for purpose" and who knew that they did not have to live the way previous generations had, Obama praised marches in general. Change, he said, did not come *from* Washington but *to* Washington.[1]

Although Obama spoke specifically about the 1963 March on Washington for Jobs and Freedom—the march judged by historians and social scientists to be the most successful of all marches on Washington—Obama's understanding of marches in general coheres with the findings of this study.[2] Contrary to the thinking that marches are a relic of yesteryear, a strategy used by leaders who have no new ideas, Obama, the former community organizer, takes the broader view and finds, like this study, that marches energize, motivate, and empower people. Even conceding that there has yet to be a march with the far-reaching impact of the 1963 march, we should acknowledge the benefit of marches and what they did for their participants at the end of the twentieth century, a time when the changes in the economy and social and political culture prompted change from individuals who found themselves uncomfortable and even unhappy in America. The marches of the 1990s and the first year of the new millennium helped people who felt lost in their own country react and adjust to an America changed by the newly inaugurated service economy; the rights movements that moved women and racial, ethnic, and sexual minorities from the periphery of American society; immigrants who held on to their native cultures and languages; and technology that altered entertainment, communication, and the individual's relationship to time and space. Known as *postmodernity* to scholars, many Americans experienced these phenomena as chaos and confusion and they tried to sort out their lives not by themselves but with others at a march or large gathering. They did not draw a straight line from, say, the rights movements to their discontent; they just knew and felt that something was wrong, that America had changed and was changing, and that life could be different and they could be happier if they made some changes in their own lives and if they helped others make America better. The various testimonies of Americans from different walks of life make this clear. Promise Keepers and Million Man marchers wanted to be different kinds of men. They wanted to relate to women and children differently, to commune with men differently, and they wanted to be more emotionally involved. Their female relatives and acquaintances wanted them to change too. Million Mom marchers wanted the culture to change so that they and their children could be safer, and they wanted more communion across races and classes; closeted lgbts wanted to live lives more truthfully, and the uncloseted wanted to live lives more fully; and African Americans wanted more community, less violence, and more brotherhood and sisterliness. They all searched for purpose, for a "thicker" experience. They all needed to be part of a majority, to feel the warmth and peace that flowed from that experience. They all needed to cry in unison and be renewed. In short, at the beginning of the new century, many Americans turned toward one another and marched for new identities and for new beginnings.

That they marched with people who they thought shared their frame of reference did not make them, ipso facto, antipostmodernist or people who resisted change; they wanted to merge the old and the new. Some, like Million Man and Woman marchers, did look back to their modern conception of "community" and long for bygone days; but they did so not to resist change but as a way to help navigate change and integrate more fully into 1990s America. Others, like lgbts, openly defended same-sex love not by toppling but by broadening traditional understandings of marriage, family, and the military. The Million Mom marchers tried to organize across race and class, and Promise Keepers did likewise while trying to update masculinity to make it more useful for the new era. In short, marchers were not reactionary. Most gathered on the basis of their modern identities in an attempt to adjust to their evolving postmodern selves. If anything, this analysis of the "identity marches" has demonstrated that turn-of-the-twenty-first-century identities were unstable and that many Americans reached back to the familiar old, not to resist the new but to reconstitute and resituate themselves in an America—indeed, a world—that demanded that they be different. It has also demonstrated that the personal is political. Lgbts and Million Mom marchers demanded specific kinds of government action and legislation, but, like Promise Keepers and Million Man and Woman marchers, they too gathered to be more whole, to heal and to be happier.

This close look at the marches also complicates theories that allege that organizations founded on identity segment Americans and destroy common dreams.[3] Nothing could be further from the truth. Besides the fact that race, gender, ethnicity, faith, wealth, poverty, and disability *do* make for different American experiences and thus different American dreams, 1990s marchers' common dream was to make America a better place for them to realize all that America had to offer. Aerial photos that show black men, black women, sexual minorities, and mothers marching in their separate marches might suggest separation, but individual testimonies paradoxically show so many dissatisfied people trying to be more inclusive; to expand beyond their personal race, class, gender, and sexual identities; to be more at peace in the home they called America; and to find the American dream. Testimonies show people gathering to find out where and how they belonged to America and, more specifically, how they could merge their needs and wants with others to make America work for them.

This made the marches anything but pure oases from postmodern reality. Although marchers found comfort from being in the majority for a day, we have seen that marches also reiterated all the complexity that confronted marchers in their daily lives. Thus, although they sought peace and happiness by marching with people who shared their identity, one of the conundrums of postmodernity that marchers could not escape was how to reconcile their various identities in an era where personal identity was fractured by faith, race, gender, class, and sexuality and where freedom and the new definition of citizenship meant being able to express every variable, sometimes all at once. Black lgbts are a perfect example of the challenges. They went to the black and lgbt marches and demanded to be recognized as full participating members of both communities—but black marchers wanted them to sublimate their sexuality and lgbts wanted them to suppress their race. Black women demonstrate another aspect of the challenges. Fractured by class and sexuality, they had difficulty enough with intraracial organizing. But added to that was the gender conflict they encountered with black men of the Million Man March and the racial conflict they encountered with Million Mom marchers. In addition to everything else, then, the marches allow us to see the turmoil unleashed by postmodernity. They show how salient race, gender, sexuality, faith, and class had become in the lives of African Americans, suburban and urban mothers, lgbts, and white and black Promise Keeper families, and how difficult it was to feel totally free in postmodern America.

All this speaks to the difficulty, though not impossibility, of organizing across identities in the postmodern age. Audre Lorde, the late black lesbian poet activist, once urged an audience of black women to embrace difference. In a talk that has become a classic manifesto—"I Am Your Sister: Black Women Organizing across Sexualities"—Lorde spoke about how heterosexism and homophobia erected barriers between black straight and lesbian women, both of whom cared deeply about racism. Black women, said Lorde, were not "one vat of homogenized chocolate milk," but they did not "have to become each other in order to work together." They did have to respect each other and meet across differences, something that required "mutual stretching." "Until you can hear me as a Black Lesbian feminist, our strengths will not be truly available to each other as Black women," she said.[4]

Though Lorde spoke to and about black women, she could just as easily have been addressing any one of the groups who marched at the turn of the twenty-first century, for each had a lot of mutual stretching to do. To their credit, Promise Keepers, lgbts, Million Man and Woman marchers, and Million Mom marchers acknowledged some of the multiple identities of their constituencies. Many stretched, or tried to, and many benefited from their effort. But, as we have seen, individuals in each group could not stretch in multiple directions at once, suggesting how hard it is to acknowledge and respect difference and still build strong alliances, much less how hard it is to be an American citizen and put that citizenship above all other identities. Also suggested is that intersectionality—the concept that individual identity is influenced by the way one's multiple frames of reference overlap and influence subjectivity—is a great analytical tool for scholars and for organizers, but it poses real problems for the latter. For while intersectionality helps scholars and organizers see how identity works and how relationships across race, class, faith, sexuality, and gender are structured, organizers who hope to build alliances across identities must develop strategies that deal not only with their particular cause for organizing but also with the stretching process. These marches show how difficult, if not impossible, that can be.

They also show that history matters. As we have seen, Americans traveled different historical roads to their particular marches and it made a difference in how much they could and did stretch. Marchers were not always aware of the difference that their history made but awareness might have helped white and black Promise Keepers grow closer to each other; changed the way urban and suburban mothers interacted and constructed their activist strategies; diluted the idealized sense of black unity; and helped lgbts at least understand their fragmented community. As this study has shown, history helps us understand how and why marchers made or did not make particular choices. Had participants grasped this history, they might have realized just how hard the task of overcoming it would be. Still, American history also shows us that the nation has survived and Americans have persevered through similar periods like that of the late twentieth century and, if nothing else, we can use this knowledge as a catalyst for building on what was done right, and for the stretching that is needed to be at peace in future America.

The first years of the new millennium brought new marches by the same groups as those analyzed here. A cursory look reveals that they spawned some of the same debates on the value of marches, some new attempts at stretching, and some failures as well. For example, the Promise Keepers continued to gather but at much smaller events. As mentioned earlier, once it dropped its admission fee of sixty dollars so that men of less means could attend their stadium events, the organization became financially insolvent. It laid off much of its staff, and PK gatherings since 1997 have been much smaller events. While the Promise Keepers were continuing to try to reach across race, class, and generations to foster change in men and their various relationships, African Americans held a Million Family March (2000), a Million More March (2005), and a twentieth-year anniversary march at which the theme of unity was reiterated. Women were encouraged to join men at all three marches, but lgbts were again denied the podium microphone. At the 2005 Million More March, for example, arrangements were made for Keith Boykin, president of the National Black Justice Coalition, to speak on homophobia in black America, but, like Cleo Manago at the Million Man March, Boykin was pulled from the program at the last minute.[5] On the Million Woman March front, the first-year anniversary found Asia Coney and Phile Chionesu in separate black women's organizations. Chionesu was heading the Million Woman March Universal Movement, and Coney joined the nine women who had walked out of organizing meetings prior to the march over issues of class and leadership. Their organization was called the Sisters of the Million Woman March. Reportedly, the two parted company over Chionesu's unapologetic dictatorial style. Although they henceforth traveled separate roads, both committed themselves to serving and speaking on behalf of black women.[6] Sexual minorities also continued to speak out for themselves. Those who went to the National Mall in 2009 marched with a crowd noticeably younger than those who had marched previously. Some older marchers wondered whether this generation, weaned as they were on Facebook and mobile phones, would choose their forebears' "antiquated" form of personal political expression. As it turned out, they marched not just because they deemed marching effective but also for the fellowship that their screens and devices could not provide.[7] And finally, though the Million Mom March folded into the Brady Campaign to Prevent Gun Violence in 2002, in 2004 another Million Mom March was held on May 9. Not nearly as well attended as the original march—reportedly only a few hundred people showed up—a greater percentage of the marchers were minorities than in 2000, and a major sponsor was the black woman's magazine *Essence*.[8] In 2015, another group, organized by Mothers for Justice United, held a Million Moms March to protest police violence against African Americans. Unaffiliated with the original Million Mom March, this group of mostly black women marched to address the pressing issue of police killings of African Americans, an issue that went unaddressed by the Brady Campaign or the original Million Mom March.[9]

Invariably, this study compels comparisons with these more contemporary marches as well as gatherings such as Occupy Wall Street and #BlackLivesMatter. In the absence of the deep research that generated this analysis, it is hard to make definitive comparisons, especially since the passing of time yields a historical perspective that is just not accessible with contemporary events. It goes without saying, though, that these gatherings helped its participants understand who they were as American citizens, assured them that their feelings were legitimate and that they were not alone with their sentiments, and encouraged them to work out a new relationship with the nation they called home. Since both Occupy Wall Street and #BlackLivesMatter were and are interracial and intergenerational, in-depth research is needed to see how difference was worked out on the ground; to discern how participants stretched to be inclusive; to determine the nature of coalition-building across identities; and to ascertain the relationship between the personal and the political.

What we do know about these latter events offers points of comparison and suggests direction for future research. For example, unlike the marches covered in this work, Occupy Wall Street and #BlackLivesMatter grew out of very specific events. The former grew from the 2008 recession, whose roots could be traced back to hedge funds and the manipulation of the market by the real estate industry, banks, and Wall Street brokers. The latter was spawned after the 2012 killing of black Florida teenager Trayvon Martin; mushroomed after the killing of Michael Brown in Ferguson, Missouri; and grew exponentially with each police killing of an unarmed black person. It could be argued that Occupy Wall Street and #BlackLivesMatter were more protest oriented than any of the marches covered here, but future research may well find that personal and interpersonal issues were just as influential in participant motivation and experience as they were in the 1990s marches. Future research will also have to take into account the impact of social media, which began to affect organizing in the early years of the new century. We know, for example, that some participants of the Million Mom March cited organizing on the Internet as a reason for the low participation of minorities. Going forward, we will have to assess the impact of texting, Facebook, Twitter, Instagram, and other social media platforms on organizing, particularly their ability to impart a "thick" experience and make people feel whole.

Analysis of these latter marches will also have to account for the effects of 9/11, which thus far for Americans is the signature event of the twenty-first century. In the 1990s, Americans could ponder the meaning of happiness and their relationship to the nation and world devoid of issues of national security. How that cataclysm changed each individual's national identity has yet to be fully analyzed by historians, who are just now beginning to understand the 1990s as a troubled decade, a time when so many American citizens felt lost and traveled to a march or gathering to resituate themselves in the nation they called home.

Notes

Introduction

1. For a lucid discussion of postmodernity, see esp. Harvey, *Condition of Postmodernity*, 284–306.

2. This book uses lowercase letters for *lgbt*. According to *The Chicago Manual of Style*, the names of government agencies, network broadcasting companies, associations, fraternal and service organization, unions, and other groups are usually set in capital letters. Because writing out *lesbian, gay, bisexual, and transgender* makes for awkward writing, and because this abbreviation does not stand for an organization, I have chosen to use lowercase letters: lgbt. *The Chicago Manual of Style*, 16th ed. (Chicago: University of Chicago Press, 2010), 490. The book does not use the abbreviation *lgbtq* because, during the 1990s, queer identity was in the process of being defined.

Chapter 1. A New-Age Search for Order

1. "Editorial/Public Pulse," sunrise ed., 6–9.

2. Hamil, "Promise Keepers Say," Metro sec., D1.

3. Melone, "Promise Keepers without Religion," City and State sec., 1B.

4. "Keep Talking," local ed., 1, 2, 3, B1.

5. Chafe, *Unfinished Journey*, 517; Stein, "Wild '90s," 10.

6. Stein, "Wild '90s," 10.

7. See, for example, Layard, *Happiness*, 30.

8. Stein, "Wild '90s," 10; Moghaddam, "Happiness, Faith, Friends, and Fortune." Moghaddam's article has an excellent review of the extensive literature on this subject. Fogel, *Fourth Great Awakening*, 176.

9. Layard, "Secrets of Happiness," 28; Ahmed, "Multiculturalism and the Promise of Happiness," 122–23.

10. H. R. Luce, "The American Century" (1941), reprinted in M. J. Hogan, *Ambiguous Legacy*, 11–29.

11. Scales, "Restoration Is Focus," national/foreign sec., A1.

12. Schaper, "Promise Keepers Can Do Real Good," Viewpoints, A49.

13. Gergen, "Promises Worth Keeping," 78.

14. Baldwin, "Speech," Editorial sec., 10A.

15. Gutierrez-Mier, "S.A. Residents to Join D.C. Gay Rights March," Metro/South Texas sec., 6B.

16. Grier, "Next Hard Steps," United States sec., 1.

17. Twomey, "Appeal of the PK," Metro sec., D1; Barker, "Group Has Promises to Keep," A1.

18. Morganfield, "Building the Million Man March," 37.

19. Eugene Robinson, *Disintegration*.

20. Fletcher and Brown, "We Are Countless in Unity," A1.

21. Janofsky, "At Million Woman March," sec. 1, 1.

22. Bryant, "Black Women Plan to March," A33.

23. Fletcher and Harris, "United They'll Stand," A1.

24. Fulwood, "Blacks Not in Lock Step," A4.

25. *Promise Keepers Men's Study Bible*, xviii.

26. Ibid., 884. In a study insert next to Ezek. 22:30, the study bible says that God's request for a man to stand in the gap "is a mighty challenge to any man who cares about the people around him." It asks, "Will you be God's man in your sphere of influence?"

27. See, for example, Murphy, "Seeking God, Man to Man," Metro sec., B1.

28. Moriwaki, "Promise Keepers Returning," A1.

29. Pettus, "Men Who Keep Their Promise," Five Star Lift ed., Editorial sec., 11B. How successful PK was in fulfilling its promises and the adequacy of the personal approach of this march and the Million Man and Woman Marches are subjects that subsequent chapters take up. The purpose for now is to acknowledge the sentiment that propelled marchers to their gatherings.

30. Centers for Disease Control and Prevention, "Gun Deaths among Children and Teens." Statistics on the number of gun deaths vary depending on who is reporting them. Pro-gun advocates minimize the number while gun-control advocates exaggerate them. This study uses statistics by government agencies such as the FBI, the General Accounting Office, and the Centers for Disease Control.

31. Tyson, "Marching Moms Come," USA sec., 1.

32. Illescas, "Moms Meet," Denver and the West sec., B1.

33. Lynn Smith, "L.A. Moms Fighting," Southern California Living sec., E1.

34. Niederberger, "Million Mom March Group Continues," South ed., Metro sec., S9.

35. Stroup, "Moms Vow to Continue," Metro sec., B1.

36. As we will see, the advocacy of gun control and gun safety was an issue that split the Million Mom movement. For now, however, it is important to note their common concern with cultural breakdown. Similarly, although anti-gun-control

groups opposed the solutions offered by the Million Moms, they too faulted the "culture."

37. Liu, "Vigil Memorializes," Metro sec., B3.

38. This is my reading of the conclusions drawn by sociologist Judith Stacey, who has written two excellent books on the postmodern family. See Stacey, *Brave New Families* and *In the Name of the Family*.

39. Monica Haynes, "Black Women Headed for Rally," State sec., A14.

40. Monica Haynes, "Marching for Little Tony," Editorial sec., A15.

41. Lesnick, "Celebrating Our Families."

42. Pettus, "Men Who Keep Their Promise," Five Star Lift ed., Editorial sec., 11B.

43. Maxwell, "Farrakhan as Seen from the Inside," City ed., Perspectives sec., 1D.

44. Berlant, *Cruel Optimism*, 24.

45. Dawson, *Blacks in and out*, 180. A deeper look at these explanations would take us far afield of the purpose of this book, hence they are purposely given only cursory notation here. However, the subject of happiness is revisited throughout this book and in the conclusion.

46. Wiebe, *Search for Order*, 44, 63, 166, 170.

47. Lears, *No Place of Grace*. Lears discusses the same period as Wiebe, but whereas Wiebe opens with the world in chaos because of the forces of modernity, Lears sees the individual in turmoil because of these forces. Whereas Wiebe proceeds to describe an era in which individuals try to control the external pressures and new society that develops in the wake of modernity, Lears sees modernity and the rational way progressives deal with it as part of the problems that turn-of-the-century Americans wrestle with. Whereas Wiebe does not concern himself as much with the internal or psychic needs of turn-of-the-century Americans, the individual and the psychic is at the center of Lears's study.

48. Lears, *No Place of Grace*, 42, 57, 58.

49. Generally identified as Great Awakenings, historians identify other periods besides that of the late nineteenth and early twentieth century as periods of extensive readjustment or "revitalization," a term used by anthropologist Anthony Wallace. As outlined and explained by William McLoughlin, these periods include: the Puritan Awakening, 1610–40; the First Great Awakening (in America), 1730–60; the Second Great Awakening 1800–30; the Third Great Awakening, 1890–1920; and the Fourth Great Awakening, circa 1960–90. See McLoughlin, *Revivals, Awakenings, and Reform*, 10. Robert Fogel outlines roughly the same dates for America's awakenings, but carries the Fourth Great Awakening through the 1990s with no ending date. See Fogel, *Fourth Great Awakening*, 19–28. For an explanation of revitalization movements, see Wallace, "Revitalization Movements."

50. Wallace, "Revitalization Movements," 265.

51. Coontz, *Way We Really Are*, 44–50; Harvey, *Condition of Postmodernity*, 330–31; Stacey, *Brave New Families*, 256; Stacey, *In the Name of the Family*, 13.

52. Stacey, *In the Name of the Family*, quote on 13; Coontz, *Way We Really Are*, 44–50; Harvey, *Condition of Postmodernity*, 330–31; Stacey, *Brave New Families*, 256.

53. For a general overview of this period in American history, see Chafe, *Unfinished Journey*, 455–524; Paul Boyer, *Promises to Keep*, 384–478.

54. See, for example, Gitlin, "Identity Politics," Metro sec., Op Ed, B9.

55. Fogel, *Fourth Great Awakening*, 193–94.

56. Cited in ibid., 194.

57. Ibid.

58. Eugene Taylor, *Shadow Culture*, 7, 287–89.

59. Comparisons have been made between McCartney and Billy Sunday, an early twentieth-century evangelical lay preacher who, like McCartney, was a sport figure—in Sunday's case, a baseball player. Sunday proselytized during the period some call the Third Great Awakening, a period that, as we have seen, had much in common with the late twentieth century.

60. Tyson, "New Stir Surrounds Men's Role," United States sec., 1.

61. "Perspective on Promise Keepers."

62. Peter Gomes, minister at the Harvard University Memorial Church in Cambridge, Massachusetts, and author of *The Good Book: Reading the Bible with Mind and Heart* stated that "people . . . have decided that they are going to really search for the Grail. You can feel it across the country: Everywhere you go . . . there is this hunger and thirsting after the deep things of life." Quoted in Marquand, "America Taps Religious Roots," United States sec., 1.

63. Murphy, "Seeking God, Man to Man," Metro sec., B1.

64. Madhubuti and Karenga, *Million Man March/ Day of Absence*, 151.

65. Statement made by Bob Law, host of a nationally syndicated call-in radio show. See Walsh, "Criticism," A22.

66. Schmoke, "Huge Family Reunion," Perspective sec., 7F.

67. Bock, "'We Are Here to Rebuild,'" News sec., 1A.

68. Chethik, "Million Man March Expands," Arts and Living sec., 5F.

69. Rojas, "Shoulder to Shoulder," final ed., News sec., A1.

70. This was a major criticism of the march, an opinion held by Earl Ofari Hutchinson, a Los Angeles–based publisher and author. See Fulwood, "Blacks Not in Lock Step," A4.

71. Jaffe, "Black Men March," Metro ed., Florida sec., 6.

72. Gross, "D.C. March Spurs," Local sec., B1.

73. Rojas, "Shoulder to Shoulder," final ed., News sec., A1.

74. Afro-America@National News. See also Mamie Locke, "Deconstruct to Reconstruct: African American Women in the Post–Civil Rights Era," in Alex-Assensoh and Hanks, *Black and Multiracial Politics*, 375–95; Radford-Hill, *Further to Fly*, 100.

75. Centers for Disease Control and Prevention, "Negative Mood and Urban versus Rural Residence," 5. Unfortunately, other minority groups were not included in the study.

76. Milloy, "Happiness Survey," Metro sec., B1.

77. Hancock, *Politics of Disgust*, 56.

78. Harris-Perry, *Sister Citizen*, 245–46.

79. Kenna, "March of 'Awakening,'" News sec., 1.

80. Brand-Williams, "What They're Saying," 7A.

81. Ibid.

82. Spratling, "Detroit's Leader," F6.

83. Lee, "Thousands of Women Share Wounds."

84. See the transcript of the "Show of Strength" segment that aired on the *PBS News-hour*: http://www.pbs.org/newshour/bb/social_issues-july-dec97-women_10-27/.

85. Bowles, "Million Woman March Will Unite."

86. Kenna, "March of 'Awakening,'" News sec., 1.

87. Winter, "Don't Like Guns," Home Front sec., 2F.

88. Crowder, "Two Mom's Stories," Local sec., 7A.

89. Gita Smith, "Georgians See Parade," News sec., 3A.

90. Knock, "Local Residents Reflect," Local sec., 3A.

91. Stone, "Thousand Gather," Front sec., A12.

92. Swanda, "From Gay Pilot to Gay Activist."

93. Rodriguez, "Gay Wichitans," Local and State sec., 9A; see also Stone, "Thousand Gather"; Ly, "Making a Public Declaration," Metro sec., C1.

94. See, for example, how Donna Dees-Thomas got involved in the movement—a subject that this work details at length in chapter 6; Dees-Thomas and Hendrie, *Looking for a Few Good Moms*, xxiii, 3–5.

95. Gerber, "Teen's Life Was Cut Short," 6A.

96. Lucy Barber, *Marching on Washington*, 3.

97. Morrow, "Why Mass Marches Have Lost."

98. Grady, "It'll Be a War," Opinion, syndicated columns, A25.

99. Chen, "Unity on the Mall," National Desk sec., A1.

100. Towns, "Potential Marchers Reluctant," E14.

101. Dickerson, "Tactics of a Bygone Era," Editorial sec., A12.

Chapter 2. Looking for a Few Good Men

1. Louis Farrakhan, "Day of Atonement," in Madhubuti and Karenga, *Million Man March/Day of Absence*, 15.

2. Bill McCartney, "Promise Makers," *Policy Review* 85 (September 1997), 14–19; Harris, "Promise Keepers Say," Metro sec., D1.

3. Newton, *From Panthers to Promise Keepers*, 214.

4. Freeman, "Go Ahead, Black Man," Five Star Lift ed., War sec., 13C.

5. Ibid.

6. See, for example, Rosen, "Feminist Send-Off," home ed., Metro sec., B9; Canellos, "Groups Making Reform," city ed., Metro/Region sec., 1; Newton, *From Panthers to Promise Keepers*, 1–26.

7. Wolf, "Men at Work," News sec., 9A; Morin and Wilson, "Men Were Driven," final ed., A1; see also a 1995 Kansas City–based National Center for Fathering survey cited in the *Washington Post* in Murphy, "Seeking God, Man to Man," Metro sec., B1.

8. Kimmel, *Manhood in America*, 240; Coontz, *Way We Really Are*, 139.

9. See Griswold, *Fatherhood in America*, 219–70; Gavanas, *Fatherhood Politics*; Cross, *Men to Boys*; and Newton, *From Panthers to Promise Keepers*, all of whom devote most of their books to this subject. See also Kimmel, *Manhood in America*, 187–282.

10. Griswold, *Fatherhood in America*, 269; Newton, *From Panthers to Promise Keepers*, 157–60.

11. Newton, *From Panthers to Promise Keepers*, 173. The description "angry white males" was used by several journalists who wrote about PK. See, for example, Terry Mattingly, "Sermons by Black Ministers," Religion/Spotlight sec., 9D.

12. Kimmel, *Manhood in America*, 240.

13. Coontz, *Way We Really Are*, 31.

14. Stacey, *Brave New Families*, 44, 101.

15. McCartney, "Promise Makers," 14–15; Gabriel Escobar, "He's the Coach for the Faithful—or the Far Right?," *Washington Post*, September 28, 1997, Sunday ed., A1.

16. *Promise Keepers Men's Study Bible*, 1170.

17. Goodstein, "Men Pack RFK," final ed., A1.

18. "Look at Promise Keepers," Outlook sec., C3.

19. Dave Condren, "Area Men to Join in Massive Rally," *Buffalo News*, September 28, 1997, Local sec., 1B; "What People Are Saying about the Baton Rouge Conference," conference testimonies—Baton Rouge, http://www.promisekeepers.org, accessed 1997; "What People Are Saying about the Milwaukee Conference," conference testimonies—Milwaukee, http://www.promisekeepers.org, accessed 1997.

20. Allen, "Promise Keepers: A Growing Movement Returns," Today's Focus sec., 1A.

21. Singhania, "About 12,000 Men Expected."

22. Jennifer Robinson, "PK Movement Is Not as Promising," Editorial/Op-Ed sec., B2.

23. Vara, "He's Ok, I'm Ok," Religion sec., 1.

24. Maller and Jones, "Men Find Mission," News sec., 1.

25. Kennedy, "Better Promise Keepers," Commentary sec., 6.

26. *Promise Keepers Men's Study Bible*, xviii.

27. Scrivener, "In Changing World," News sec., A1.

28. Ballingrud, "Keeping the Faith," City and State sec., 1B.

29. Wolf, "Men at Work," News sec., 9A.

30. Stowe, "Promise Keepers Keeping the Faith," Town News Extra sec., H1; Rico, a Cape Verdean, discusses his minority status in PK, an issue taken up shortly.

31. Wolf, "Men at Work," News sec., 9A.

32. Romano, "Promise Keepers Helps," Local sec., 5A.

33. Scrivener, "In Changing World," News sec., A1.

34. *Promise Keepers Men's Study Bible*, John 13:5–12, 1165.

35. Herrmann, "Promise Keepers Grapple," News sec., 17.

36. Both cited in Gray, "Promise, Promises," metropolitan ed., FYI sec., F1.

37. Hodges, "Promise Keeper Turns," St. Bernard sec., 6G.

38. Putney, *Muscular Christianity*, 24.

39. Ibid. See also Bederman, *Manliness and Civilization*, 77–120; Rotundo, *American Manhood*, 222–46.

40. Susan Hogan, "Keepers' Good-Guy Image," metro ed., Faith and Values sec., 5B.

41. Bright et al., *Seven Promises of a Promise Keeper*.

42. Bright et al., *Seven Promises*, 73–81. Scholar Judith Newton also notes that Evans was more the exception than the rule. See Newton, *From Panthers to Promise Keepers*, 226–27.

43. Murphy, "Seeking God, Man to Man," Metro sec., B1.

44. Uhlenhuth and Gray, "70,000 Jam," National/World sec., A1.

45. McNamara, "They Have Promises to Keep."

46. Raleigh Washington, Glen Kehrein, and Claude V. King, "Help Me Understand," in Bright et al., *Seven Promises*, 163.

47. Renfroe, "Promise Keepers Say Rally Promotes," metro ed., Polk sec., 1.

48. Moriwaki, "Promise Keepers Returning," final ed., News sec., A1.

49. B. Maria Baldridge, "The Definitions behind the Discourse: Analysis of the Public Discourse Surrounding the Promise Keepers," Incidental.org, accessed November 10, 2003, http://www.incidental.org/citizenjane/writing/promise_keepers .html; Emerson and Smith, *Divided by Faith*, 65–66.

50. Herrick, "Promise Keepers Targeting," Two Star ed., Religion sec., 1.

51. Akizuki, "Promise Keeper Hires," Saturday 2D ed., A22.

52. Hogan-Albach, "Promise Keepers Say Prayer," metro ed., News sec., 1A.

53. Joseph McCormick 2d and Sekou Franklin, "Expressions of Racial Consciousness in the African American Community: Data from the Million Man March," in Alex-Assensoh, and Hanks, *Black and Multiracial Politics in America*, 322.

54. Tidwell, *State of Black America*, 249.

55. Tucker, "That Old-Time Religion."

56. "Surveys Show Few Black Men," 32.

57. McCormick and Franklin, "Expressions of Racial Consciousness," 315–36; Brossard and Fletcher, "Last Year's Gathering," A14; "Surveys Show," 32; McCormick, "How African American Men View."

58. Given the myriad reasons that men gave for attending, the most consistent answers came down to this: almost 30 percent said they attended to show support for black families. Twenty-five percent said they participated because they wanted to show support for black men taking more responsibility for their families and communities, and another 25 percent participated to demonstrate black unity.

59. Eugene Robinson, *Disintegration*, 7.

60. For a comprehensive analysis of these issues, see the articles in Tucker and Mitchell-Kernan, *Decline in Marriage*.

61. Lochhead, "Civil Rights Leader Won't Support," News sec., A4; O'Hare et al., "African Americans in the 1990s," 14.

62. Alexander, *New Jim Crow*, 96. For an analysis of the effect that incarceration has on marriage, families, and child development, see Robert J. Sampson, "Unemployment and Imbalanced Sex Ratios: Race-Specific Consequences for Family Structure and Crime," and William A. Darity Jr. and Samuel I. Myers Jr., "Family Structure and the Marginalization of Black Men: Policy Implications," both in Tucker and Mitchell-Kernan, *Decline in Marriage*, 229–54, 263–308.

63. Terry, "Black Man March Is Cheered, Jeered," Sunday third ed., National sec., A27.

64. Cose, *Rage of a Privileged Class*, 6–8.

65. Superville, "Marchers See Rally," Final Markets ed., News sec., 1.

66. See, for example, Green, "Board Resist Call," Connecticut sec., A3; Yusuf Davis, "Around Town," Extra sec., 1D; Ripley, "Pride, Peace Reign," 3B; Eric Young, "San Diegans Step Off Bus," News sec., A1. See also the heartfelt testimonies in Sadler, *Atonement*.

67. "Remarks before One Million Men by Reverend Jesse L. Jackson, Sr., Monday, October 16, 1995," in Madhubuti and Karenga, *Million Man March/Day of Absence*, 34–35.

68. Dickerson, "Tactics of a Bygone Era," Editorial sec., 12A; Fulwood, "Blacks Not in Lock Step," National Desk, A4.

69. Sadler, *Atonement*, 131.

70. Jaffe, "Black Men March," Metro ed., Florida sec., 6.

71. Edward Boyer, "Black Leaders Seek to Sign Up," home ed., Metro sec., B1.

72. Sadler, *Atonement*, 133–34.

73. Biers and Brimberg, "Sobering Event," A10.

74. Maxwell, "Farrakhan as Seen from the Inside," City ed., Perspectives sec., 1D.

75. Sanchez, "Men Invigorated," Metropolitan ed., Metropolitan sec., C1.

76. Rojas, "Shoulder to Shoulder," final ed., News sec., A1.

77. Best, "Area Marchers Reflect," Five Star Lift ed., News 1A.

78. Childress, "Portraits," final ed., A19.

79. Rojas, "Shoulder to Shoulder," final ed., News sec., A1.

80. Loeb, "Portraits," final ed., A23.

81. Freeman, "Go Ahead, Black Man," Five Star Lift ed., War sec., 13C.

82. Dwyer, "Numbers Don't Tally," News sec., 4.

83. Linda Wheeler, "I'm Going to Keep At It," A24.

84. Ripley, "Pride, Peace Reign," 3B; Maxwell, "Farrakhan as Seen from the Inside," City ed., Perspectives sec., 1D.

85. Millner, "Journey Brings Hope," News sec., 21.

86. For this history, see Muhammad, *Condemnation of Blackness*, and Stabile, *White Victims, Black Villains*.

87. Stabile, *White Victims, Black Villains*, 162–64.

88. Byfield, *Savage Portrayals*, 1–2, 169–71, 183–85.

89. See, for example, Swedenburg, "Homies in the Hood."

90. Shepard, "Fathers and Sons Revel," National sec., 9A.

91. Bock, "'We Are Here to Rebuild,'" News sec., 1A.

92. Scholars and journalists have compared the two. See Boyd, *Black Men Worshipping*, 64, 67; Newton, *From Panthers to Promise Keepers*, 29; Canellos, "Groups Making Reform," city ed., Metro/Region sec., 1; O'Clery, "Now White Males Take," city ed., World News Letter from America, 10; "Really Late Show," News sec., 14A; Rosen, "Feminist Send-Off," home ed., Metro sec., B9.

93. See, for example, Coontz, *Way We Really Are*, 139.

94. Gutman, *Family in Slavery and Freedom*, 185–229, 432–76.

95. Wilgoren, "In the Land of Promise," final ed., Metro sec., B1.

96. Conference Testimonies, Milwaukee Conference, accessed August 1, 2001, http://www.promisekeepers.org.

97. Uhlenhuth and Gray, "70,000 Jam 'Pep Rally,'" National/World sec., A1.

98. Norris P. West, "High Goal Set," final ed., Telegraph (News) sec., 7A.

99. Penn and Sanchez, "KC Crowd Marches," Metropolitan ed., B1.

100. Rodriguez, "Show of Unity," A1.

101. Edward Boyer, "Million Man May End Up Short," A29.

102. Rodriguez, "Show of Unity," A1.

103. Ibid.

104. Milloy, "Stepping In," final ed., Metro sec., B1.

105. Nate Smith, "One in a Million," sooner ed., Editorial sec., A7.

106. Quoted in Roediger, *Wages of Whiteness*, 28.

107. Ibid., 23–40, 55–64, 95–131; Bederman, *Manliness and Civilization*, 1–44.

108. Quoted in Bederman, *Manliness and Civilization*, 34.

109. Quoted in ibid., 210.

110. Ibid., 50.

111. Hood, *Begrimed and Black*, 182.

112. Winthrop Jordan, *White over Black*, 94.

113. Ibid., 17–20; Gen. 9:21–25, the Official King James Bible online, http://www.kingjamesbibleonline.org/Genesis-Chapter-9/.

114. Boyd, *Black Men Worshipping*, 24–32.

115. Douglass, *Narrative*, 89.

116. James Oliver Horton and Lois E. Horton, "Violence, Protest, and Identity," in Horton, *Free People of Color*, 83.

117. Kimmel, *Manhood in America*, 54.

118. Quoted in Harding, Kelley, and Lewis, *We Changed the World*, 28.

119. Estes, *I Am a Man!*, 4.

120. Horton and Horton, "Violence, Protest, and Identity," in Horton, *Free People of Color*, 95.

121. Giddings, *When and Where I Enter*, 318.

122. See, for example, Summers, *Manliness and Its Discontents*.

123. Estes, *I Am a Man!*, 62.

124. Ibid., 63.

125. Rojas, "Shoulder to Shoulder," final ed., News sec., A1.

126. Bright et al., *Seven Promises*, 73–75.

127. Dickerson, "Tactics of a Bygone Era," Editorial sec., A12.

128. "Farrakhan's Mixed Message," final ed., Editorial sec., 10A.

129. Fletcher and Brossard, "Poll," Three Star ed., A6.

130. See Earl Ofari Hutchinson, *The Assassination of the Black Male Image* (New York: Touchstone, 1994).

131. Fletcher and Brossard, "Poll," Three Star ed., sec. A6.

132. Shaffer, "Surprising Many," National News sec., 19A.

133. Du Bois, *Souls of Black Folk*, 102.

134. Sanchez, "Men Invigorated by March," Metropolitan ed., Metropolitan sec., C1.

135. Penn and Sanchez, "KC Crowd Marches," Metropolitan ed., B1; see also Grier, "Next Hard Steps," United States sec., 1.

136. West, "Baltimore Men Flock," final ed., Telegraph sec., 6A.

137. Stricker, "New Racial Ideology," 61.

138. Stammer, "Promise Keepers Dodges Skeptics," home ed., Metro sec., B4.

139. Boyd, *Black Men Worshipping*, 65; Stricker, "New Racial Ideology," 10. Stricker cites Emerson and Smith, *Divided by Faith*, 68.

140. Stricker, "New Racial Ideology," 16; Bartkowski, *Promise Keepers*, 2–4.

141. Stricker, "New Racial Ideology," 99.

142. Ibid., 89–115.

143. Emerson and Smith, *Divided by Faith*, 69–92, 170–71.

144. Sharn, "Ministers' Promise," final ed., News sec., 2A.

145. Nolan, "Promise Land," Metro sec., B1.

146. Hamblin, "Patronizing Promise," first ed., Denver and the West B07.

147. Stricker, "New Racial Ideology," 5.

148. Morganfield, "Each One, Reach One," Two Star ed., sec. A33. See also Rodgers-Melnick, "Making Their Promises," Two Star ed., Local sec., A1.

149. Goodstein, "For Christian Men's Group," late ed., National Desk sec., A12.

150. Nolan, "30,000 Men Gathering," National sec., A1.

151. Pettus, "Men Who Keep Their Promise," Five Star Lift ed., Editorial sec., 11B.

152. Moriwaki, "Promise Keepers Returning," Sunday final ed., News sec., A1.

153. Page, "NOW Suggestion a Promise Worth Keeping," Three Star ed., sec. A18.

154. Moriwaki, "Promise Keepers Returning," Sunday final ed., News sec., A1.

155. Emerson and Smith, *Divided by Faith*, 105–7, 115–34.

156. Ibid.; Merrill, "How Could Women Fear," final ed., Editorial sec., 2H.

157. Mike Barber, "Men's Group Rallies," final ed., News sec., A1.

158. Nolan, "Promise Land," Metro sec., B1.

159. Goodstein, "For Christian Men's Group," late ed., National Desk sec., A12.

160. Lewis, "Black-White Differences in Attitudes toward Homosexuality and Gay

Rights," 66; Herek and Capitanio, "Black Heterosexuals' Attitudes toward Lesbians and Gay Men in the United States," 96, 100; Lemelle Jr. and Battle, "Black Masculinity in Attitudes toward Gay Males," 39–51.

161. Boyd, *Black Men Worshipping*, 64; Bartkowski, *Promise Keepers*, 80.

162. Nolan, "30,000 Men Gathering," National sec., A1; see also Stricker, "New Racial Ideology," 18–19.

163. "Farrakhan Speaks on Homosexuality: Is It Natural?," YouTube video, 6:37, posted by Ahmad 770 on May 31, 2012, https://www.youtube.com/watch?v =VCDfqXN9AHw, originally aired in 1972 on SOUL TV, New York, NY. Accessed July 13, 2016.

164. Cited by Monroe, "Louis Farrakhan's Ministry," 275.

165. Cleo Manago, founder of the Black Men's Xchange, an organization of gay and bisexual males, had been slated to speak but was pulled from the program at the last minute. Cleo Manago, "A Day of Replenishment from a Reflecting Pool of Black," *Whazzup Magazine*, n.d., Schomberg Center for Research in Black Culture, Black Gay and Lesbian Archive, New York Public Library (hereafter cited as Schomberg BGLA).

166. Bartkowski, "Breaking Walls."

167. Becker, *Gay TV and Straight America*, 23–37; Sedgwick, *Epistemology of the Closet*, 182–212.

Chapter 3. Standing By Their Men

1. Newton, *From Panthers to Promise Keepers*, 31–32.

2. "Public Pulse," 24.

3. Lambert, "Much to Fear," A12.

4. Malveaux, "A Woman's Place," C12.

5. Williams, "Absent from the March," E1.

6. A. Leon Higginbotham Jr., "I Couldn't Separate," A34.

7. Newton, *From Panthers to Promise Keepers*, 31–32.

8. Although there are many different kinds of feminism, I use the term here the way my subjects use the term. Sometimes they used the term *radical feminism* to distinguish what they perceived as extreme views, but often they just used the word *feminism* or *feminist*. As you will see, as this essay proceeds it problematizes the term.

9. Fisher, "Million Man March; Behind the Scenes," final ed., Style sec., D1.

10. Fletcher, "Black Men Jam Mall," A1.

11. Madhubuti and Karenga, *Million Man March/Day of Absence*, 140–54.

12. Fletcher and Brossard, "March Has Solid Support," A1.

13. "How Black Academics Viewed," 61.

14. Parrott, "Dale Came Home," in Claussen, *Standing on the Promises*, 161.

15. Barker, "Group Has Promises to Keep," Final Chaser sec., B1.

16. Fields, "Power of a Promise," final ed., Nation/World sec., 19.

17. Unless otherwise noted, throughout this chapter the term *family* is used to describe the two-parent, heterosexual, nuclear family.

18. Cantave and Harrison, "Marriage and African Americans." See also the Associated Press report stating that at the end of the 1990s, 27 percent of those describing themselves as born-again Christians were currently or had previously been divorced, compared to 24 percent among other adults. Baptists had the highest divorce rate of any Christian denomination (34 percent) and were more likely to be divorced than atheists and agnostics. See Associated Press, "Baptists Have Highest Divorce Rate."

19. "Letters from Readers," News sec., 18A; Maller and Jones, "Men Find Mission," News sec., 1.

20. Stammer, "Teaching Patriarchs," Metro Desk sec., 1.

21. Gray, "What Promise to Keep?," FYI sec., E1.

22. Allen, "Promise Keepers: A Growing Movement," Focus sec., 1A.

23. Vara, "He's Ok, I'm Ok," Religion sec., 1.

24. Tarjanyi, "Men Flock to Learn," Religion sec., 2.

25. Cimons and Zeuthen, "Participants, Doubters Ponder Meaning," National Desk sec., A5.

26. Gray, "What Promises to Keep?," FYI sec., E1.

27. Allen, "Promise Keepers: A Growing Movement," Focus sec., 1A.

28. Gray, "What Promises to Keep?," FYI sec., E1. See also Kenaga, "Fulfilling God's Role," in Claussen, *Standing on the Promises*, 168.

29. Iris Marion Young, "Logic of Masculinist Protection," 2–5.

30. Ibid.

31. Kandiyoti, "Bargaining with Patriarchy," 274–90. Historian Jacqueline Dowd Hall made this point somewhat differently. Describing the dynamic at work when chivalric white men came to the rescue of white women who were supposedly violated by black male rapists, Hall described the trade-off implicit in the protection the white woman received. According to Hall, "the right of the southern lady to protection presupposed her obligation to obey." In other words, men only rescued proper women—women who kept their place and behaved according to rules established by patriarchs. The protection, like the pedestal, thus became a prison, one that white Southern women escaped at their peril. See Hall, "'Mind That Burns in Each Body,'" in Snitow, Stansell, and Thompson, *Powers of Desire*, 335–36.

32. Romano, "Keeping the Promise of God," News/National/International sec., 16A.

33. Hamblin, "Roles of God and Responsible Fathers," Denver and the West sec., B7.

34. Eph. 5:22–25 in the King James Bible reads: "Wives, submit yourselves unto your own husbands, as unto the Lord. For the husband is the head of the wife, even as Christ is the head of the church; and he is the savior of the body. Therefore as the church is subject unto Christ, so let the wives be to their own husbands in every thing. Husbands, love your wives, even as Christ also loved the church, and gave himself for it." This verse reads differently in different bibles.

35. Butler, "Keeping Promises for Men Only," Editorials and Forum sec., B11.

36. Gray, "What Promises to Keep?," FYI sec., E1.

37. Valerie Bridgeman Davis, "Womanist/Feminist Lives with a Promise Keeper," in Claussen, *Standing on the Promises*, 154–60.

38. Stingl, "Journey of Spirit," News sec., 1.

39. Kenaga, "Fulfilling God's Role," in Claussen, *Standing on the Promises*, 167–68.

40. Stingl, "Journey of Spirit," News sec., 1.

41. Vara, "He's Ok, I'm Ok," Religion sec., 1.

42. Schaper, "Promise Keepers Can Do Real Good," Viewpoints sec., A49. This idea of complementary roles was not new. For example, in the nineteenth century, Sarah Grimke expressed the view that men and women were different but coequal. She resented the fact that men discriminated against women in the antislavery movement. She argued that women's childbearing and mothering made them different from men in the realm of the family, domestic, and social life. But in public and political matters, women were coequals. See Parker, *Articulating Rights*, 84–85.

43. In theorizing the nation, several scholars have made the point that the nation is imagined and configured like a family. Both are hierarchal and men control both. As hearth keepers, women birth children and transmit culture and thus reproduce the family and the nation. When men circumscribe the behavior of women, they simultaneously police the boundaries of family and nation and thereby control who is included and/or excluded in both. See, for example, the work of Anne McClintock and Nira Yuval-Davis: McClintock, "Family Feuds," and Yuval-Davis, "Gender and Nation."

44. Winner, "Wives, Daughters, Mothers, and Sisters," in Claussen, *Standing on the Promises*, 150–51.

45. Ibid.

46. "Christian Women's Declaration."

47. Ibid.

48. It is tempting to see PK women as theological feminists, yet there are several reasons to resist categorizing them as such. For one, theological feminists are a varied group themselves. Some are critical of racism, sexism, classism, and heterosexism, and some are not. Many endorse reproductive freedom and same-sex marriage, and some do not. Another reason to resist categorizing PK women as theological feminists has to do with the source material mined for this study. It allows for an analysis of PK women and the Promise Keepers but does not easily lend itself to an analysis of PK women and the church and/or religion.

49. Hutchins, "Papering Over a Rift."

50. Stacey, *Brave New Families*, 139–45, 260.

51. Griffith, *God's Daughters*, 208–9.

52. Fisher, "Million Man March; Behind the Scenes," final ed., Style sec., D1.

53. Battista, "FSU Women Unite."

54. Harris, "Despite Paradox," final ed., Metro sec., B1.

55. Cantave and Harrison, "Marriage and African Americans"; "Topics in Minority Health Homicide among Young Black Males—United States, 1978–1987," CDC,

Morbidity and Mortality Weekly Report 39, 869–73; Camp, "Incarceration Rates by Race"; Fingerhaut, Ingram, and Feldman, "Homicide Rates among US Teenagers and Young Adults"; Lichter et al., "Race and the Retreat from Marriage"; Collins, *Black Sexual Politics*, 80–81.

56. Fisher, "Million Man March; Behind the Scenes," final ed., Style sec., D1. Between 1950 and 2000 the percentage of never-married black women doubled from 20.7 percent to 42.4 percent. The percentage of African American women who were married declined from 62 percent to 36.1 percent between 1950 and 2000. Among white women the corresponding decline was from 66 percent to 57 percent. Trends in divorce have shown less difference between the races, rising from 3 percent to 11.7 percent among blacks and from 2 percent to 10.2 percent among whites. See Cantave and Harrison, "Marriage and African Americans."

57. Kerrill, "Black Women Split," late sports final ed., News sec., 14.

58. Asimov and Olszewski, "Hundreds of Bay Area Students Stay Home," News, 7. See also Mays and Davis, "Women's Reactions," News sec., A3.

59. Geneva Smitherman, "A Womanist Looks at the Million Man March," in Madhubuti and Karenga, *Million Man March/Day of Absence*, 105.

60. Kerrill, "Black Women Split," late sports final ed., News sec., 14.

61. Paul Shepard, "Exclusion Bothers Some Women," Metro sec., B8.

62. Kimberly Hayes Taylor, "Million Woman March," News sec., A1.

63. Longwood, "One Million Strong."

64. A work that takes up the issue of Stewart and Truth and the intersection of race and sex is Martha Jones, *All Bound Up Together*, 23–85. On stereotypes of black women and charges of being a race traitor, see White, *Ar'n't I a Woman?*, 2nd ed., 27–61, 176–77; White, *Too Heavy a Load*, 56–68, 216–23. For a discussion of recent charges against black women, see Alexander-Floyd, *Gender, Race, and Nationalism*, 109–45. Most of the essays in Toni Morrison's edited book *Race-ing Justice, Engendering Power* deal with some aspect of the idea of black women as race traitors.

65. Kerrill, "Black Women Split," late sports final ed., News sec., 14.

66. Paul Shepard, "Exclusion Bothers Some Women," Metro sec., B8.

67. "Many Women Attended March . . .," News sec., A8.

68. Charshee McIntyre, "Why Focus on the Men?," in Madhubuti and Karenga, *Million Man March/Day of Absence*, 114.

69. DeWitt, "Themes from the March," National Desk sec., B9.

70. Alexander-Floyd, *Gender, Race, and Nationalism*, 3.

71. Ibid., 75–107.

72. Geneva Smitherman, "A Womanist Looks at the Million Man March," in Madhubuti and Karenga, *Million Man March/Day of Absence*, 104.

73. Fisher, "Million Man March; Behind the Scenes," final ed., Style sec., D1.

74. Reed, "Buck Passing," in Madhubuti and Karenga, *Million Man March/Day of Absence*, 129–33. For a more extensive discussion of the way black feminists have been villainized, see Alexander-Floyd, *Gender, Race, and Nationalism*, 71–74, 109–45.

75. Shaw, *What a Woman Ought to Be*, 14, 92.

76. Editorial, *Baltimore Afro-American*, November 8, 1997. "From the AFRO website."

77. Harris, "Despite Paradox," final ed., Metro sec., B1.

78. Paul Shepard, "Exclusion Bothers Some Women," Metro sec., B8.

79. Haynes, "Million Woman March Powering Up," Local sec., B5.

80. Marita Golden, *Saving Our Sons: Raising Black Children in a Turbulent* World (New York: Anchor Books, 1995) 8; Milloy, "Stepping In," Metro sec., B1.

81. Golden, *Saving Our Sons*, 7. This subject is taken up in greater detail in the final chapter of this book.

82. Geneva Smitherman, "A Womanist Looks at the Million Man March," in Madhubuti and Karenga, *Million Man March/Day of Absence*, 104–5.

83. Greene, "Welcome for Women," A21.

84. "Many Women Attended March . . .," News sec., A8.

85. McCraven, "Day of Unity," Perspective sec., E1.

86. Harris, "Despite Paradox," final ed., Metro sec., B1.

87. Hutchins, "Papering Over a Rift."

88. Alexander-Floyd, *Gender, Race, and Nationalism*, 73.

89. Carol Mattingly, *Well-Tempered Women*, 13–38, 96–120.

90. Ibid., 17. For an example of a black women who used this tactic, see Martha Jones, *All Bound Up Together*, 153.

91. Stacey, *Brave New Families*, 263.

92. Ibid.; Aronson, "Feminist or 'Postfeminist'?"; Machung, "Talking Career, Thinking Job."

93. See, for example, Freedman, *No Turning Back*, 48–54.

94. Quoted in DeBerg, *Ungodly Women*, 45. This opinion was also expressed by some black ministers. See Martha Jones, *All Bound Up Together*, 190–99.

95. Quoted in DeBerg, *Ungodly Women*, 66, 43–74. See also Carol Mattingly, *Well-Tempered Women*, 97.

96. Hutchins, "Papering Over a Rift."

97. For a discussion of these ideas, see Alexander-Floyd, *Gender, Race, and Nationalism*, esp. 51–74; Giddings, *When and Where I Enter*, 314–24; White, *Too Heavy a Load*, 216–20; Martha Jones, *All Bound Up Together*. For a comprehensive understanding of these issues, see the following: Horton, *Free People of Color*, esp. "Violence, Protest, and Identity: Black Manhood in Antebellum America," written with Lois E. Horton, and "Freedom's Yoke: Gender Conventions among Free Blacks." Other aspects of these issues can be found in Hernton, *Sex and Racism in America*, 128–55; Grier and Cobbs, *Black Rage*, 41, 47; Cleaver, *Soul on Ice*, esp. part 4, "White Woman, Black Man."

98. For a discussion of these ideas, see the following: Stabile, *White Victims, Black Villains*, 85–104; Fredrickson, *Black Image in the White Mind*, 256–82; White, *Ar'n't I a Woman*, 2nd ed., 176–77; Giddings, *When and Where I Enter*, 85–94.

99. For a discussion of these issues, see Carby, *Reconstructing Womanhood*, 89–94;

Carby, *Race Men*, 9–41; Gaines, *Uplifting the Race*, 67–99; Gatewood, *Aristocrats of Color*, 332–48; Evelyn Brooks Higginbotham, *Righteous Discontent*, esp. 185–230; White, *Too Heavy a Load*, 56–109.

100. See, for example, the illustrations in Martha Jones, *All Bound Up Together*, 127–28. See also Wahneema Lubiano's discussion of Anita Hill and the representations of black women in "Black Ladies, Welfare Queens, and State Minstrels," in Morrison, *Race-ing Justice, En-gendering Power*.

101. This issue is taken up at length by works on tensions between black and white women in the feminist movement and among black women in the civil rights and feminist movements. See, for example, Breines, *Trouble between Us*. See also Roth, *Separate Roads to Feminism*.

Chapter 4. The Fierce Urgency of Unity

1. Stephens, "It Was a Day of Atonement," News, Local and National sec., 5B.

2. Janofsky "When a Rally's Strength," Saturday late final ed., A7.

3. Foege and Miller, "Philadelphia Story," 123.

4. Estes-Hicks, "Way We Were," 11.

5. Benedict Anderson, *Imagined Communities*, 6–7.

6. Centers for Disease Control and Prevention, "Negative Mood and Urban versus Rural Residence," 5, 9.

7. See chapter 2.

8. Bajwa, "NU Students to Participate."

9. King, "Show of Sisters," News sec., A1.

10. Britt, "Black Women's Dilemma," B1.

11. Ibid.

12. "Crowds Gather," 5.

13. Quoted in Pardo, "Million Woman Rally," 314.

14. Milloy, "For One Woman," sec. D, B1.

15. "Sisters Challenging the Stereotypes," accessed August 8, 2016, www.home-phillynews.com/packages/wmill/opin/DN/.

16. "Million Woman March—Media Didn't Give Gathering," letter to the editor, Editorial sec., B5.

17. Britt, "Black Women's Dilemma," B1.

18. Moore, "Drill Is Shaky."

19. Mitchell, "Road to Sisterhood," Sunday ed., News sec., 4.

20. Gilliam, "Time Will Tell," Metro sec., B1.

21. Ibid.

22. Afro-America@National News, http://www.afroam.org/information/news/10-27-97//nationaltext/htlm, accessed August 1, 1999.

23. Fletcher and Brown, "We Are Countless in Unity," A1.

24. See, for example, Dill, "Race, Class, and Gender"; Evelyn Brooks Higginbotham, *Righteous Discontent*, 1–46; Julie Des Jardins, *Women and the Historical Enterprise*, 118–76; White, *Too Heavy a Load*, 21–55.

25. See the Million Woman March mission statement in "Million Woman March, Philadelphia, PA, October 1997: A Commemoration," unpublished compilation, ed. Darlene Clark Hine, Michigan State University.

26. Patricia Smith, "In Spirit, There Were Millions," National/Foreign sec., A1.

27. Brown, "Away from Home," A14.

28. Mitchell, "Women's March a Well-Kept Secret," Commentary sec., 33.

29. Patricia Smith, "In Spirit, There Were Millions," National/Foreign sec., A1.

30. Lee, "Thousands of Women Share," National Desk sec., 22. See also Dare, *1.3 Million Marched*, 42, 46, 48–49, 52, 53.

31. Kee, "Black Women Get on Their Own Bus," Editorial sec., C11.

32. Fletcher and Brown, "We Are Countless in Unity," A1.

33. Brown, "Away from Home," A14.

34. Fletcher and Brown, "We Are Countless in Unity," A1.

35. Brown, "Away from Home," A14.

36. "Million Woman March a Misstep," letter to the editor, n.p., accessed August 8, 2016, http://articles.philly.com/1997-10-22/news/25539758_1_black-men-black-women-black-art.

37. Peterman, "Million Woman March Fails," Commentary sec., 1D.

38. Brown, "My Bumpy Ride Back," Outlook sec., C1.

39. June Jordan, "Gathering Purpose," 33–34.

40. Brown, "My Bumpy Ride Back," Outlook sec., C1. See also Britt, "Inspired by the Words of the Future," Metro sec., C1; Bernstein, "Achieving Sisterhood," Everywoman sec., 1E.

41. Fulwood, "Blacks Not in Lock Step," National Desk, A4.

42. C-SPAN and other news organizations recorded the Million Man March. The Million Woman March received limited coverage.

43. White, *Let My People Go*, 94–95.

44. Audrey Elisa Kerr, *The Paper Bag Principle: Class, Colorism, and Rumor and the Case of Black Washington, D.C.* (Knoxville: University of Tennessee Press, 2006).

45. White, *Too Heavy a Load*, 72.

46. NOI (Nation of Islam), CORE (Congress of Racial Equality), SCLC (Southern Christian Leadership Conference), SNCC (Student Nonviolent Coordinating Committee), NAACP (National Association for the Advancement of Colored People), COFO (Council of Federated Organizations), OAAU (Organization of Afro-American Unity), MFDP (Mississippi Freedom Democratic Party), BPP (Black Panther Party), RAM (Revolutionary Action Movement), US (Us black people).

47. Cooper, *Voice from the South*, 30–31; White, *Too Heavy a Load*, 215–20.

48. Du Bois, "Conservation of the Races," in Levering, *W. E. B. Du Bois: A Reader*, 20–27.

49. Foege and Miller, "Philadelphia Story."

50. Police estimates were generally lower than organizers.' Reporters were generally in between.

51. Quoted in Foege and Miller, "Philadelphia Story," 123.

52. Fletcher and Brown, "Anticipation, Hopes Build," A3.

53. Quoted in Fletcher and Brown, "We Are Countless in Unity," A1.

54. Janofsky, "When a Rally's Strength," A7.

55. Dennis, "'If You Want the World to Change.'"

56. Janofsky, "When a Rally's Strength," A7.

57. Britt, "Desperately Seeking Sisterhood," 84.

58. Ibid.

59. See esp. chap. 5 in Alexander-Floyd, "From Endangerment to Atonement."

60. Religion News Service, "Million Man Plan Divides Churches," Metro sec.; Millner, "Marchers Feel Like a Million"; Golab, "14 Ministers Endorse"; Fulwood, "Blacks Not in Lock Step," National Desk, A4; Wilgoren and Harris, "In Last-Minute Switch," Metro sec.

61. McCormick 2d and Franklin, "Expressions of Racial Consciousness"; Fletcher and Brossard, "Poll: Many Blacks Back March but Find Organizers Troubling," *Houston Chronicle*, October 6, 1995, Three Star ed., A6; Brossard and Morin, "Leader Popular among Marchers," A01.

62. "'Million Man' Plan," Metro sec., B4.

63. Bock, "We Are Here to Rebuild." *Baltimore Sun*, News sec., 1A.

64. Rivera, "Normal Day at Office," News 6A.

65. Walsh, "Criticism," A22; Fisher, "Million Man March; Behind the Scenes," final ed., Style sec., D1.

66. Tate, *From Protest to Politics*, 168–69; Robert C. Smith, *We Have No Leaders*, 103–5, 279.

67. "African American Women in Defense of Ourselves," n.p.; Morrison, *Race-ing Justice, En-gendering Power*, xxx.

68. Quoted in Wallace and Dent, *Black Popular Culture*, 328.

69. Berry, "I Have Not Endorsed the March," Op-Ed sec., A12.

70. Jahn, "Many Blacks See March," News sec., A27.

71. John D'Emilio, *Lost Prophet: The Life and Times of Bayard Rustin* (Chicago: University of Chicago Press, 2004), 3, 338–39.

72. Tracy Baim, "Activists Denied Right to March in African-American Parade," *Outlines* 7, no. 3 (August 1993): 19, Randy Shilts Collection, James C. Hormel LGBTQIA Center, San Francisco Public Library.

73. Salim Muwakkil, "Fear of a Gay Planet," *In These Times*, August 23, 1993, 8, acc. #4511-001, box 3, folder 1, Religious Right and Blacks and Gays, University of Washington Suzzallo and Allen Libraries, Gay and Lesbian Issues Collection.

74. Earnest E. Hite Jr., "Lift the Ban on Gay Men and Lesbians in the Black Community," *Outlines* 7, no. 3 (August 1993): 26, Randy Shilts Collection, James C. Hormel LGBTQIA Center, Gay Papers, San Francisco Public Library.

75. "Gay Blacks Anxious," 5A.

76. Chandler and Bryant, "Farrakhan Criticizes Black Lesbians," 7.

77. Quoted in Darren Lenard Hutchinson, "'Claiming' and 'Speaking' Who We Are," in Carbado, *Black Men on Race, Gender, and Sexuality*, 28.

78. Quoted in ibid., 38.

79. Ibid., 34–35, 36.

80. Dunlap, "Gay Blacks in Quandary," National Desk sec., 24.

81. Quoted in Darren Lenard Hutchinson, "'Claiming' and 'Speaking' Who We Are," in Carbado, *Black Men on Race, Gender, and Sexuality*, 28.

82. Barbara Smith, unpublished pamphlet, GLC-VF/Subjects, March on Washington 1993, folder 1, San Francisco GLBT Historical Society, Archives and Research Center, San Francisco.

83. Cleo Manago, "Over a Million Men Came," *Alternatives* 4, no. 7 (November/December n.d. [circa 1995]): 24–25, Schomberg Center for Research in Black Culture, Black Gay and Lesbian Archive, New York Public Library (hereafter, Schomberg BGLA). Sources from the BGLA were accessed before the collection was processed. Therefore, there are no folders or box numbers attached to these citations.

84. Sheila Alexander-Reid and Straight from L.A., "Marching to the Beat of a Different Drummer," *Women in the Life* 5, no. 9 (November 1997): 10, Schomberg BGLA.

85. "Anti-Gay Gospel Song Sparks Debate," 9.

86. See, for example, Dare, *1.3 Million Woman Marched*, 55.

87. Jesse Jackson, "What Do Gay Rights Have to Do with Civil Rights?," *Advocate*, February 12, 1991, #570, acc. #4511–001, box 3, Gay and Lesbian Politics folder, University of Washington Suzzallo and Allen Libraries, Gay and Lesbian Issues Collection. Jackson spoke at the 1993 march but did so before C-SPAN picked up coverage.

88. "Resolution Passed Unanimously by the Board of Directors of the NAACP," *NAACP News*, acc. #4511–001, box 3, folder 1, Religious Right and Blacks and Gays folder, University of Washington Suzzallo and Allen Libraries, Gay and Lesbian Issues Collection.

89. "1993 March on Washington Draws Record Support from Black Leaders," *Bay Area Reporter* 23, no. 13 (April 1, 1993), Periodical Collection, vol. 23, no. 8–no. 29, 2/25/93–7/22/93, San Francisco GLBT Historical Society, Archives and Research Center.

90. See C-SPAN coverage of the march: http://www.c-span.org/video/?67630-1/million-man-march, at the 2:44 mark, accessed July 13, 2016. .

91. Ibid., 4:50 mark.

92. Madhubuti and Karenga, *Million Man March/Day of Absence*, 32–36. See esp. p. 35.

93. See C-SPAN coverage of the march: http://www.c-span.org/video/?67630-1/million-man-march, accessed July 13, 2016. Jackson speaks at the 5:00 mark.

94. Oliver, "Inside Cover Statement," in "'Post-Black,' 'Post-Soul,' or Hip Hop Iconography?," n.p.

95. Fox, "National Black Arts Festival," Features sec., 4F.

96. Byrd, "Is There a 'Post-Black' Art?," 37.

97. Golden, "Introduction, " in *Freestyle, the Studio Museum of Harlem* (catalog), 14.

98. Ibid., 15.

99. Brockington, "After Representation"; Oliver, "Inside Cover Statement," in "'Post-Black,' 'Post-Soul,' or Hip Hop Iconography?"

100. Brockington, "After Representation," 46; Oliver, "Inside Cover Statement," in "'Post-Black,' 'Post-Soul,' or Hip Hop Iconography?," n.p.

101. These conclusions are broad summaries of lengthy books and articles on this subject. For the details of their analyses, see Tate, *From Protest to Politics*, esp. chap. 2; Dawson, *Behind the Mule*. Four sociological studies are Elijah Anderson, *Streetwise*; Feagin and Sikes, *Living with Racism*; Waters, *Black Identities*; William Julius Wilson, *Declining Significance of Race*. Contemporary evidence presented by Melissa Harris-Lacewell shows that these trends still persist today. For a post-2000 look at the relationship of race and class, see Harris-Lacewell, "Liberation to Mutual Fund"; Grynaviski and Harris-Lacewell, "Shifting Alliances."

102. Sugrue, *Sweet Land of Liberty*, 537.

103. Ibid.; Wiese, *Places of Their Own*; MacLean, *Freedom Is Not Enough*, 13–117.

104. See Tate, *From Protest to Politics*, esp. chap. 2; Dawson, *Behind the Mule*.

105. "Two Nations of Black America."

106. Kent, "Immigration and America's Black Population"; Scruggs, "What Kind of Black Are We?"

107. Eugene Robinson, *Disintegration*, 139–63. This is a very simplified and reductive description of biracial identity, which intersects with other identity delineators such as gender and sexuality. See, for example, Fordham, "Passin' for Black."

108. Johnson, "End of the Black American Narrative."

109. Eugene Robinson, "Which Black America?," *Washington Post*, October 9, 2007, accessed August 8, 2016, http://www.washingtonpost.com/wp-dyn/content/article/2007/10/08/AR2007100801324.html. Robinson's book *Disintegration: The Splintering of Black America* explicates his argument.

110. Touré, *Who's Afraid of Post-Blackness*, 5.

Chapter 5. Things Fall Apart; the Center Holds

1. Margaret Cerullo, "Hope and Terror: The Paradox of Gay and Lesbian Politics in the 90s," *Radical America* 24, no. 3 (1993):10–16, acc. #4511–001, box 3, Lesbian and Gay Politics folder, University of Washington Suzzallo and Allen Libraries, Gay and Lesbian Issues Collection (hereafter, Suzzallo and Allen GLIC).

2. Loree Cook-Daniels, "We Need Every Tool in the Box," *March on Washington Newspaper*, n.d., San Francisco GLBT Historical Society, GLC-VF/Subjects, March on Washington 1993 folder.

3. Roger Doughty and Rebecca LePere, "Why Another March?," *March on Washington Newspaper*, n.d., San Francisco GLBT Historical Society, Ephemera Collection/Protest, etc./Marches on Washington folder.

4. See, for example, "Editorial: Pride in Numbers" and "March Recount in Works" in *Outlines* 7, no. 1 (June 1993): 13, 27–28, in Randy Shilts Papers (GLC 43), series 3, Gay Research Files, LGBTQIA Center, San Francisco Public Library, (hereafter, Shilts Papers, series 3, SFPL).

5. The 1987 march was very well attended, bringing about 500,000 to Washington, but organizers complained that it was virtually ignored by the press. They were determined that that would not happen again. See, for example, Tracy Baim, "March Momentum Picks Up Steam," *Outlines* 6, no. 1 (April 1993): n.p., in Shilts Papers, series 3, SFPL.

6. "Message about Gay Power," final ed., A20.

7. Ibid.

8. Roger Doughty and Rebecca LePere, "Why Another March?," *March on Washington Newspaper*, n.d., Ephemera Collection/Protest, etc./Marches on Washington folder, San Francisco GLBT Historical Society.

9. Jewelle Gomez, "Telling the World: A Retrospective Look at the Marches," *Breakthrough* 17, no. 1 (Spring 1993): 3–6, acc. #4511-001, box 5, Magazines folder, Suzzallo and Allen GLIC.

10. Letters, *Front Page* 14, no. 10 (May 28, 1993): 5, Shilts Papers, series 3, SFPL.

11. Mimi Hall, "'You Can't Ignore Us,' Say Marchers," *USA Today*, April 26, 1993, acc. #4511-001, box 5, Clippings folder, Suzzallo and Allen GLIC.

12. Ly, "Making a Public Declaration," Sunday final ed., Metro sec., C1.

13. Letters, *Front Page* 14, no. 10 (May 28, 1993): 5, Shilts Papers, series 3, SFPL.

14. Experts agree that "little can be said with any certainty about the extent of suicide deaths among LGB youth," and that the 30 percent figure, though cited frequently, is based on questionable scientific grounding. Still, researchers have found that lgbt youth are at a greater risk than other youth. See Suicide Prevention Resource Center, "Suicide Risk and Prevention."

15. Jason Shepard, "Sunday's Gay March," Communities sec., 1B.

16. Ibid.

17. Stone, "Thousands Gather," final ed., Front sec., A12.

18. Ibid.

19. Gutierrez-Mier, "S.A. Resident to Join D.C. Gay Rights March," Metro ed., South Texas sec., 6B.

20. Dart, "Gay Communities March," News sec., 3A.

21. Worthington and Hamlin, "Doesn't Speak for Us," letter to the editor, Editorial sec., A22.

22. Tracy Baim, "Million March for Gay, Lesbian, Bi Rights," *Outlines* 6, no. 12 (May 1993): n.p., Ephemera Collection/Protest, etc./Marches on Washington folder, San Francisco GLBT Historical Society.

23. Mixner, "Millennium March Will Help."

24. D'Emilio and Freedman, *Intimate Matters*, 354.

25. Some AIDS activists, like Larry Kramer, did not think AIDS was being given enough attention. He urged activist to cease marching and instead participate in a "die-in" in front of the White House. See "Pay Attention America," *Front Page* 14, no. 8 (April 30, 1993): 6, Shilts Papers, series 3, SFPL.

26. Elise Harris, "What Do Gay Men and Lesbians Want? Be Careful What You Wish For," *Out*, April/May 1993, 31, acc. #4511-001, box 5, Suzzallo and Allen GLIC.

27. Michael Nava, "The Whying Game," *Frontiers* (n.d.), Ephemera Collection/ Protest, etc./Marches on Washington folder, San Francisco GLBT Historical Society.

28. "Pay Attention America," *Front Page* 14, no. 8 (April 30, 1993): 6, Shilts Papers, series 3, SFPL.

29. Herb King, "Marching Together—to a Different Drumbeat," *Bocage '93*, Periodical Collection, 2/25/93–7/22/93, San Francisco GLBT Historical Society.

30. "Pay Attention America," *Front Page* 14, no. 8 (April 30, 1993): 8, Shilts Papers, series 3, SFPL.

31. Herb King, "Marching Together—to a Different Drumbeat," *Bocage '93*, Periodical Collection, 2/25/93–7/22/93, San Francisco GLBT Historical Society.

32. Karen Ocamb, "Building on D.C.'s Momentum," *Lesbian News* 18, no. 10 (May 1993): n.p., Shilts Papers, series 3, SFPL.

33. Hammonds, "Where Do We Go from Here?," Editorial sec., A-15.

34. Vicki Torres, "Making History in Washington," *Lesbian News* 18, no. 10 (May 1993): 44–45, Shilts Papers, series 3, SFPL.

35. Victor Raymond and Laura Perez, "We're Here, We're Queer, Bisexuals Included!," *March on Washington Newspaper*, n.d., GLC-VF/Subjects/March on Washington 1993 folder, San Francisco GLBT Historical Society.

36. "Flexing Political Muscle," Nation sec., A12.

37. Meyerowitz, *How Sex Changed*, 256.

38. Victor Raymond and Laura Perez, "We're Here, We're Queer, Bisexuals Included!," *March on Washington Newspaper*, n.d., GLC-VF/Subjects/March on Washington 1993 folder, San Francisco GLBT Historical Society.

39. Meyerowitz, *How Sex Changed*, 9–10.

40. Ibid., 259–62.

41. Marcus, *Making Gay History*, 154–55.

42. Phyllis Randolph Frye, "Transgendered People at the March on Washington," *March on Washington Newspaper*, n.d., GLC-VF/Subjects/March on Washington 1993 folder, San Francisco GLBT Historical Society.

43. Thom Bean, "Queer Monoculture on Parade," *Outlines* 7, no. 3 (August 1993): 4, GLC 43, Shilts Papers, series 3, SFPL.

44. Wright, "Black, Gay, at Risk," 32.

45. Letter from the Editor's Desk, *Angel Herald*, July 2000, 2, Gay Men of African Descent (GMAD), G-Mag folder, Schomberg Center for Research in Black Culture, Black Gay and Lesbian Archive, New York Public Library (hereafter cited as Schomberg BGLA).

46. Wright, "Black, Gay, at Risk," 32.

47. Don Thomas, "Liberty and Justice for All," *Advocate* 693 (October 5, 1993): 8, acc. #4511-001, box 3, folder 1, Religious Right and Blacks and Gays, Suzzallo and Allen GLIC.

48. See, for example, Keith Boykin, "A Poem for the Millennium March," *Angel Herald* 13, no. 10 (June 2000), GMAD, G-Mag folder, Schomberg BGLA.

49. Letter from the Editor's Desk, *Angel Herald*, July 2000, 2, GMAD, G-Mag folder, Schomberg BGLA.

50. *Whazzup Magazine*, n.d. (ca. 1999), picture with caption, 24, SBC box, Schomberg BGLA.

51. SGL is here capitalized because it was capitalized by same gender loving people who embraced the term.

52. Cleo Manago, "The SGL Nation," *Wazzup Magazine*, n.d., SBC box, Schomberg BGLA.

53. "Affirming Black Diversity," *Wazzup Magazine*, n.d., SBC box, Schomberg BLGA.

54. Gabriel Gomez, "The Queer March on Washington," *Thing*, Spring 1993, 20–23, A–G, Schomberg BGLA.

55. Michael Crawford, "To Be Young, Black, Gay and Marching," *Wazzup Magazine* 4, no. 9 (March 2000): 16, Schomberg BGLA.

56. Scales, "Weekend Gay Rights March," 3rd ed., National/Foreign sec., A3.

57. Marcus, *Making Gay History*, 56.

58. D'Emilio, *Sexual Politics, Sexual Communities*, 105; Faderman, *Odd Girls and Twilight Lovers*, 211.

59. D'Emilio, *Sexual Politics, Sexual Communities*, 229.

60. Faderman, *Odd Girls and Twilight Lovers*, 211.

61. Schneider, "Lesbian Politics and AIDS Work," in Plummer, *Modern Homosexualities*, 163–66.

62. Ibid., 172.

63. Marcus, *Making Gay History*, 261.

64. Schneider, "Lesbian Politics and AIDS Work," in Plummer, *Modern Homosexualities*, 170–71.

65. Ibid., 173.

66. Letters, *Front Page* 14, no. 9 (May 14, 1993): 5, Shilts Papers, series 3, SFPL.

67. Miller, "Gay White Males," in Bawer, *Beyond Queer*, 31.

68. Monroe, "Prophetic Voices."

69. Michael Crawford, "To Be Young, Black, Gay and Marching," *Wazzup Magazine* 4, no. 9 (March 2000): 16, Schomberg BGLA.

70. Kreisher, "San Diego Gay Rights Activist," n.p.

71. Editorial, "Queer Rights Are Human Rights Are Queer Rights," *Breakthrough* 17, no. 1 (Spring 1993): 1, acc. #4511–001, box 5, Lesbian and Gay Politics folder, Suzzallo and Allen GLIC.

72. Ibid.; "Don't Ask Don't Tell Me to Be in Your Army," originally published by Anonymous Queers, June 1992, Ephemera Collection/Protests, etc./Marches on Washington, 1993, folder 2 of 2, San Francisco GLBT Historical Society.

73. Warner, *Trouble with Normal*, 36.

74. "Don't Ask Don't Tell Me to Be in Your Army," originally published by Anonymous Queers, June 1992, Ephemera Collection/Protests, etc./Marches on Washington, 1993, folder 2 of 2, San Francisco GLBT Historical Society.

75. Lee Lynch, "Bringing the March Back Home," *Lesbian News* 18, no. 10 (May 1993): n.p., in Shilts Papers, series 3, SFPL.

76. Nannery, "Wrong Picture of Gay Rally," Nassau and Suffolk ed., Currents sec., 42.

77. *New York Times*, April 27, 1993, Opinion sec., A20.

78. Castaneda, "Day to Take Pride," final ed., Metro sec., D3.

79. Joe Rodriguez, "Gay Wichitans Part of March," Local and State sec., 9A.

80. McKay, "Calling for Legislation," final ed., sec. A, 1A.

81. Miller, "Gay White Males," in Bawer, *Beyond Queer*, 25.

82. Ibid., 24–37.

83. Miller, "March On?"; see also Miller, "Uninspiring March"; Miller, "Baiting Game."

84. "Editorial, Jim Crow for Queers," *Outlines* 7, no. 3 (August 1993): 4, Shilts Papers, series 3, SFPL.

85. Quoted in "'Some of My Closest Advisors Are Gay' Syndrome, or Don't Be Fooled by Bill," in "Why I Hated the March on Washington" published by QUASH (Queers United Against Straight-acting Homosexuals) [ad-hoc newspaper], Ephemera Collection/Protests, etc./Marches on Washington, 1993, folder 2 of 2, San Francisco GLBT Historical Society.

86. Edward Cone and Lisa Scheer, "Queen of the Right," *Mirabella*, February 1993, 86, acc. #4511–001, box 4, Concerned Women for America folder, Suzzallo and Allen GLIC.

87. Memo from Concerned Women for America, n.d., acc. #4511–001, box 2, Concerned Women for America folder, Suzzallo and Allen GLIC.

88. Edward Cone and Lisa Scheer, "Queen of the Right," *Mirabella*, February 1993, 93, acc. #4511–001, box 4, Concerned Women for America folder, Suzzallo and Allen GLIC.

89. Beverly LaHaye, "The Hidden Homosexual Agenda," acc. #4511–001, box 4, Concerned Women for America 1991 folder, Suzzallo and Allen GLIC.

90. Robert Davis, "Rights Issue Still Divides," *USA Today*, April 26, 1993, 1A; Robert Davis, "Poll: Women More Tolerant," *USA Today*, April 26, 1993, 10A, acc. #4511–001, box 5, Clippings folder, Suzzallo and Allen GLIC.

91. Becker, *Gay TV and Straight America*, 103.

92. Ibid., 1–3, 104.

93. Ibid., 108–35.

94. Robert Davis, "Rights Issue Still Divides" *USA Today*, April 26, 1993, 1A, acc. #4511–001, box 5, Clippings folder, Suzzallo and Allen GLIC.

95. See, for example, Ralph Z. Hallow, "Christian Coalition to Court Minorities," *Washington Times*, September 10, 1993, and Farai Chideya, "How the Right Stirs Black Homophobia," *Time*, October 18, 1993, acc. #4511–001, box 5, Clippings folder, Suzzallo and Allen GLIC.

96. All quotes from Eric Washington, "Freedom Rings: The Alliance between

Blacks and Gays Is Threatened by Mutual Inscrutability," *Village Voice*, June 29, 1993, acc. #4511–001, box 5, Clippings folder, Suzzallo and Allen GLIC.

97. Edwards, "Religion," in Jarrett, *Impact of Macro Social Systems*, 237–38.

98. Ibid., 239–41.

99. *Gay Rights, Special Rights*. According to the film, which supports its claims with visuals and "expert" testimony, if special rights are granted to lgbts, the following will happen: homosexual teachers will teach a homosexual orthodoxy that will encourage their children to become homosexuals; boys will be co-opted so they won't want to be with boys, which will lead to the destruction of the family; taxpayers will have to pay for transvestite sex-change operations and artificial insemination for lesbians; churches who refuse to marry same-sexed couples will lose their tax-exempt status; private businesses will be forced to hire homosexuals; sexual practices like fisting, defecation, and sadomasochism will become the norm; AIDS will spread; children will be assaulted in parks; and the political power of gays will escalate while America degenerates into decay. Gays can be rehabilitated, and learn to be heterosexuals, says the narrator. Legislation is not the answer; neither are special rights. Only Christ can save this population, says the narrator. In Christ all things are possible, including the salvation of lgbts and the nation.

100. *Gay Rights, Special Rights*.

101. "Special Rights: A Code Word for Campaigns of Discrimination," flyer, People for the American Way Action Fund, acc. #4511–001, box 4, Gay Rights, Special Rights folder, Suzzallo and Allen GLIC.

102. Ralph Z. Hallow, "Christian Coalition to Court Minorities," *Washington Times*, September 10, 1993, Nation sec., acc. #4511–001, box 5, Clippings folder, Suzzallo and Allen GLIC.

103. Ibid.

104. Gamson, "Whose Millennium March?," 16.

105. Taormino, "Sex and Silence in D.C.," Hot Spot sec., 154.

106. Quoted in Gamson, "Whose Millennium March?," 16.

107. Ibid., 20.

108. Kim Diehl, "Here's the Movement, Let's Start Building" in *Colorlines*, November 2, 2000, accessed August 11, 2016, http://www.colorlines.com/articles/heres -movement-lets-start-building.

109. Goldstein, "Millennium March."

110. "Gay Rights Activists' Millennium March on Washington."

111. Sciolino, "Gays Set to Flex Political Muscle," News sec., A8.

112. Scales, "Weekend Gay-Rights March," National/Foreign sec., A3.

113. Morris, "Age of Dissonance," sec. 9, Style Desk, 1; "Breakdown in the Instinct for Self-Preservation."

114. "Mock Marriages Highlight Gay Rights Rally," *Pantagraph* (Bloomington, IL), April 30, 2000, News sec., A1; "Breakdown in the Instinct for Self-Preservation."

115. "Breakdown in the Instinct for Self-Preservation."

116. Christopher Smith, "Sparks Fly."

117. The advertisement appeared in the September 18, 1998, issue of the *Washington Blade*, http://gaytoday.badpuppy.com/garchive/events/092298ev.htm, accessed July 13, 2016.

118. Sandalow, "Millennium March: Gay Rally Bares."

119. Armas, "Mock Same Sex Wedding Staged," Domestic sec., non-Washington general news item.

120. "Gay Rights Movement in the New Millennium," Editorial sec., 6.

121. Phillips and O'Brien, "Supporters of Gay Rights March," News, Domestic sec.

122. Nelson and Snow, "Thousands in Washington."

123. Dart, "Gay Activist Rally," Washington General News sec.

124. Helmore, "College Football Hero Corey Johnson," Observer News Pages sec., 26.

125. Vanasco, "Boring Is Beautiful."

126. See, for example, Chauncey, *Gay New York*, 299; Kennedy and Davis, *Boots of Leather, Slippers of Gold*, 91–92, 374.

127. *New York Times*, April 27, 1993, Opinion sec., A20.

Chapter 6. Guns and Motherhood

1. Million Mom March transcript, speeches by Gale Thorson, Madella Marsh-Williams, and Veronica McQueen; Million Mom March profiles from the national website, http://www.millionmommarch.org/mam/index.asp?record=28; Stroup, "Moms Vow to Continue," Metro ed., Metro sec., B1.

2. Garrison and Olivo, "Protest Takes Aim," Metro sec., B1.

3. Million Mom March transcript, speeches by Yvonne Pope, Patty Nielson, and Dawn Anna.

4. Jetter, Orleck, and Taylor, *Politics of Motherhood*, 3–20.

5. Centers for Disease Control and Prevention, "Gun Deaths among Children and Teens." Statistics on the number of gun deaths vary depending on who is reporting them. Pro-gun advocates minimize the number while gun-control advocates exaggerate them. This study uses statistics by government agencies such as the FBI, the General Accounting Office, and the Centers for Disease Control.

6. Haynes, "Local Women Join," local ed., 21.

7. Morrison and Bowles, "Do Marches Make a Difference?," News sec., A1.

8. Toner, "Nation Pulling Strings," sec. 4, 1.

9. Galloway, "When Mothers Get Mad," Perspective sec., 1E.

10. This is a very long and complicated history. See, for example, Roth, *Separate Roads to Feminism*, and Roberts, *Killing the Black Body*. Roth reports that when radical white feminists met at Sandy Spring, Maryland, in 1968 to hammer out a radical feminist agenda, they admitted that they had "problems dealing with black people." They believed that black women "want to discuss different things, have different concerns." While describing a meeting of black and white welfare workers, a white feminist expressed her fear of black women: "Black militant women ruled the day.

... They set the tone and they managed to completely cow the white women. ... I don't want to go to a conference to hear a black militant woman tell me she is more oppressed and what am I going to do about it."

11. Morrison, "What the Black Woman Thinks." As Nobel laureate Tony Morrison put it in this article, black women see white women "and think of the enemy." They have "no abiding admiration of white women as competent, complete people," but rather see them as "willful children, pretty children, mean children, ugly children, but never as real adults." According to political scientist Melissa Harris-Perry, a poll taken of black women in December 2005 at the Black Women's Expo revealed that black women still held similar negative opinions about white women; (fall 2005 presentation at the Woodrow Wilson International Center, Division of United States Studies).

12. Goodwin, Jasper, and Polletta, "Introduction: Why Emotions Matter," in Goodwin, Jasper, and Polletta, *Passionate Politics*, 1–24.

13. Dees-Thomases, *Looking for a Few Good Moms*, 3–5, xxiii.

14. Sansbury, "Million Mom March," News sec., 6A.

15. Dees-Thomases, *Looking for Few Good Moms*, 150.

16. Ibid., 174, 78.

17. Ibid., 107.

18. Galloway, "When Mothers Get Mad," Perspective sec., 1E; *Guns and Mothers*.

19. Pagano, "Moms See Bigger Picture," Viewpoints sec., 3B.

20. Wolff, "Can Million Moms Be Wrong?," Editorial sec., 47.

21. Dratch and Dorfman, "Moms on a Mission."

22. DeFao, "Moms' March in Oakland," News sec., A15.

23. Sweet, "Some Stay Behind," News sec., 7.

24. Galloway, "When Mothers Get Mad," Perspective sec., 1E.

25. Norton, "Evolution of White Women's Experience," 617.

26. Million Mom March transcript, speeches by Mieko Hattori and Rosie O'Donnell.

27. Kerber, "Republican Mother," in Kerber and De Hart, *Women's America*, 87–95; Degler, *At Odds*, 298–327.

28. See Bederman, *Manliness and Civilization*. For other instances of mother-blaming, see Ladd-Taylor and Umansky, *"Bad" Mothers*.

29. Wylie, "Common Women," in *Generation of Vipers*, 184–96.

30. Frazier, *Negro Family in the United States*, 89–113, 209–24, 265, 256–67, 349–50; Moynihan, *Negro Family: The Case for National Action*.

31. Pollitt, "Moms to NRA."

32. Johnson, "Letter to the Editor."

33. Dresser, "Lest We Forget," Outlook sec., 4.

34. For a lay history of the issues, see Burkett, *Baby Boon*, esp. 147–75. For a quick scholarly review and personal stories, see Reti, *Childless by Choice*. See also Jetter, Orleck, and Taylor, *Politics of Motherhood*, esp. 349–81.

35. See Cobble, *Other Women's Movement*, 60.

36. Pollitt, "Moms to NRA." See also Ruddick, "Rethinking 'Maternal' Politics," in Jetter, Orleck, and Taylor, *Politics of Motherhood*, 369–81.

37. See, for example, Porter, "Moms Should Stay Home," Editorial and Comment sec., 2B; Burroughs, "NRA Moms," News sec. 1; Bernstein, "Pro-Gun Women," Everywoman sec., 6.

38. Sanborn, "Million Mom March," Editorial sec., B11.

39. Kruse, "Public Pulse," Editorial sec., B11.

40. Stroupe, "Reader Responses," Editorial sec., 8A.

41. Dlouhy, "Public Pulse," Editorial sec., 24.

42. See the Urban Dictionary's definition of *soccer mom*: http://www.urbandictionary.com/define.php?term=soccer+mom.

43. Fields, "Moms Should Redirect," Forum Opinion and Ideas sec., 7B.

44. Monsen, "Letters," Nation/World sec., 10.

45. Paglia, "Million Mom March."

46. Goodwin, Jasper, and Polletta, "Introduction: Why Emotions Matter," in Goodwin, Jasper, and Polletta, *Passionate Politics*, 14–15.

47. Halbwachs, *On Collective Memory*, 50–51, 174–75, 194; Kaplan, *Taking Back the Streets*, esp. 1–14.

48. See, for example, Guy, "175 Gun Advocates Protest," Denver and the West sec., B3.

49. Brower, "Logic and Facts Necessary," Editorial sec., E3.

50. "NRA Answers Moms Rally," A3.

51. See, for example, Charlton Heston's speech before an NRA convention in Colorado: https://www.youtube.com/watch?v=BWCzEwWNNIc, n.d., accessed August 12, 2016.

52. Gammerman, "Million Mom March Evokes Power," Telegraph sec., 1A.

53. *Guns and Mothers.*

54. Stuttaford, "Moms Away," 22.

55. Mize, "Reader Responses," Editorial sec., 4E.

56. See, for example, Fields, "Moms Should Redirect"; Stuttaford, "Moms Away."

57. Burroughs, "NRA Moms Get Their Say," Midwest sec., 1.

58. Fields, "Women Are Fairly Split," B9; Monsen, "Letters," Nation/World sec., 10.

59. McCullen, "Boulder Gun Debate," local ed., 32A.

60. Ibid.; Fields, "Women Are Fairly Split, B9; "Letter Hearing Held."

61. Kopel, "Rapists Like Gun Control."

62. Jacoby, "Guns for Rapists."

63. Huebert, "Open Fire."

64. While some might think *manhood* and *masculinity* are synonymous, Gail Bederman reminds us that they are distinct. See Bederman, *Manliness and Civilization*, 5–10, 17–19.

65. To understand the racial and gender dynamics of rape, see Fredrickson, *Black Image in the White Mind*, 256–82; Hall, "'The Mind That Burns in Each Body,'"

in Snitow, Stansell, and Thompson, *Powers of Desire*, 328–49; Hall, *Revolt against Chivalry*.

66. Monica Haynes, "Local Women Join," local ed., 21.

67. Hart, "Shooting Victim's Mother Fights," metro ed., B12.

68. "Gun-Toting Mothers," News sec., A7.

69. *Guns and Mothers.*

70. Fields, "Women Are Fairly Split," B9.

71. Stabile, *White Victims, Black Villains*, 11–28, 177, see also n. 43.

72. For a sociological study on white fears of young black males, see Elijah Anderson, *Streetwise*, 163–89; "Media Matters Exposes Bennett."

73. Lubiano, "Black Ladies, Welfare Queens, and State Minstrels," in Morrison, *Race-ing Justice, En-gendering Power*. See also Feldstein, *Motherhood in Black and White*, 57, 98–102; Hancock, *Politics of Disgust*; Roberts, *Killing the Black Body*, 104–49; White, *Ar'n't I a Woman?*

74. For example, when Emmett Till was murdered, his mother, Mamie Till Bradley, went to great lengths to raise sympathy for her son. See Feldstein, *Motherhood in Black and White*, 86–110.

75. Quoted in Monica Haynes, "Local Women Join," local ed., 21.

76. Monica Haynes, "Marching for Little Tony," Editorial sec., A15.

77. On the few minority women who participated, see Cocco, "Moms Face a Stiffer Challenge," Nassau and Suffolk ed., Viewpoints sec., A35; "Free for All," final ed., Op-Ed sec.; Dejevsky, "500,000 'Moms' Rally," Foreign News sec.; Gamerman, "Moms and Minivans," Telegraph sec.; Galloway, "When Mothers Get Mad," Perspective sec., 1E.

78. Monica Haynes, "Local Women Join," local ed., 21.

79. Garrison and Olivo, "Protest Takes Aim," Metro sec., B1.

80. *Guns and Mothers.*

81. Leonard, "'Million Mom March' against Guns," A1.

82. Gerber, "Bus Brings Moms," News sec., 3A.

83. Karima Haynes, "Los Angeles: Mothers Push Fight," B3; see also Harden, "Moms Take Anti-Gun Fight"; Niederberger, "Million Mom March Group Continues," South ed., Metro sec., S9; Borger, "U.S. Faces Its Biggest Anti-Gun March."

84. Dratch and Dorfman, "Moms on a Mission"; Dees-Thomases, *Looking for a Few Good Moms*, 31.

85. Lynn Smith, "L.A. Moms Fighting," Southern California Living sec., E1.

86. Monica Haynes, "Local Women Join," local ed., 21.

87. "Million Mom Impact," Editorial sec., A22.

88. Ibid.

89. Galloway, "When Mothers Get Mad," Perspective sec., 1E.

90. Dejevsky, "500,000 'Moms' Rally," Foreign News sec., 13; see also Karima Haynes, "Los Angeles: Mothers Push Fight," B3.

91. Garrison, "Rift over Location," Metro sec., B1.

92. Garrison and Olivo, "Protest Takes Aim," Metro sec., B1; Garrison, "Rift over Locations," Metro sec., B1; Simon and Anderson, "Mothers March," B1.

93. Garrison, "Rift over Locations," Metro sec., B1; Lynn Smith, "L.A. Moms Fighting," Southern California Living sec., E1; see also Karima Haynes, "Los Angeles: Mothers Push Fight," B3; Garrison and Olivo, "Protest Takes Aim," Metro sec., B1.

94. See Roth, *Separate Roads to Feminism*, 195–200. Roth describes a similar phenomenon in the 1960s–1970s feminist movement.

95. Dees-Thomases, *Looking for a Few Good Moms*, 56, 31, 158.

96. Terborg-Penn, *African American Women and the Struggle for the Vote*, 107–35.

97. Dees-Thomases, *Looking for a Few Good Moms*, 156–59, 56–57, 79. Dees-Thomases also noted that the "malcontents," who she euphemistically calls the 151s, consistently asked to be paid for their work and complained that Moms were being pushed out of organizing as more and more professionals assumed greater responsibilities.

98. Statistics for other minority women are spotty at best. Even for Hispanic males the statistics are incomplete because sometimes Hispanics are put in either the black or white group without distinguishing Hispanic origin.

99. The statistics on homicide and suicide for juveniles and for adults vary according to the agency doing the reporting. The facts in this paragraph are not disputed, although different agencies may give different numbers. See Office of Justice and Delinquency Prevention, "Promising Strategies to Reduce Gun Violence; "Homicide One of Leading Causes"; U.S. Census Bureau, *Statistical Abstract of the United States: 2000*; Bilchik, *1999 National Report Series*; "Methods of Suicide."

100. Baum, "Mom Marches On," National Desk sec., A22.

101. Guinier and Torres, *The Miner's Canary*.

102. Spitzer, *Politics of Gun Control*, 96–97.

103. Ruddick. "Rethinking 'Maternal' Politics," 371.

104. Hancock, *Politics of Disgust*.

105. Stabile, *White Victims, Black Villains*, 153–89.

106. For histories of recent discordant relationships between black and white women, see Breines, *Trouble between Us*, and Roth, *Separate Roads to Feminism*. Guinier and Torres suggest that it is possible for blacks, whites, and Hispanics to come together if a strategy of what they call political race is adopted. See Guinier and Torres, *Miner's Canary*, especially 67–107. David Plotke suggests a tactic different from that suggested by Guinier and Torres; see Plotke, "Racial Politics and the Clinton-Guinier Episode."

Epilogue

1. See his speech at https://www.youtube.com/watch?v=y0z87SKSyyw, accessed August 13, 2016.

2. For an in-depth examination of the 1963 march, see William Jones, *March on Washington*.

3. See, for example, Gitlin, *Twilight of Common Dreams*. Gitlin alleges that identity politics keep Americans from seeing commonalities. Gitlin's particular argument is that identity politics fractured the leftist coalition of the 1960s. If this work were about

the 1960s or if it were more concerned with the *politics* of the 1990s, it would argue that such a coalition was tenuous at best and that the politics of difference has always stood between African Americans and the so-called '60s leftist coalition of antiwar students, left-wing labor, and liberal white civil rights advocates. Postmodernity has made it difficult to build coalitions but the fault lies in the postmodern condition itself—not in one group or another's failure to see commonalities.

4. Lorde, *I Am Your Sister*. https://www.marxists.org/subject/lgbtq/pamphlets /I%20Am%20Your%20Sister-Audrey%20Lorde.pdf, accessed July 13, 2016.

5. Bartkowski, *Promise Keepers*, 2–4; Nathan Riley, "Gay Millions More Role Nixed," *Gay City News* 75, no. 42 (October 20–26, 2005), http://gaycitynews.nyc/gcn_442 /gaymillionsmorerole.html, accessed July 13, 2016; "More on Keith Boykin's Banning from the Podium and the Millions More March," *Shadowproof*, October 16, 2005, http://shadowproof.com/2005/10/16/more-on-keith-boykins-banning-from-the -podium-at-the-millions-more-march/, accessed July 13, 2016.

6. Karen E. Quinones Miller, "A Year Later, Marching Apart the Million Woman March's Leaders Have Split Up but Still Believe in the Basic Cause," *Philly.com*, October 25, 1998, http://articles.philly.com/1998–10–25/news/25762553_1_million -woman-march-phile-chionesu-black-women, accessed July 13, 2016.

7. Cloud, "Postcard: Washington," 10.

8. Jo Freeman, "The 2004 Million Mom March," May 11, 2004, http://www.jofreeman .com/photos/MomMarch.html, accessed July 13, 2016.

9. Mothers for Justice United, http://www.mothersforjusticeunited.org/, accessed July 13, 2016.

Bibliography

Archival Collections

James C. Hormel LGBTQIA Center, Gay Papers, San Francisco Public Library, San Francisco, California
Black Gay and Lesbian Archive, Schomburg Center for Research in Black Culture, New York Public Library
GLBT Historical Society Archives and Museum, San Francisco
  GLC-VF/Subjects
  Ephemera Collection/Protests, etc.
  Periodical Collection
The James C. Hormel LGBTQIA Center, San Francisco Public Library
  GLBT Historical Society collections (on deposit)
  Randy Shilts Papers
University of Washington Suzzallo and Allen Libraries, Seattle, Washington
  Black Gay, and Lesbian Archive
  Gay and Lesbian Issues Collection

Books, Articles, Dissertations

"African American Women in Defense of Ourselves." *New York Times*, November 17, 1991.
Afro-America@National News. Accessed August 1, 1999. http://www.afroam.org /information/news/10-27-97//nationaltext/htlm
Ahmed, Sara. ""Multiculturalism and the Promise of Happiness." *New Formations* 63 (Winter 2007–8): 121–37.
Akizuki, Dennis. "Promise Keeper Hires Asian Leader 'Forgotten' Ethnic Group Welcomed Aboard." *Denver Post*, September 27, 1997.
Alex-Assensoh, Yvette Marie, and Lawrence J. Hanks, eds. *Black and Multiracial Politics in America*. New York: New York University Press, 2000.

Alexander-Floyd, Nikol G. "From Endangerment to Atonement: Reading Gender, Race and Nationalism in the Million Man March." PhD diss., Rutgers, the State University of New Jersey, 1999.

———. *Gender, Race, and Nationalism in Contemporary Black Politics.* New York: Palgrave Macmillan, 2007.

Alexander, Michelle. *The New Jim Crow: Mass Incarceration in the Age of Colorblindness.* New York: New Press, 2010.

Alexander-Reid, Sheila, and Straight from L.A. "Marching to the Beat of a Different Drummer." *Women in the Life* 5, no. 9 (1997): 10.

Allen, Martha Sawyer. "Promise Keepers: A Growing Movement Returns to Minnesota; They're Coming to the Metrodome." *Minneapolis Star Tribune,* May 9, 1996.

Anderson, Benedict. *Imagined Communities: Reflections on the Origin and Spread of Nationalism.* 1983. Repr., London: Verso, 1991.

Anderson, Elijah. *Streetwise: Race, Class, and Change in an Urban Community.* Chicago: University of Chicago Press, 1990.

"Anti-Gay Gospel Song Sparks Debate." *Outlook Magazine: The Voice of Waterloo Regions Gay and Lesbian Community* 26 (November 1997): 8–9.

Armas, Genaro C. "Mock Same-Sex Wedding Staged." *Associated Press Online,* April 30, 2000. https://www.highbeam.com/doc/1P1-26261673.html.

Aronson, Pamela. "Feminist or 'Postfeminist'?: Young Women's Attitudes towards Feminism and Gender Relations." *Gender and Society* 17, no. 6 (December 2003): 903–22.

Asimov, Nanette, and Lori Olszewski. "Hundreds of Bay Area Students Stay Home, Some Take Time Out to Fast, Reflect." *San Francisco Chronicle,* October 17, 1995.

Associated Press. "Baptists Have Highest Divorce Rate." ReligiousTolerance.org, December 30, 1999. Accessed July 13, 2016. http://www.religioustolerance.org/chr_dira.htm.

Bajwa, Hena. "NU Students to Participate in Million Woman March." *Daily Northwestern,* October 7, 1997.

Baldwin, Tammy. "Speech: Keep Flame Alive for Rights." *Capital Times* (Madison, WI), May 15, 2000.

Ballingrud, David. "Keeping the Faith: Resuscitated Promise Keepers Back, Man to Man." *St. Petersburg Times,* June 13, 1998.

Barber, Lucy G. *Marching on Washington: The Forging of an American Political Tradition.* Berkeley: University of California Press, 2002.

Barber, Mike. "Men's Group Rallies 'Round Racial Unity." *Seattle Post-Intelligencer,* April 27, 1996.

Barker, Jeff. "Group Has Promises to Keep; Men's Organization Plans Giant Gathering in Washington." *Arizona Republic,* September 2, 1997.

Bartkowski, John. "Breaking Walls, Raising Fences: Masculinity, Intimacy and Accountability among the Promise Keepers." *Sociology of Religion* 61, no. 1 (2000): 33–53.

———. *The Promise Keepers: Servants, Soldiers, and Godly Men.* New Brunswick, NJ: Rutgers University Press.

Battista, Elena. "FSU Women Unite, Join Historic March of Millions." *Florida Flambeau* via U-Wire, October 22, 1997.

Baum, Geraldine. "Mom Marches On to Keep Ban on Weapons." *Los Angeles Times,* May 9, 2004.

Becker, Ron. *Gay TV and Straight America.* New Brunswick, NJ: Rutgers University Press, 2006.

Bederman, Gail. *Manliness and Civilization: A Cultural History of Gender and Race in the United States, 1880–1917.* Chicago: University of Chicago Press, 1995.

Berlant, Lauren. *Cruel Optimism.* Durham, NC: Duke University Press, 2011.

Bernstein, Margaret. "Achieving Sisterhood." *Cleveland Plain Dealer,* October 28, 1997, Everywoman sec. 1E.

Bernstein, Margaret. "Pro-Gun Women Plan Counterdemonstration." *Cleveland Plain Dealer,* May 2, 2000.

Berry, Mary Frances. "I Have Not Endorsed the March." *Washington Post,* October 10, 1997.

Best, Kathleen. "Area Marchers Reflect on the Day's Meaning." *St. Louis Post-Dispatch,* October 17, 1995.

Biers, John M., and Judith Brimberg. "Sobering Event a Turning Point for Denverites." *Denver Post,* October 17, 1995.

Bilchik, Shay. *1999 National Report Series: Juvenile Justice Bulletin: Kids and Guns,* March 2000. Washington, DC: National Criminal Justice Reference Service.

Bock, James. "'We Are Here to Rebuild.'" *Baltimore Sun,* October 17, 1995.

Borger, Julian. "U.S. Faces Its Biggest Anti-Gun March as Moms Say 'No More.'" *Guardian* (U.S. edition), May 12, 2000.

Boyd, Stacy. *Black Men Worshipping: Intersecting Anxieties of Race, Gender, and Christian Embodiment.* New York: Palgrave Macmillan, 2011.

Boyer, Edward J. "Black Leaders Seek to Sign Up 1 Million Men for October Rally." *Los Angeles Times,* September 1, 1995.

———. "Million Man May End Up Short." *Houston Chronicle,* September 17, 1995.

Boyer, Paul S. *Promises to Keep: The United States Since World War II.* Boston: Houghton Mifflin, 2005.

Bowles, Laurian. "Million Woman March Will Unite Voices of Black Women." *Daily Collegian* (Pennsylvania State University) via U-Wire, September 11, 1997.

Brand-Williams, Oralander. "What They're Saying." *Detroit News,* October 24, 1997.

"A Breakdown in the Instinct for Self-Preservation: Saddle Sores Goes to the Not-Yet-the-Millennium March on Washington." Saddle Sores.org, May 1, 2000. Accessed July 13, 2016. http://www.saddlesores.org/meow.html.

Breines, Winifred. *The Trouble Between Us: An Uneasy History of White and Black Women in the Feminist Movement.* New York: Oxford University Press, 2006.

Bright, Bill, et al. *Seven Promises of a Promise Keeper.* Nashville: Thomas Nelson, 1999.

Britt, Donna. "Black Women's Dilemma: Do We Also March?" *Washington Post,* October 24, 1997.

———. "Desperately Seeking Sisterhood," *Essence,* January 1998.

————. "Inspired by the Words of the Future," *Washington Post*, October 31, 1997, Metro sec. Cl.

Brockington, Horace. "After Representation." *International Review of African American Art* 16, no. 4 (2000): 42–52.

Brossard, Mario, and Michael A. Fletcher. "Last Year's Gathering Has Lasting Effects, Poll Says." *Washington Post*, October 16, 1996.

Brossard, Mario, and Richard Morin. "Leader Popular among Marchers; but Most Came to Support Black Family, Show Unity, Survey Finds," *Washington Post*, October 17, 1995.

Brower, Shane. "Logic and Facts Necessary." *Pittsburgh Post-Gazette*, June 11, 2000.

Brown, DeNeen L. "Away from Home, Marchers Find Mix of Kinship, Disappointment." *Washington Post*, October 26, 1997.

————. "My Bumpy Ride Back from a Day of Sisterhood." *Washington Post*, November 2, 1997.

Bryant, Salatheia. "Black Women Plan to March by the Million." *Houston Chronicle*, October 1, 1997.

Burkett, Elinor. *The Baby Boon: How Family-Friendly America Cheats the Childless*. New York: Free Press, 2000.

Burroughs, Rusty. "NRA Moms Get Their Say." *Chicago Sun-Times*, May 22, 2000.

Butler, Diana. "Keeping Promises for Men Only." *Cleveland Plain Dealer*, April 30, 1997.

Byfield, Natalie. *Savage Portrayals: Race, Media, and the Central Park Jogger Story*. Philadelphia: Temple University Press, 2014.

Byrd, Cathy. "Is There a 'Post-Black' Art? Investigating the Legacy of the 'Freestyle' Show." *Art Papers* 26 (November/December 2002): 37.

Camp, David A. "Incarceration Rates by Race." *Journal of the Oklahoma Criminal Justice Research Consortium* 1 (August 1994): 117–24.

Canellos, Peter S. "Groups Making Reform Next 'Guy' Thing." *Boston Globe*, October 21, 1995.

Cantave, Cassandra, and Roderick Harrison. "Marriage and African Americans." Joint Center for Political and Economic Studies, October 2001. Accessed September 2009. http://www.jointcenter.org/DB/factsheet/marital.htm

Carby, Hazel. *Race Men*. Cambridge, MA: Harvard University Press, 1998.

————. *Reconstructing Womanhood: The Emergence of the Afro-American Women Novelist*. New York: Oxford University Press, 1987.

Castaneda, Ruben. "A Day to Take Pride in the Gay Family: Thousands Celebrate at D.C. Parade, Fest." *Washington Post*, June 21, 1993.

Centers for Disease Control and Prevention. *Morbidity and Mortality Weekly Report* 39, no. 48 (December 1990): 869–73.

Centers for Disease Control and Prevention, National Center for Health Statistics. "Gun Deaths among Children and Teens Drop Sharply." *HHS News*, U.S. Department of Health and Human Services, July 24, 2000. Accessed July 13, 2016. http://www.cdc.gov/nchs/pressroom/00news/finaldeath98.htm.

———. "Negative Mood and Urban versus Rural Residence: Using Proximity to Metropolitan Statistical Areas as an Alternative Measure of Residence." By Bruce S. Jonas and Ronald W. Wilson, U.S. Department of Health and Human Services, Advance Data, Vital and Health Statistics, no. 281, March 6, 1997, 1–12.

Chafe, William H. *The Unfinished Journey: America since World War II*, 5th ed. New York: Oxford University Press, 2003.

Chandler, John, and Rebecca Bryant. "Farrakhan Criticizes Black Lesbians in CSUN Appearance," *Los Angeles Times*, November 5, 1993, 7.

Chang, Jeani, Cynthia Berg, Linda E. Saltzman, and Joy Herndon. "Homicide: A Leading Cause of Injury Deaths among Pregnant and Postpartum Women in the United States, 1991–1999." *American Journal of Public Health* 95, no. 3 (March 2005): 471–77.

Chauncey, George. *Gay New York: Gender, Urban Culture, and the Making of the Gay Male World, 1890–1940*. New York: Basic Books, 1994.

Chen, Edwin. "Unity on the Mall Provokes Divided Opinions Elsewhere." *Los Angeles Times*, October 17, 1995.

Chethik, Neil. "Million Man March Expands Movement." *Cleveland Plain Dealer*, October 29, 1995.

Childress, Deidre M. "Portraits: I Want the Memory." *Washington Post*, October 17, 1995.

"Christian Women's Declaration." Juicy Ecumenism: The Institute on Religion and Democracy's Blog. February 20, 2014. Accessed July 13, 2016. http://juicyecumenism .com/2014/02/20/ecumenical-christian-womens-declaration/.

Cimons, Marlene, and Kasper Zeuthen. "Participants, Doubters Ponder Meaning of Promise Keepers Movement." *Los Angeles Times*, September 30, 1997.

Cleaver, Eldridge. *Soul on Ice*. New York: Random House, 1968.

Cloud, John. "Postcard: Washington," *Time*, 174, no. 16 (October 26, 2009): 10.

Cobble, Dorothy Sue. *The Other Women's Movement: Workplace Justice and Social Rights in Modern America*. Princeton, NJ: Princeton University Press, 2004.

Cocco, Marie. "Moms Face a Stiffer Challenge after Their March." *New York Newsday*, May 16, 2000.

Collins, Patricia Hill. *Black Sexual Politics: African Americans, Gender, and the New Racism*. New York: Routledge, 2004.

Coontz, Stephanie. *The Way We Really Are: Coming to Terms with America's Changing Families*. New York: Basic Books, 1997.

Cooper, Anna J. *A Voice from the South*. 1892. Repr., Oxford: Oxford University Press, 1988.

Cose, Ellis. *The Rage of a Privileged Class: Why Are Middle-Class Blacks Angry? Why Should America Care?* New York: HarperCollins, 1993.

Crawford, Michael. "To Be Young Black, Gay, and Marching." PlanetOut.com. MMOW: About the March: Stories. Accessed December 8, 2003. htttp://www .planetout.com/mmow/about/stories/triangle.html.

Cross, Gary. *Men to Boys: The Making of Modern Immaturity*. New York: Columbia University Press, 2008.

Crowder, Carla. "Two Mom's Stories." *Denver Rocky Mountain News,* May 14, 2000.

"Crowds Gather in Philadelphia to Take Part in Million Woman March." *Los Angeles Times,* October 25, 1997.

Dare, G. D. *1.3 Million Woman Marched: Get a Glimpse of the Feeling of the Day.* Amherst, MA: Butterfly Press, 1998.

Dart, Bob. "Gay Activist Rally at Capitol." Cox News Service, April 30, 2000.

———. "Gay Communities March on Washington: Synergism Thwarted by Boycott." *Atlanta Journal-Constitution,* April 29, 2000.

Dawson, Michael C. *Behind the Mule: Race and Class in African American Politics.* Princeton, NJ: Princeton University Press, 1994.

———. *Blacks in and out of the Left.* Cambridge, MA: Harvard University Press, 2013.

Davis, Valerie Bridgeman. "A Womanist/Feminist Lives with a Promise Keeper and Likes It." In *Standing on the Promises: The Promise Keepers and the Revival of Manhood,* edited by Dane S. Claussen, 154–55. Cleveland, OH: Pilgrim Press, 1999.

Davis, Yusuf. "Around Town: Atlanta Rallies 'Round Million Man March." *Atlanta Journal-Constitution,* October 5, 1995.

DeBerg, Betty A. *Ungodly Women: Gender and the First Wave of American Fundamentalism.* Macon, GA: Mercer University Press, 2000.

Dees-Thomases, Donna, with Alison Hendrie. *Looking for a Few Good Moms: How One Mother Rallied a Million Others against the Gun Lobby.* Emmaus, PA: Rodale Press, 2004.

DeFao, Janine. "Moms' March in Oakland Draws 5,000 People." *San Francisco Chronicle,* May 15, 2000.

Degler, Carl N. *At Odds: Women and the Family in America from the Revolution to the Present.* New York: Oxford University Press, 1980.

Dejevsky, Mary. "500,000 'Moms' Rally for Tougher Controls on Guns." *London Independent,* May 15, 2000.

D'Emilio, John. *Lost Prophet: The Life and Times of Bayard Rustin.* Chicago: University of Chicago Press, 2004.

D'Emilio, John. *Sexual Politics, Sexual Communities: The Making of a Homosexual Minority in the United States, 1940–1970,* 2nd ed. Chicago: University of Chicago Press, 1998.

D'Emilio, John, and Estelle B. Freedman. *Intimate Matters: A History of Sexuality in America,* 2nd ed. Chicago: University of Chicago Press, 1997.

Dennis, Yvonne. "'If You Want the World to Change You Have to Do It': To March or Not to March? Many Are Still Undecided." *Philadelphia Daily News,* October 24, 1997. Accessed July 13, 2016. http://articles.philly.com/1997-10-24/news /25536997_1_black-women-black-men-men-of-other-races.

Des Jardins, Julie. *Women and the Historical Enterprise in America: Gender, Race, and the Politics of Memory, 1880–1945.* Chapel Hill: University of North Carolina Press, 2003.

DeWitt, Karen. "Themes from the March Resonate." *New York Times,* October 18, 1995.

Dickerson, Jeff. "Tactics of a Bygone Era, Why Should I Attend the Million Man March?" *Atlanta Journal-Constitution*, September 13, 1995.

Diehl, Kim. "Here's the Movement, Let's Start Building." *Colorlines*, November 2, 2000. Accessed August 11, 2016. http://www.colorlines.com/articles/heres-movement -lets-start-building.

Dill, Bonnie Thornton. "Race, Class, and Gender: Prospects for an All-Inclusive Sisterhood," *Feminist Studies* 9, no. 1 (Spring 1983): 67–85.

Dlouhy, Dallas. "Public Pulse." *Omaha World-Herald*, May 17, 2000.

Douglass, Frederick. *Narrative of the Life of Frederick Douglass, an American Slave, Written by Himself, with Related Documents*, edited by David W. Blight. Boston: Bedford/St. Martin's, 2003.

Dratch, Dana, and Shelli Liebman Dorfman. "Moms on a Mission." *Atlanta Jewish Times*, May 12, 2000.

Dresser, Jannie. "Lest We Forget the Contributions of Non-Moms." *Houston Chronicle*, May 14, 2000.

Du Bois, W. E. B. "The Conservation of the Races." American Negro Academy, *Occasional Papers*, no. 2, 1897. In *W. E. B. Du Bois: A Reader*, edited by David Levering Lewis, 20–27. New York: Henry Holt, 1995.

———. *The Souls of Black Folk* in *The Oxford W. E. B. Du Bois Reader*, edited by Eric J. Sundquist, 97–240. New York: Oxford University Press, 1996.

Dunlap, David W. "Gay Blacks in Quandary over Farrakhan's March." *New York Times*, October 8, 1995.

Dwyer, Jim. "Numbers Don't Tally." *New York Daily News*, October 17, 1995.

Echols, Alice. *Daring to Be Bad: Radical Feminism in America 1967–1975*. Minneapolis: University of Minnesota Press, 1989.

"Editorial/Public Pulse." *Omaha World-Herald*, May 22, 2000.

Edwards, Andrew W. "Religion." In *The Impact of Macro Social Systems on Ethnic Minorities in the United States*, edited by Alfred A. Jarrett, 229–66. Westport, CT: Praeger, 2000.

Emerson, Michael O., and Christian Smith. *Divided by Faith: Evangelical Religion and the Problem of Race in America*. New York: Oxford University Press, 2000.

Escobar, Gabriel. "He's the Coach for the Faithful—or the Far Right?" *Washington Post*, September 28, 1997.

Estes-Hicks, Onita. "The Way We Were: Precious Memories of the Black Segregated South." *African American Review* 27, no. 1 (Spring 1993): 9–18.

Estes, Steve. *I Am a Man! Race, Manhood, and the Civil Rights Movement*. Chapel Hill: University of North Carolina Press, 2005.

Faderman, Lillian. *Odd Girls and Twilight Lovers: A History of Lesbian Life in Twentieth-Century America*. New York: Penguin Group, 1992.

Farber, Jim. "Sing Out! Concert's Focus Is Gay Issues." *New York Daily News*, April 28, 2000.

"Farrakhan's Mixed Message: Million Man March: Despite the Demagogy, an Important Truth." *Baltimore Sun*, October 17, 1996.

Feagin, Joe R., and Melvin P. Sikes. *Living with Racism: The Black Middle-Class Experience*. Boston: Beacon Press, 1994.

Feldstein, Ruth. *Motherhood in Black and White: Race and Sex in American Liberalism, 1930–1965*. Ithaca, NY: Cornell University Press, 2000.

Fields, Suzanne. "Moms Should Redirect Their March in Line with the Facts." *Cleveland Plain Dealer*, May 22, 2000.

———. "The Power of a Promise." *Tampa Tribune*, December 26, 1996.

———. "Women Are Fairly Split on Issue of Gun Control." *Reading (PA) Eagle*, May 24, 2000.

Fingerhaut, Lois A., Deborah D. Ingram, and Jacob J. Feldman. "Homicide Rates among U.S. Teenagers and Young Adults: Differences by Mechanism, Level of Urbanization, Race, and Sex, 1987 through 1995." *Journal of the American Medical Association* 280, no. 5 (August 1998): 423–27.

Fisher, Marc. "Million Man March; Behind the Scenes, the Women Count." *Washington Post*, October 14, 1995.

Fletcher, Michael. "Black Men Jam Mall for a 'Day of Atonement': Fiery Rhetoric, Alliances, Skepticism Mark March." *Washington Post*, October 17, 1995.

Fletcher, Michael, and Mario Brossard. "March Has Solid Support of Blacks, Poll Finds." *Washington Post*, October 5, 1995.

———. "Poll: Many Blacks Back March but Find Organizers Troubling." *Houston Chronicle*, October 6, 1995.

Fletcher, Michael A., and DeNeen L. Brown. "Anticipation, Hopes Build for Million Woman March." *Washington Post*, October 24, 1997.

———. "We Are Countless in Unity." *Washington Post*, October 26, 1997.

Fletcher, Michael, and Hamil R. Harris. "United They'll Stand." *Washington Post*, September 10, 1995.

"Flexing Political Muscle." *Akron (OH) Beacon Journal*, April 30, 2000.

Foege, Alec, and Karen Quinones Miller. "Philadelphia Story." *People Weekly* 48, no. 19 (November 10, 1997): 123.

Fogel, Robert William. *The Fourth Great Awakening and the Future of Equalitarianism*. Chicago: University of Chicago Press, 2000.

Fordham, Signithia. "Passin' for Black: Race, Identity, and Bone Memory in Postracial America." *Harvard Educational Review* 80, no. 1 (2010): 13–23.

Fox, Catherine. "National Black Arts Festival: Role of Race in Black Art Debated." *Atlanta Journal-Constitution*, July 25, 2003.

Frazier, E. Franklin. *The Negro Family in the United States*. 1939. Repr., Chicago: University of Chicago Press, 1966.

Fredrickson, George M. *The Black Image in the White Mind: The Debate on Afro-American Character and Destiny, 1817–1914*. New York: Harper and Row, 1971.

Freedman, Estelle B. *No Turning Back: The History of Feminism and the Future of Women*. New York: Random House, 2002.

"Free for All." *Washington Post*, May 20, 2000.

Freeman, Greg. "Go Ahead, Black Man, the Magic Can Last. *St. Louis Post-Dispatch*, October 20, 1995.

Fulwood, Sam, III. "Blacks Not in Lock Step as Washington March Nears." *Los Angeles Times*, October 7, 1995.

Gaines, Kevin. *Uplifting the Race: Black Leadership, Politics, and Culture in the Twentieth Century*. Chapel Hill: University of North Carolina Press, 1996.

Galloway, Jim. "When Mothers Get Mad." *Atlanta Journal-Constitution*, May 14, 2000.

Gammerman, Ellen. "Million Mom March Evokes Power, Pathos." *Baltimore Sun*, May 15, 2000.

———. "Moms and Minivans versus Lawyers, Guns and Money." *Baltimore Sun*, May 11, 2000.

Gamson, Joshua. "Whose Millennium March?" *Nation*, March 30, 2000.

Garrison, Jessica. "Rift over Locations Yields 2 Anti-Gun Protest Marches." *Los Angeles Times*, May 12, 2000.

Garrison, Jessica, and Antonio Olivo. "Protest Takes Aim at Guns." *Los Angeles Times*, May 15, 2000.

Gatewood, Willard B. *Aristocrats of Color: The Black Elite, 1880–1920*. Bloomington: Indiana University Press, 1990.

Gavanas, Anna. *Fatherhood Politics in the United States: Masculinity, Sexuality, Race, and Marriage*. Urbana: University of Illinois Press, 2004.

"Gay Blacks Anxious about Joining March," *Gainesville (FL) Sun*, October 8, 1995.

"Gay Rights Activists' Millennium March on Washington." Anchor, Carole Simpson; reporter, Jim Sciutto. *ABC World News Tonight*, April 30, 2000.

"A Gay Rights Movement in the New Millennium." *San Francisco Chronicle*, April 30, 2000.

Gay Rights, Special Rights: Inside the Homosexual Agenda. Hernet, CA: Traditional Values Coalition/Jeremiah Films, 1993.

Gerber, Alison. "Bus Brings Moms Together for Rally." *USA Today*, May 15, 2000.

———. "Teen's Life Was Cut Short Just as He Regained Feeling in His Legs." *USA Today*, May 12, 2000.

Gergen, David. "Promises Worth Keeping." *U.S. News and World Report*, September 29, 1997.

Giddings, Paula. *When and Where I Enter: The Impact of Black Women on Race and Sex in America*. New York: William Morrow, 1984.

Gilliam, Dorothy. "Time Will Tell True Impact of March." *Washington Post*, November 1, 1997.

Gitlin, Todd. "Identity Politics Takes an Awful Toll." *Los Angeles Times*, December 7, 1995.

———. *The Twilight of Common Dreams: Why America Is Wracked by Culture Wars*. New York: Metropolitan Books, 1995.

Golab, Art. "14 Ministers Endorse Million Man March; Farrakhan's Role Keeps Many Black Churches Away." *Chicago Sun-Times*, October 6, 1995.

Golden, Marita. *Saving Our Sons: Raising Black Children in a Turbulent World*. New York: Anchor Books, 1995.

Golden, Thelma. "Introduction." *Freestyle, the Studio Museum of Harlem* (catalog). New York: Studio Museum of Harlem, 2001.

Goldstein, Richard. "The Millennium March: A Gay March on Washington Spawns a Major Movement Rift." *Village Voice*, April 25, 2000. Accessed August 12, 2016. http://www.commondreams.org/headlines/042500-03.htm.

Gomes, Peter. *The Good Book: Reading the Bible with Mind and Heart.* New York: Harper One, 2002.

Goodstein, Laurie. "For Christian Men's Group, Racial Harmony Starts at the Local Level." *New York Times*, September 29, 1997.

———. "Men Pack RFK on Promise of Religious Renewal." *Washington Post*, May 28, 1995.

Goodwin, Jeff, James M. Jasper, and Francesca Polletta. "Introduction: Why Emotions Matter." In *Passionate Politics: Emotions and Social Movements*, edited by Jeff Goodwin, James M. Jasper, and Francesca Polletta, 1–26. Chicago: University of Chicago Press, 2001.

Grady, Sandy. "It'll Be a War to Get Gun-Law Changes." *Contra Costa (CA) Times*, May 18, 2000.

Gray, Helen. "Promise, Promises; They're Not Easy to Keep, but Men Who Attended Promise Keepers Conference Are Trying Hard." *Kansas City (MO) Star*, August 1, 1996.

———. "What Promises to Keep?" *Kansas City (MO) Star*, April 25, 1996.

Greene, Marcia Slacum. "A Welcome for Women on the Mall." *Washington Post*, October 17, 1995.

Green, Rick. "Board Resist Call to Close City Schools for March." *Hartford Courant*, October 3, 1995.

Grier, Peter. "Next Hard Steps of Turning March Euphoria into Action." *Christian Science Monitor*, October 17, 1995.

Grier, William H., and Price M. Cobbs. *Black Rage.* New York: Basic Books, 1968.

Griffith, R. Marie. *God's Daughters: Evangelical Women and the Power of Submission.* Berkeley: University of California Press, 1997.

Griswold, Robert L. *Fatherhood in America: A History.* New York: HarperCollins, 1993.

Gross, Greg. "D.C. March Spurs Local Action at Meeting." *San Diego Union-Tribune*, October 22, 1995.

"Group Has Promises to Keep; Men's Organization Plans Giant Gathering in Washington." *Arizona Republic*, September 2, 1997.

Grynaviski, Jeffrey, and Melissa Harris-Lacewell. "Shifting Alliances: Are Black Voters Ready to Rethink Allegiance to the Democratic Party?" Paper prepared for presentation at the annual meeting for the Political Science Association, Washington DC, September 2005.

Guinier, Lani, and Gerald Torres. *The Miner's Canary: Enlisting Race, Resisting Power.* Cambridge, MA: Harvard University Press, 2002.

"Gun-Toting Mothers 'Want to Be Safe at Home.'" *Ottawa Citizen*, May 22, 2000.

Guns and Mothers. Thom Powers, dir. DVD. Brooklyn, NY: First Run/Icarus Films, 2003.

Gutierrez-Mier, John. "S.A. Residents to Join D.C. Gay Rights March." *San Antonio Express News,* April 28, 2000.

Gutman, Herbert. *The Black Family in Slavery and Freedom, 1750–1925.* New York: Pantheon Books, 1976.

Guy, Andrew, Jr. "175 Gun Advocates Protest Group's Agenda at Hotel." *Denver Post,* September 16, 2000.

Halbwachs, Maurice. *On Collective Memory,* edited and translated by Lewis A. Cosner. Chicago: University of Chicago Press, 1992.

Hall, Jacquelyn Dowd. "'The Mind That Burns in Each Body': Women, Rape, and Racial Violence." In *Powers of Desire: The Politics of Sexuality,* edited by Ann Snitow, Christine Stansell, and Sharon Thompson, 328–49. New York: Monthly Review Press, 1983.

———. *Revolt against Chivalry: Jesse Daniel Ames and the Women's Campaign against Lynching.* New York: Columbia University Press, 1979.

Hamblin, Ken. "A Patronizing Promise." *Denver Post,* June 25, 1996.

———. "The Roles of God and Responsible Fathers." *Denver Post,* August 2, 1994.

Hammonds, Donald I. "Where Do We Go from Here?" *Pittsburgh Post-Gazette,* May 10, 2000.

Hancock, Ange-Marie. *The Politics of Disgust: The Public Identity of the Welfare Queen.* New York: New York University Press, 2004.

Harden, Mike. "Moms Take Anti-Gun Fight on the Road." *Columbus (OH) Dispatch,* May 14, 2000.

Harding, Vincent, Robin Kelley, and Earl Lewis. *We Changed the World: African Americans 1945–1970.* New York: Oxford University Press, 1997.

Harris, Hamil R. "Despite Paradox, Black Women Support March." *Washington Post,* October 1, 1995.

———. "Promise Keepers Say They're Halfway to Goal." *Washington Post,* August 29, 1997.

Harris-Lacewell, Melissa. "Liberation to Mutual Fund: The Political Consequences of Differing Conceptions of Christ in the African American Church" (unpublished paper).

Harris-Perry, Melissa V. *Sister Citizen: For Colored Girls Who've Considered Politics When Being Strong Isn't Enough.* New Haven, CT: Yale University Press, 2011.

Hart, James. "Shooting Victim's Mother Fights for Tougher Gun Laws." *Kansas City (MO) Star,* October 12, 2000.

Harvey, David. *The Condition of Postmodernity: An Enquiry into the Origins of Cultural Change.* Malden, MA: Blackwell, 1990.

Haynes, Karima. "Los Angeles: Mothers Push Fight against Gun Violence." *Los Angeles Times,* August 5, 2002.

Haynes, Monica. "Black Women Headed for Rally." *Pittsburgh Post-Gazette,* October 26, 1997.

———. "Local Women Join Million Mom March Next Sunday to Fight Guns." *Pittsburgh Post-Gazette,* May 7, 2000.

———. "Marching for Little Tony; One of the Million Moms Has a Personal Reason to Take a Stand Against Gun Violence." *Pittsburgh Post-Gazette*, May 10, 2000.

———. "Million Woman March Powering Up." *Pittsburgh Post-Gazette*, September 23, 1997.

Helmore, Edward. "College Football Hero Corey Johnson Came Out and No One Was Outraged: America Rallies to Teenage Gay Icon." *Guardian* (U.S. edition), April 30, 2000. Accessed August 14, 2016. https://www.theguardian.com/world/2000/apr/30/gayrights.theobserver.

Herek, Gregory M., and John P. Capitanio. "Black Heterosexuals' Attitudes Toward Lesbians and Gay Men in the United States," *Journal of Sex Research* 32, no. 2 (1995):96, 100.

Herndon, Lucia. "March with a Million Memories." *Denver Post*, October 28, 1997.

Hernton, Calvin C. *Sex and Racism in America*. New York: Doubleday, 1965.

Herrick, Thaddeus. "Promise Keepers Targeting Hispanic Males." *Houston Chronicle*, November 30, 1996.

Herrmann, Andrew. "Promise Keepers Grapple with Men's Role in Family." *Chicago Sun-Times*, February 10, 1996.

Heston, Charlton. Speech before the Free Congress Foundation, December 7, 1997. Violence Policy Center. Accessed August 12, 2016. https://www.youtube.com/watch?v=BWCzEwWNNIc.

Higginbotham, A. Leon, Jr. "I Couldn't Separate the Message from the Messenger." *Newsday*, October 18, 1995.

Higginbotham, Evelyn Brooks. *Righteous Discontent: The Woman's Movement in the Black Baptist Church, 1880–1920*. Cambridge, MA: Harvard University Press, 1993.

Hine, Darlene Clark. "Million Woman March, Philadelphia, PA, October 1997: A Commemoration," unpublished compilation, 1998.

Hodges, Earl. "Promise Keeper Turns Life Around." *New Orleans Times-Picayune*, September 29, 1996.

Hogan, M. J., ed. *The Ambiguous Legacy*. Cambridge: Cambridge University Press, 1999.

Hogan-Albach, Susan. "Promise Keepers Say Prayer, Not Power Is Force." *Minneapolis Star Tribune*, September 28, 1997.

Hogan, Susan. "Keepers' Good-Guy Image Attracts Critics' Jabs." *Minneapolis Star Tribune*, August 9, 1997.

Hood, Robert E. *Begrimed and Black: Christian Traditions on Blacks and Blackness*. Minneapolis, MN: Fortress Press, 1994.

Horton, James Oliver. *Free People of Color: Inside the African American Community*. Washington, DC: Smithsonian Institution Press, 1993.

"How Black Academics Viewed the Million Man March." *Journal of Blacks in Higher Education* 10 (Winter 1995–96): 59–63.

Huebert, J. H. "Open Fire on Chicago's Gun Law." *Chicago Maroon*, July 12, 2002. Accessed April 24, 2006. www.jhhuebert.com/articles/chicagoguns.html.

Hutchinson, Darren Lenard. "'Claiming' and 'Speaking' Who We Are: Black Gays and Lesbians, Racial Politics and the Million Man March." In *Black Men on Race, Gender, and Sexuality: A Critical Reader,* edited by Devon W. Carbado, 28–45. New York: New York University Press, 1999.

Hutchinson, Earl Ofari. *The Assassination of the Black Male Image.* New York: Touchstone, 1994.

Hutchins, S. M. "Papering Over a Rift." *Touchstone, a Journal of Mere Christianity* 12, no. 3 (May/June 1999). Accessed August 14, 2016. http://www.touchstonemag.com/archives/article.php?id=12-03-014-o.

Illescas, Carlos. "Moms Meet to Organize." *Denver Post,* September 16, 2000.

Jacoby, Jeff. "Guns for Rapists, but Not for Potential Victims." *Capitalism,* October 6, 2002. Accessed July 13, 2016. http://www.capmag.com/article.asp?ID=1949.

Jaffe, Susan. "Black Men March for Community." *Tampa Tribune,* September 17, 1995.

Jahn, Ed. "Many Blacks See March as Step in Right Direction." *San Diego Union-Tribune,* October 18, 1997.

Janofsky, Michael. "At Million Woman March, Focus Is on Family." *New York Times,* October 25, 1997.

———. "Million Women March Is Set with High Hopes." *New York Times,* October 23, 1997.

———. "When a Rally's Strength Is Seen as Its Weakness." *New York Times,* October 25, 1997.

Jetter, Alexis, Annelise Orleck, and Diana Taylor, eds. *The Politics of Motherhood: Activist Voices from Left to Right.* Hanover, NH: University Press of New England, 1997.

Johnson, Charles. "The End of the Black American Narrative: A New Century Calls for New Stories Grounded in the Present, Leaving Behind the Painful History of Slavery and Its Consequences." *American Scholar* 77, no. 3 (Summer 2008): 32–42.

———. "Letter to the Editor." *Geekery Today,* May 11, 2000. Accessed April 17, 2006. http:/radgeek.com/gt/2000/05/11/on

Jones, Martha S. *All Bound Up Together: The Woman Question in African American Public Culture, 1830–1900.* Chapel Hill: University of North Carolina Press, 2007.

Jones, William P. *The March on Washington: Jobs, Freedom, and the Forgotten History of Civil Rights.* New York: W. W. Norton, 2013.

Jordan, June. "A Gathering Purpose." *Progressive* (Madison, WI), 62, no. 1 (January 1998): 33–34.

Jordan, Winthrop D. *White over Black: American Attitudes toward the Negro, 1550–1812.* Baltimore: Penguin Books, 1969.

Kandiyoti, Deniz. "Bargaining with Patriarchy." *Gender and Society* 2, no. 3 (1988): 274–90.

Kaplan, Temma. *Taking Back the Streets: Women, Youth, and Direct Democracy.* Berkeley: University of California Press, 2003.

Kee, Lorraine. "Black Women Get on Their Own Bus." *St. Louis Post-Dispatch,* November 7, 1997.

"Keep Talking." *San Diego Union-Tribune,* October 30, 1995.

Kenaga, Marilyn. "Fulfilling God's Role for the Woman Is the Most Rewarding Feeling." In *Standing on the Promises: The Promise Keepers and the Revival of Manhood*, edited by Dane S. Claussen, 169–84. Cleveland, OH: Pilgrim Press, 1999.

Kenna, Kathleen. "March of 'Awakening' Black Women Set to Reaffirm Their Sisterhood." *Toronto Star*, October 24, 1997.

Kennedy, Elizabeth Lapovsky, and Madeline D. Davis. *Boots of Leather, Slippers of Gold: A History of a Lesbian Community*. New York: Routledge, 1993.

Kennedy, Morris. "Better Promise Keepers Than Promise Breakers." *Tampa Tribune*, August 13, 1995.

Kent, Mary Mederios. "Immigration and America's Black Population." *Population Bulletin: A Publication of the Population Reference Bureau* 62, no. 4 (December 2007): 1–16.

Kerber, Linda. "The Republican Mother." In *Women's America: Refocusing the Past*, edited by Linda Kerber and Jane Sherron De Hart, 3rd ed., 87–95. New York: Oxford University Press, 1991.

Kerr, Audrey Elisa. *The Paper Bag Principle: Class Colorism, and Rumor and the Case of Black Washington, D.C.* Knoxville: University of Tennessee Press, 2006.

Kerrill, Tamara. "Black Women Split on Staying Out of March." *Chicago Sun-Times*, October 5, 1995.

Kimmel, Michael. *Manhood in America: A Cultural History*, 3rd ed. New York: Oxford University Press, 2012.

King, Marsha. "Show of Sisters from Seattle-Local Women to Join Million Woman March in Philadelphia." *Seattle Times*, October 24, 1997.

Knock, Michael. "Local Residents Reflect on D.C. Millennium March." *Iowa City Press-Citizen*, June 1, 2000.

Kopel, Dave. "Rapists Like Gun Control." *National Review*, April 14, 2000. Accessed August 14, 2016. http://www.davekopel.com/NRO/2000/Rapists-Like-Gun-Control .htm.

Kreisher, Otto. "San Diego Gay Rights Activist Leads National March." Copley News Service, Washington, DC, April 28, 2000.

Kruse, Steve. "Public Pulse." *Omaha World-Herald*, May 17, 2000.

Ladd-Taylor, Molly, and Lauri Umansky, eds. *"Bad" Mothers: The Politics of Blame in Twentieth-Century America*. New York: New York University Press, 1998.

Lambert, Alice. "Much to Fear from Promise Keepers." *Hartford (CT) Courant*, September 14, 1999.

Layard, Richard. *Happiness: Lessons from a New Science*. New York: Penguin Press. 2008.

———. "The Secrets of Happiness." *New Statesman* 132, no. 4627 (March 2003): 25–29.

Lears, T. J. Jackson. *No Place of Grace: Antimodernism and the Transformation of American Culture, 1880–1920*. Chicago: University of Chicago Press, 1981.

Lee, Felicia R. "Thousands of Women Share Wounds, and Celebrate." *New York Times*, October 26, 1997. Accessed July 15, 2016. http://www.nytimes.com/1997/10/26/us /thousands-of-women-share-wounds-and-celebrate.html.

Lemelle, Anthony J. Jr., and Juan Battle. "Black Masculinity in Attitude toward Gay Males," *Journal of Homosexuality* 47, no. 1 (2004): 39–51.

Leonard, Mary. "'Million Mom March' against Guns on Mother's Day, May 14." *Boston Globe*, May 14, 2000.

Lesnick, Delores. "Celebrating Our Families at the Millennium March on Washington." PlanetOut.com. April 30, 2000. Accessed December 8, 2003. http://www.planetout.com/mmow/about/stories/lesnick.html.

"Letter Hearing Held to Gather Comments." *Denver Rocky Mountain News*, June 22, 2000.

"Letters from Readers." *Minneapolis Star Tribune*, August 24, 1997.

Lewis, Gregory B. "Black-White Differences in Attitudes toward Homosexuality and Gay Rights," *Public Opinion Quarterly* 67, no. 1 (2003): 66.

Lichter, Daniel T., Diane K. McLaughlin, George Kephart, David J. Landry et al. "Race and the Retreat from Marriage: A Shortage of Marriageable Men?" *American Sociological Review* 57, no. 6 (December 1992): 781–99.

Liu, Caitlin. "Vigil Memorializes Gun Violence Victims." *Los Angeles Times*, December 11, 2000.

Lochhead, Carolyn. "Civil Rights Leader Won't Support March." *San Francisco Chronicle*, October 11, 1995.

Loeb, Vernon. "Portraits, the Million Man March: 'I Will Have a Different Outlook.'" *Washington Post*, October 17, 1995.

Longwood, Dyann. "One Million Strong: An Insider's Diary of the Million Woman March." *Contemporary Women's Issues* 4, no. 1 (Winter 1998): 15–19.

"A Look at Promise Keepers; the Men Speak for Themselves." *Washington Post*, September 9, 1997.

Lorde, Audre. *I Am Your Sister: Black Women Organizing across Sexualities.* New York: Kitchen Table/Women of Color Press, 1985.

Lubiano, Wahneema. "Black Ladies, Welfare Queens, and State Minstrels: Ideological War by Narrative Means." In *Race-ing Justice, En-gendering Power: Essays on Anita Hill, Clarence Thomas, and the Construction of Social Identity*, edited by Toni Morrison, 323–61. New York: Pantheon Books, 1992.

Ly, Phuong. "Making a Public Declaration." *Washington Post*, April 30, 2000.

Machung, Anne. "Talking Career, Thinking Job: Gender Differences in Career and Family Expectations of Berkeley Seniors." *Feminist Studies* 15, no. 1 (Spring 1989): 35–58.

MacLean, Nancy. *Freedom Is Not Enough: The Opening of the American Workplace.* New York: Russell Sage Foundation, 2006.

Madhubuti, Haki R., and Maulana Karenga, eds. *Million Man March/Day of Absence: A Commemorative Anthology—Speeches, Commentary, Photography, Poetry, Illustrations and Documents.* Chicago: Third World Press, 1996.

Maller, Peter, and Meg Jones. "Men Find Mission in Promise Keepers' Vows." *Milwaukee Journal Sentinel*, February 15, 1996.

Malveaux, Julianne. "A Woman's Place Is in the March; Why Should I Stand By My Man, When He's Trying to Step Over Me?" *Washington Post*, October 8, 1995.

"Many Women Attended March. . . ." *St. Louis Post-Dispatch*, October 17, 1995.

"Marching for Little Tony; One of the Million Moms Has a Personal Reason to Take a Stand against Gun Violence." *Pittsburgh Post-Gazette*, May 10, 2000.

Marcus, Eric. *Making Gay History: The Half-Century Fight for Lesbian and Gay Equal Rights*. New York: HarperCollins, 2002.

Marquand, Robert. "America Taps Religious Roots in Year of Spiritual Questing." *Christian Science Monitor*, December 31, 1996.

Mattingly, Carol. *Well-Tempered Women: Nineteenth-Century Temperance Rhetoric*. Carbondale: Southern Illinois University Press, 1998.

Mattingly, Terry. "Sermons by Black Ministers Appeal to Angry White Males." *Denver Rocky Mountain News*, June 10, 1995.

Maxwell, Bill. "Farrakhan as Seen from the Inside." *St. Petersburg Times*, October 22, 1995.

Mays, Andrea L., and Robert Davis. "Women's Reactions Run from Elation to Disdain." *USA Today*, October 17, 1995.

McClintock, Anne. "Family Feuds: Gender, Nationalism and the Family." *Feminist Review* 44 (Summer 1993): 61–79.

McCormick, Joseph P., 2d. "How African American Men View Various African American Leadership Types: Findings from the Million Man March." In *Overview of Black and Latina/o Politics: Issues in Political Development in the United States*, edited by William Nelson and Jessica Perez-Monforti, 143–55. Miami: Barnhardt and Ash, 2005.

McCormick, Joseph P., 2d. and Sekou. "Expressions of Racial Consciousness in the African American Community: Data from the Million Man March." *Black and Multiracial Politics in America*, Yvette U. Alex-Assenson and Lawrence J. Hanks, eds. New York: New York University Press, 2000.

McCraven, Marilyn. "Day of Unity, Civility, Kindness." *Baltimore Sun*, October 22, 1995.

McCullen, Kevin. "Boulder Gun Debate Lures Crowd." *Denver Rocky Mountain News*, June 22, 2000.

McKay, Rick. "Calling for Legislation, Gay People and Their Supporters Crowd onto National Mall on Sunday." *Palm Beach Post*, May 1, 2000.

McLoughlin, William G. *Revivals, Awakenings, and Reform: An Essay on Religion and Social Change in America, 1607–1977*. Chicago: University of Chicago Press, 1978.

McNamara, Bill. "They Have Promises to Keep: Diocese Organizes 'Wake-Up Call' for Catholic Men." *South Coast Today* (New Bedford, MA), August 4, 1994, updated January 10, 2011. Accessed July 16, 2016. REFS.http://www.southcoasttoday.com /article/19970804/News/308049930.

"Media Matters Exposes Bennett: '[Y]ou Could Abort Every Black Baby in This Country, and Your Crime Rate Would Go Down.'" By Andrew Seifter. September

28, 2005. Accessed July 26, 2015. http://mediamatters.org/video/2005/09/28
/media-matters-exposes-bennett-you-could-abort-e/133904.

Melone, Mary Jo. "Promise Keepers without Religion." *St. Petersburg Times*, February 20, 1997.

Merrill, Scott. "How Could Women Fear the Woman-Friendly Agenda of the Promise Keepers." *Buffalo News*, January 4, 1998.

"A Message about Gay Power." Editorial, *San Francisco Chronicle*, May 2, 2000.

"Methods of Suicide among Persons Aged 10–19 Years—United States 1992–2001." CDC, *Morbidity and Mortality Weekly Report* 53, no. 22 (June 11, 2004): 471–74. Accessed July 13, 2016. http://www.cdc.gov/mmwr/preview/mmwrhtml/mm5322a2.htm.

Meyerowitz, Joanne. *How Sex Changed: A History of Transsexuality in the United States.* Cambridge, MA: Harvard University Press, 2002.

Miller, Stephen H. "The Baiting Game." Independent Gay Forum Culture Watch. Accessed August 10, 2016. https://igfculturewatch.com/1999/11/30/the-baiting-game/.

———. "Gay White Males: PC's Unseen Target." In *Beyond Queer: Challenging Gay Left Orthodoxy*, edited by Bruce Bawer, 24–37. New York: Free Press, 1996.

———. "March On?" Independent Gay Forum Culture Watch. Accessed August 11, 2016. https://igfculturewatch.com/?s=March+On+.

———. "An Uninspiring March on Washington." Independent Gay Forum Culture Watch. Accessed August 10, 2016. https://igfculturewatch.com/2000/01/27/an-uninspiring-march-on-washington/Accessed August 10, 2016.

"Million Man March Sent Strong Messages." *Baltimore Sun*, October 21, 1995.

"'Million Man' Plan Divides Churches; Some African Americans View March as Effort to Legitimize Farrakhan." *Los Angeles Times*, October 7, 1995.

"The Million Mom Impact." *San Francisco Chronicle*, May 16, 2000.

"Million Woman March a Misstep for Black Community." *Philadelphia Daily News*, October 22, 1997.

"Million Woman March—Media Didn't Give Gathering the Coverage It Afforded Similar Men-Oriented Events." *Seattle Times*, November 4, 1997.

Millner, Denene. "Journey Brings Hope for Future Pilgrimage." *New York Daily News*, October 17, 1995.

———. "Marchers Feel Like a Million." *New York Daily News*, October 8, 1995.

Milloy, Courtland. "Awakened by Spirits of Change." *Washington Post*, October 18, 1995.

———. "For One Woman, a Million Fond Memories." *Washington Post*, October 29, 1997.

———. "Happiness Survey Yields Painful Truth." *Washington Post*, March 23, 1997.

———. "Stepping In to Stop the Heartbreak." *Washington Post*, September 10, 1995.

Mitchell, Mary A. "Road to Sisterhood Starts aboard a Bus to Philadelphia." *Chicago Sun-Times*, October 26, 1997.

———. "Women's March a Well-Kept Secret." *Chicago Sun-Times,* October 9, 1997.
Mixner, David. "Millennium March Will Help Generate Political Power." MMOW: About the March: Stories. PlanetOut.com. Accessed December 8, 2003. http://planetout.com/mmow/about/stories/mixner.html.
Mize, Scott. "Reader Responses: Mom Marchers Ignoring Statistics." *Atlanta Journal-Constitution,* May 14, 2000.
Moghaddam, Masoud. "Happiness, Faith, Friends, and Fortune—Empirical Evidence from the 1998 US Survey Data." *Journal of Happiness Studies* 9 (2008): 577–87.
Monroe, Irene. "Louis Farrakhan's Ministry of Misogyny and Homophobia." In *The Farrakhan Factor: African-American Writers on Leadership, Nationhood, and Minister Louis Farrakhan,* edited by Amy Alexander. New York: Grove Press, 1998.
———. "Prophetic Voices of the New Millennium." MMOW: About the March: Stories. PlanetOut.com. Accessed December 8, 2003. htttp://www.planetout.com/mmow/about/stories/Monroe.html.
Monsen, Sonja. "Letters." *Tampa Tribune,* May 30, 2000.
Moore, Linda Wright. "The Drill Is Shaky, but the March Is Strong." *Philadelphia Online,* October 23, 1997. Accessed July 13, 2016. http://articles.philly.com/1997–10–23/news/25541093_1_black-women-asia-coney-million-woman-march.
Morganfield, Robbie. "Building the Million Man March, Christians Split on Supporting." *Houston Chronicle,* October 8, 1995.
———. "Each One, Reach One: Growing Men's Group Promotes Racial Reconciliation." *Houston Chronicle,* May 29, 1995.
Morin, Richard, and Scott Wilson. "Men Were Driven to Confess Their Sins." *Washington Post,* October 5, 1997.
Moriwaki, Lee. "Promise Keepers Returning." *Seattle Times,* April 21, 1996.
Morris, Bob. "The Age of Dissonance." *New York Times,* April 30, 2000.
Morrison, Blake, and Scott Bowles. "Do Marches Make a Difference?" *USA Today,* May 12, 2000.
Morrison, Toni, ed. *Race-ing Justice, En-gendering Power: Essays on Anita Hill, Clarence Thomas, and the Construction of Social Reality.* New York: Pantheon Books, 1992.
———. "What the Black Woman Thinks about Women's Lib." *New York Times Magazine,* August 22, 1971.
Morrow, Lance. "Why Mass Marches Have Lost Their Meaning." *Time,* May 15, 2000. Accessed July 16, 2016. http://content.time.com/time/magazine/article/0,9171,45210,00.html.
Moynihan, Daniel Patrick. *The Negro Family: The Case for National Action.* Office of Policy, Planning and Research, United States Department of Labor. U.S. Government Printing Office, 1965.
Muhammad, Khalil Gibran. *The Condemnation of Blackness: Race, Crime, and the Making of Modern Urban America.* Cambridge, MA: Harvard University Press, 2010.

Murphy, Caryle. "Seeking God, Man to Man; Promise Keepers See Group as an Emotional Response to Troubled Times." *Washington Post*, September 21, 1997.

Nannery, Matt. "A Wrong Picture of Gay Rally." *Newsday*, May 2, 1993.

Nelson, Brian, and Kate Snow. "Thousands in Washington for Gay and Lesbian Rights." *CNN Worldview*, April 30, 2000.

Newton, Judith. *From Panthers to Promise Keepers: Rethinking the Men's Movement.* Lanham, MD: Rowman and Littlefield, 2005.

Niederberger, Mary. "Million Mom March Group Continues Fight for Gun Control." *Pittsburgh Post-Gazette*, June 7, 2000.

Nolan, Bruce. "Promise Land—Racial Forgiveness Keepers' Message." *New Orleans Times-Picayune*, July 28, 1996.

———. "30,000 Men Gathering to Restore Moral Bonds." *New Orleans Times-Picayune*, July 26, 1996.

Norton, Mary Beth. "The Evolution of White Women's Experience in Early America." *The American Historical Review* 89, no. 3 (1984): 593–619.

"NRA Answers Moms Rally." *St. Louis Post-Dispatch*, May 22, 2000.

O'Clery, Conor. "Now White Males Take the Moral Stage." *Irish Times*, October 21, 1995.

Office of Juvenile Justice and Delinquency Prevention, U.S. Department of Justice. "Promising Strategies to Reduce Gun Violence." Accessed on July 13, 2016. http://www.ojjdp.gov/pubs/gun_violence/contents.html.

O'Hare, William P., Kelvin M. Pollard, Taynia L. Mann, and Mary M. Kent. "African Americans in the 1990s." *Population Bulletin* 46, no. 1 (1991): 14. Washington, DC: Population Reference Bureau.

Oliver, Valerie Cassel. "Inside Cover Statement." In "'Post-Black,' 'Post-Soul' or Hip Hop Iconography? Defining the New Aesthetics." *International Review of African American Art* 20, no. 2 (2005): n.p.

Pagano, Doni. "Moms See Bigger Picture about Guns." *Buffalo News*, May 16, 2000.

Page, Clarence. "NOW Suggestion a Promise Worth Keeping," *Houston Chronicle*, September 9, 1997, Three Star ed., sec. A18.

Paglia, Camille. "The Million Mom March: What a Crock!" *Salon.com*, May 17, 2000. Accessed July 13, 2016. http://www.salon.com/2000/05/17/cpmillionmom/.

Pardo, Steve. "Million Woman Rally in Detroit Stresses Unity." *Detroit Sunday News*, November 16, 1997.

Parker, Alison. *Articulating Rights: Nineteenth-Century American Women on Race, Reform, and the State.* DeKalb: Northern Illinois University Press, 2010.

Parrott, Jeanne. "Dale Came Home a Different Husband and Father." In *Standing on the Promises: The Promise Keepers and the Revival of Manhood*, edited by Dane S. Claussen, 161–62. Cleveland, OH: Pilgrim Press, 1999.

Penn, Steven, and Mary Sanchez. "KC Crowd Marches in Step with Men in Washington." *Kansas City (MO) Star*, October 17, 1995.

"A Perspective on Promise Keepers." United States Conference of Catholic Bishops' Committee on Laity, Marriage, Family Life, and Youth. Accessed July 13, 2016.

http://www.usccb.org/about/laity-marriage-family-life-and-youth/upload
/USCCB-FLWY-A-Perspective-on-Promise-Keepers.pdf.

Peterman, Erika D. "Million Woman March Fails to Hit Its Stride." *St. Petersburg Times*, October 28, 1997.

Pettus, Tim. "Men Who Keep Their Promise to Families." *St. Louis Post-Dispatch*, May 21, 1996.

Phillips, Kyra, and Miles O'Brien. "Supporters of Gay Rights March on Washington in Millennium March for Equality." April 30, 2000. Accessed July 13, 2016. http://www.cnn.com/TRANSCRIPTS/0004/30/sm.03.html XQQ\.

Plotke, David. "Racial Politics and the Clinton-Guinier Episode." *Dissent* 42 (Spring 1995): 221–35.

Pollitt, Katha. "Moms to NRA: Grow Up!" *Nation*, May 25, 2000. Accessed July 13, 2016. http://www.thenation.com/article/moms-nra-grow.

Porter, Rita. "Moms Should Stay Home and Focus on Raising Kids." *Columbus (OH) Dispatch*, May 21, 2000, editorial and comment, 2B.

Promise Keepers Men's Study Bible: King James Version. Grand Rapids, MI: Zondervan, 1997.

"Public Pulse." *Omaha World-Herald*, August 14, 1998.

Putney, Clifford. *Muscular Christianity: Manhood and Sports in Protestant America, 1880–1920*. Cambridge, MA: Harvard University Press, 2001.

Radford-Hill, Sheila. *Further to Fly: Black Women and the Politics of Empowerment*. Minneapolis: University of Minnesota Press, 2000.

"The Really Late Show." *USA Today*, October 28, 1997.

Reed, Ishmael. "Buck Passing: The Media, Black Men, O.J. and the Million Man March." In *Million Man March/Day of Absence: A Commemorative Anthology— Speeches, Commentary, Photography, Poetry, Illustrations and Documents*, edited by Haki R. Madhubuti, and Maulana Karenga, 129–33. Chicago: Third World Press, 1996.

Renfroe, Donna. "Promise Keepers Say Rally Promotes Family Unity." *Tampa Tribune*, September 19, 1997.

Reti, Irene, ed. *Childless by Choice: A Feminist Anthology*. Santa Cruz, CA: HerBooks, 1992.

Ripley, Jackie. "Pride, Peace Reign at March for Black Men." *St. Petersburg Times/ Tampa Today*, September 17, 1995.

Rivera, John. "Normal Day at Office, Even with Many Gone." *Baltimore Sun*, October 17, 1995.

Roberts, Dorothy. *Killing the Black Body: Race, Reproduction, and the Meaning of Liberty*. New York: Random House, 1997.

Robinson, Eugene. *Disintegration: The Splintering of Black America*. New York: Doubleday, 2010.

Robinson, Jennifer. "PK Movement Is Not as Promising as It Seems." *Montreal Gazette*, October 10, 1997.

Rodgers-Melnick, Ann. "Making Their Promises: 44,000 Christian Men Pray for Racial Unity as Promise Keepers." *Pittsburgh Post-Gazette*, July 14, 1996.

Rodriguez, Joe. "Gay Wichitans Part of March." *Wichita Eagle*, April 29, 2000.

Rodriguez, Lori. "Show of Unity, Message of Hope." *Houston Chronicle*, October 17, 1995.

Roediger, David R. *The Wages of Whiteness: Race and the Making of the American Working Class*. London: Verso, 1991.

Rojas, Aurelio. "Shoulder to Shoulder, with a Common Concern." *San Francisco Chronicle*, October 17, 1995.

Rodgers, Daniel T. *Age of Fracture*. Cambridge, MA: Harvard University Press, 2011.

Romano, Michael. "Keeping the Promise of God." *Denver Rocky Mountain News*, July 17, 1994.

———. "Promise Keepers Helps Promise Breakers." *Denver Rocky Mountain News*, June 18, 1995.

Rosen, Ruth. "A Feminist Send-Off for a Million Men: Farrakhan Aside, the March in Washington Holds Promise for the Needs of Women, Children. *Los Angeles Times*, October 12, 1995.

Roth, Benita. *Separate Roads to Feminism: Black, Chicana, and White Feminist Movements in America's Second Wave*. New York: Cambridge University Press, 2004.

Rotundo, E. Anthony. *American Manhood: Transformations in Masculinity from the Revolution to the Modern Era*. New York: Basic Books, 1993.

Ruddick, Sara. "Rethinking 'Maternal' Politics." In *The Politics of Motherhood: Activist Voices from Left to Right*, edited by Alexis Jetter, Annelise Orleck, and Diana Taylor, 369–82. Hanover, NH: University Press of New England, 1997.

Sadler, Kim Martin, ed. *Atonement: The Million Man March*. Cleveland, OH: Pilgrim Press, 1996.

Sanborn, Charles. "Million Mom March—Where Do Comments Differ?" *Seattle Times*, May 14, 2000.

Sanchez, Mary. "Men Invigorated by March." *Kansas City (MO) Star*, October 19 1995.

Sandalow, Marc. "Millennium March: Gay Rally Bares Deep Divisions." *San Francisco Chronicle*, April 29, 2000. Accessed July 13, 2016. http://www.commondreams.org /headlines/042900–01.htm.

Sansbury, Jen. "Million Mom March: Georgia Marchers Urge Common Sense." *Atlanta Journal-Constitution*, May 15, 2000.

Scales, Ann. "Restoration Is Focus of Women's March." *Boston Globe*, October 24, 1997.

———. "Weekend Gay-Rights March Doesn't Sit Well with Some Grassroots Activists." *Boston Globe*, April 29, 2000.

Schaper, Donna. "Promise Keepers Can Do Real Good." *New York Newsday*, October 2, 1997.

Schmoke, Kurt. "A Huge Family Reunion at the March." *Baltimore Sun*, October 29, 1995.

Schneider, Beth E. "Lesbian Politics and AIDS Work." In *Modern Homosexualities: Fragments of Lesbian and Gay Experience*, edited by Ken Plummer, 160–74. New York: Routledge, 1992.

Sciolino, Elaine. "Gays Set to Flex Political Muscle in Today's Washington March." *Contra Costa (CA) Times*, April 30, 2000.

Scrivener, Leslie. "In Changing World, Men Flock to Jesus." *Toronto Star*, September 24, 1995.

Scruggs, Afi-Odelia E. "What Kind of Black Are We?" *Washington Post*, July 29, 2007.

Sedgwick, Eve Kosofsky. *Epistemology of the Closet*. 1990; repr. Berkeley: University of California Press, 2008.

Shaffer, Erica. "Surprising Many, Million Man March Now Looms as Big Event." *Atlanta Journal-Constitution*, October 1, 1995.

Sharn, Lori. "Ministers' Promise: Shed All-White Image." *USA Today*, February 13, 1996.

Shaw, Stephanie J. *What a Woman Ought to Be and to Do: Black Professional Women Workers during the Jim Crow Era*. Chicago: University of Chicago Press, 1996.

Shepard, Jason. "Sunday's Gay March Divides Local Activists." *Capital Times* (Madison, WI), April 27, 2000.

Shepard, Paul. "Exclusion Bothers Some Women." *Cleveland Plain Dealer*, October 1, 1995.

———. "Fathers and Sons Revel in Sun-Drenching Scene." *Cleveland Plain Dealer*, October 17, 1995.

"Show of Strength: The Million Woman March." *PBS Newshour*, October 27, 1997, transcript. Accessed July 13, 2016. http://www.pbs.org/newshour/bb/social_issues -july-dec97-women_10-27/.

Simon, Richard, and Nick Anderson. "Mothers March against Guns." *Los Angeles Times*, May 15, 2000.

Singhania, Lisa. "About 12,000 Men Expected to Attend First-Ever Promise Keeper Event in Grand Rapids." Associated Press state and local wire, August 14, 1998.

Singh, Nikhil Pal. *Black Is a Country: Race and the Unfinished Struggle for Democracy*. Cambridge, MA: Harvard University Press, 2005.

"Sisters Challenging the Stereotypes." *Philadelphia Daily News*, October 24, 1997.

Smith, Christopher. "Sparks Fly over National Gay Rally Plans: Queers of Color and Radicals Demand a Voice in the 'Millennium March.'" *Freedom Socialist* 20, no. 2 (July–September 1999). Accessed July 13, 2016. http://www.socialism.com/ drupal-6.8/articles/sparks-fly-over-national-gay-rally-plans-queers-color-and -radicals-demand-voice.

Smith, Gita M. "Georgians See Parade Leading to Political Clout." *Atlanta Journal-Constitution*, April 29, 2000.

Smith, Lynn. "L.A. Moms Fighting Guns on a Local Level." *Los Angeles Times*, May 1, 2000.

Smith, Nate. "One in a Million; Why I'm Going to the Million Man March." *Pittsburgh Post-Gazette*, October 7, 1995.

Smith, Patricia. "In Spirit, There Were Millions." *Boston Globe*, October 26, 1997.

Smith, Robert C. *We Have No Leaders: African Americans in the Post–Civil Rights Era*. Albany: State University of New York Press, 1996.

Spitzer, Robert. *The Politics of Gun Control*, 3rd ed. Washington, DC: CQ Press, 2004.

Spratling, Cassandra. "Detroit's Leader for Million Woman March." *Detroit Free Press*, November 19, 1997.

Stabile, Carole A. *White Victims, Black Villains: Gender, Race, and Crime News in US Culture*. New York: Routledge, 2006.

Stacey, Judith. *Brave New Families: Stories of Domestic Upheaval in Late-Twentieth-Century America*. Berkeley: University of California Press, 1990.

———. *In the Name of the Family: Rethinking Family Values in the Postmodern Age*. Boston: Beacon Press, 1996.

Stammer, Larry B. "Promise Keepers Dodges Skeptics in Dodging Bid for Rose Bowl Rally." *Los Angeles Times*, December 7, 1996.

———. "Teaching Patriarchs to Lead." *Los Angeles Times*, June 19, 1994.

Stein, Charles. "The Wild '90s: The Pleasures and Perils of Prosperity." *Boston Globe*, January 17, 1999.

Stephens, Steve. "It Was a Day of Atonement in Local Churches as Well." *Columbus (OH) Dispatch*, October 17, 1995.

Stingl, Jim. "Journey of Spirit Begins with a Jet to Washington." *Milwaukee Journal Sentinel*, September 28, 1997.

Stone, Steve. "Thousand Gather, Demanding Right to Live, Love." *Norfolk Virginian-Pilot*, May 1, 2000.

Stowe, Stacey. "Promise Keepers Keeping the Faith." *Hartford Courant*, March 8, 1998.

Stricker, Mary. "A New Racial Ideology for the New Christian Right? The Meanings of Racial Reconciliation within the Promise Keepers Movement." PhD diss., unpublished, Temple University, 2001.

Stroupe, Susan. "Reader Responses: Million Mom March." *Atlanta Journal-Constitution*, May 16, 2000.

Stroup, Sheila. "Moms Vow to Continue Their March." *New Orleans Times-Picayune*, May 18, 2000.

Stuttaford, Andrew. "Moms Away: The New Brand of Gun Nut." *National Review*, June 5, 2000.

Sugrue, Thomas J. *Sweet Land of Liberty: The Forgotten Struggle for Civil Rights in the North*. New York: Random House, 2008.

Suicide Prevention Resource Center. "Suicide and Prevention among Gay, Lesbian, Bisexual and Transgender Youth." U.S. Department of Health and Human Services, 2007. Accessed July 13, 2016. http://www.sprc.org/resources-programs/suicide -prevention-among-gay-lesbian-bisexual-transgender-youth.

Summers, Martin. *Manliness and Its Discontents: The Black Middle Class and the Transformation of Masculinity, 1900–1930*. Chapel Hill: University of North Carolina Press, 2004.

Superville, Darlene. "Marchers See Rally as a Step Forward; Participants Pledge to Rebuild the Country." *Chicago Sun-Times*, October 17, 1995.

"Surveys Show Few Black Men Attending Church." *Jet*, July 30, 1990.

Swanda, Ron. "From Gay Pilot to Gay Activist." Millennium March on Washington. PlanetOut.com. Accessed December 8, 2003. http://www.planetout.com/mmow/about/stories/ngpa.html

Swedenburg, Ted. "Homies in the Hood: Rap's Commodification of Insubordination." In *That's the Joint! The Hip-Hop Studies Reader*, edited by Murray Forman and Mark Anthony Neal, 579–92. New York: Routledge, 2004.

Sweet, Laurel J. "Some Stay Behind to Rally Troops Near Home." *Boston Herald*, May 15, 2000.

Taormino, Tristan. "Sex and Silence in D.C." *Village Voice*, May 16, 2000.

Tarjanyi, Judy. "Men Flock to Learn How to Be All They Can Be." *St. Petersburg Times*, September 18, 1993.

Tate, Katherine. *From Protest to Politics: The New Black Voters in American Elections*. New York: Russell Sage Foundation, 1993.

Taylor, Eugene. *Shadow Culture: Psychology and Spirituality in America*. Washington, DC: Counterpoint, 2000.

Taylor, Kimberly Hayes. "Black Women Gather to Show Strength and Unity." *Minneapolis Star Tribune*, October 25, 1997.

———. "Million Woman March." *Minneapolis Star Tribune,* October 26, 1997.

Taylor, Robert Joseph, and Karen D. Lincoln, "The Million Man March: Portraits and Attitudes." *African American Research Perspectives* 3, no. 1 (Winter 1997): n.p., accessed July 13, 2016, http://www.rcgd.isr.umich.edu/prba/perspectives/winter1997/rtaylor1.pdf.

Terborg-Penn, Rosalyn. *African American Women and the Struggle for the Vote: 1850–1920*. Bloomington: Indiana University Press, 1998.

Terry, Don. "Black Man March Is Cheered, Jeered." *New Orleans Times-Picayune*, October 8, 1995.

"Thousands of Women Jam Philadelphia Rally." *Vancouver Sun* (New York Times News Service), October 27, 1997.

Tidwell, Billy J., ed. *The State of Black America, 1993*. New York: National Urban League, 1993.

Toner, Robin. "The Nation Pulling Strings: Invoking the Moral Authority of Moms." *New York Times*, May 7, 2000.

Touré. *Who's Afraid of Post-Blackness? What It Means to Be Black Now*. New York: Free Press, 2011.

Towns, Hollis R. "Potential Marchers Reluctant to Sign On." *Atlanta Journal-Constitution*, October 18, 1997.

Tucker, Carlson. "That Old-Time Religion." *Policy Review* 61 (1992): 13–18.

Tucker, M. Belinda, and Claudia Mitchell-Kernan, eds. *The Decline in Marriage among African Americans: Causes, Consequences, and Policy Implications*. New York: Russell Sage Foundation, 1995.

Twomey, Steve. "Appeal of the PK Way Hits Home." *Washington Post*, October 2, 1997.

"The Two Nations of Black America." *Frontline*. PBS, February 10, 1998. Accessed July 13, 2016. http://www.pbs.org/wgbh/pages/frontline/shows/race/.

Tyson, Ann Scott. "Marching Moms Come from All Walks of Life." *Christian Science Monitor*, May 12, 2000.

———. "A New Stir Surrounds Men's Role." *Christian Science Monitor*, September 17, 1997.

Uhlenhuth, Karen, and Helen Gray. "70,000 Jam 'Pep Rally with a Purpose': Christ and Camaraderie Draw Promise Keepers." *Kansas City (MO) Star*, April 27, 1996.

U.S. Census Bureau. *Statistical Abstract of the United States: 2000*. Accessed July 13, 2016. http://www.census.gov/prod/2001pubs/statab/sec02.pdf.

Vanasco, Jennifer. "Boring Is Beautiful." IGF Culture Watch.com. June 10, 2000. Accessed July 13, 2016. http://igfculturewatch.com/2000/06/10/boring-is-beautiful/.

Vara, Richard. "He's Ok, I'm Ok; These Wives Staunchly behind Husbands as Promise Keepers." *Houston Chronicle*, June 22, 1996.

Wallace, Anthony F. C. "Revitalization Movements." *American Anthropologist* 58, no. 2 (1956): 264–81.

Wallace, Michelle, and Gina Dent. *Black Popular Culture: Discussions in Contemporary Culture*. New York: Dia Center for the Arts, 1992.

Walsh, Edward. "Criticism of Farrakhan's Million Man March Muted: Nation of Islam Leader's Effort Pushing Him to Forefront of Black Leadership." *Washington Post*, October 8, 1995.

Warner, Michael. *The Trouble with Normal: Sex, Politics, and the Ethics of Queer Life*. New York: Free Press, 1999.

Waters, Mary C. *Black Identities: West Indian Immigrant Dreams and American Realities*. Cambridge, MA: Harvard University Press, 1999.

West, Norris P. "Baltimore Men Flock to Demonstrate in D.C." *Baltimore Sun*, October 17, 1995.

———. "High Goal Set for State; 200,000 MD Black Men Predicted for D.C. Rally." *Baltimore Sun*, October 6, 1995.

"What Promise to Keep: Stadium Faith Events Sexist?" *Kansas City (MO) Star*, April 25, 1996.

Wheeler, Linda. "I'm Going to Keep At It." *Washington Post*, October 17, 1995.

White, Deborah Gray. *Ar'n't I a Woman? Female Slaves in the Plantation South*. 1985. Repr., New York: W. W. Norton, 1999.

———. *Let My People Go: African Americans 1804–1860*. New York: Oxford University Press, 1996.

———. *Too Heavy a Load: Black Women in Defense of Themselves, 1894–1994*. New York: W. W. Norton, 1999.

Wiebe, Robert H. *The Search for Order, 1877–1920*. New York: Hill and Wang, 1967.

Wiese, Andrew. *Places of Their Own: African American Suburbanization in the Twentieth Century*. Chicago: University of Chicago Press, 2004.

Wilgoren, Debbi. "In the Land of Promise; Christian Crusade Leads Men to God, Family." *Washington Post*, May 24, 1996.

Wilgoren, Debbi, and Hamil Harris. "In Last-Minute Switch, Ministers Disown March." *Washington Post*, October 3, 1995.

Williams, Rhonda. "Absent from the March; a Woman Wonders about the Agenda." *Baltimore Sun*, October 22, 1995.

Wilson, Rita. "We Are Countless in Unity." *Washington Post*, October 26, 1997.

Wilson, William Julius. *The Declining Significance of Race: Blacks and Changing American Institutions*. Chicago: University of Chicago Press, 1978.

Winner, Lauren F. "Wives, Daughters, Mothers, and Sisters as Kept Women." In *Standing on the Promises: The Promise Keepers and the Revival of Manhood*, edited by Dane S. Claussen, 150–51. Cleveland, OH: Pilgrim Press, 1999.

Winter, Mary. "Don't Like Guns, Walk the Walk." *Denver Rocky Mountain News*, May 14, 2000.

Wolff, Paula. "Can Million Moms Be Wrong?" *Chicago Sun-Times*, May 19, 2000.

Wolf, Richard. "Men at Work: On the Power of Prayer." *USA Today*, August 8, 1995.

"Word of Mouth Draws Throngs to March." *Christian Science Monitor*, October 27, 1997.

Worthington, Kathy, and Sara Hamlin. "Doesn't Speak for Us." *Pittsburgh Post-Gazette*, May 17, 2000.

Wright, Kaj. "Black, Gay, at Risk." *Village Voice*, June 27, 2000.

Wylie, Philip. "Common Women." In *Generation of Vipers*. 1942. Repr., New York: Pocket Books, 1955.

Young, Eric. "San Diegans Step Off Bus into Sea of Unity." *San Diego Union-Tribune*, October 17, 1995.

Young, Iris Marion. "The Logic of Masculinist Protection: Reflections on the Current Security State." *Signs, the Journal of Women in Culture and Society* 29, no. 1 (2003): 2–5.

Yuval-Davis, Nira. "Gender and Nation." *Ethnic and Racial Studies* 16, no. 4 (October 1993): 621–32.

Index

DEBORAH GRAY WHITE is Board of Governors
Distinguished Professor of history at Rutgers University.
Her books include *Too Heavy a Load: Black Women in
Defense of Themselves, 1894–1994*, *Let My People Go:
African Americans 1804–1860*, and *Ar'n't I a Woman?:
Female Slaves in the Plantation South*.

Women, Gender, and Sexuality in American History

Gendered Strife and Confusion: The Political Culture of Reconstruction
Laura F. Edwards
The Female Economy: The Millinery and Dressmaking Trades, 1860–1930
Wendy Gamber
Mistresses and Slaves: Plantation Women in South Carolina, 1830–80
Marli F. Weiner
A Hard Fight for We: Women's Transition from Slavery to Freedom in
South Carolina   *Leslie A. Schwalm*
The Common Ground of Womanhood: Class, Gender, and Working Girls'
Clubs, 1884–1928   *Priscilla Murolo*
Purifying America: Women, Cultural Reform, and Pro-Censorship Activism,
1873–1933   *Alison M. Parker*
Marching Together: Women of the Brotherhood of Sleeping Car Porters
Melinda Chateauvert
Creating the New Woman: The Rise of Southern Women's Progressive Culture
in Texas, 1893–1918   *Judith N. McArthur*
The Business of Charity: The Woman's Exchange Movement, 1832–1900
Kathleen Waters Sander
The Power and Passion of M. Carey Thomas   *Helen Lefkowitz Horowitz*
For Freedom's Sake: The Life of Fannie Lou Hamer   *Chana Kai Lee*
Becoming Citizens: The Emergence and Development of the California
Women's Movement, 1880–1911   *Gayle Gullett*
Selected Letters of Lucretia Coffin Mott   *Edited by Beverly Wilson Palmer
with the assistance of Holly Byers Ochoa and Carol Faulkner*
Women and the Republican Party, 1854–1924   *Melanie Susan Gustafson*
Southern Discomfort: Women's Activism in Tampa, Florida, 1880s–1920s
Nancy A. Hewitt
The Making of "Mammy Pleasant": A Black Entrepreneur in Nineteenth-
Century San Francisco   *Lynn M. Hudson*
Sex Radicals and the Quest for Women's Equality   *Joanne E. Passet*
"We, Too, Are Americans": African American Women in Detroit and
Richmond, 1940–54   *Megan Taylor Shockley*
The Road to Seneca Falls: Elizabeth Cady Stanton and the First Woman's
Rights Convention   *Judith Wellman*
Reinventing Marriage: The Love and Work of Alice Freeman Palmer and
George Herbert Palmer   *Lori Kenschaft*
Southern Single Blessedness: Unmarried Women in the Urban South,
1800–1865   *Christine Jacobson Carter*
Widows and Orphans First: The Family Economy and Social Welfare Policy,
1865–1939   *S. J. Kleinberg*
Habits of Compassion: Irish Catholic Nuns and the Origins of the Welfare
System, 1830–1920   *Maureen Fitzgerald*

The University of Illinois Press
is a founding member of the
Association of American University Presses.

Composed in 10.5/13 Minion Pro
with Gill Sans display
by Jim Proefrock
at the University of Illinois Press
Cover designed by Dustin J. Hubbart
Cover photo: Aerial view of the Million Man March.
*Library of Congress, Prints and Photograph Division,
LC-DIG-ppmsca-38892.*
Manufactured by Cushing-Malloy, Inc.

University of Illinois Press
1325 South Oak Street
Champaign, IL 61820-6903
www.press.uillinois.edu